The Free Church and the Early Church

The Free Church and the Early Church

BRIDGING THE HISTORICAL
AND THEOLOGICAL DIVIDE

Edited by

D. H. Williams

WILLIAM B. EERDMANS PUBLISHING COMPANY
GRAND RAPIDS, MICHIGAN / CAMBRIDGE, U.K.

© 2002 Wm. B. Eerdmans Publishing Co.
All rights reserved

Wm. B. Eerdmans Publishing Co.
255 Jefferson Ave. S.E., Grand Rapids, Michigan 49503 /
P.O. Box 163, Cambridge CB3 9PU U.K.

Printed in the United States of America

07 06 05 04 03 02   7 6 5 4 3 2 1

ISBN 0-8028-4986-5

www.eerdmans.com

Contents

TRADITION AND THE CHURCH

Preface

To embark on a study that addresses the faith of the patristic or early church from the perspective of the free (or believer's) church is to discover how high is the historical and theological wall that separates the two. Even to say that free church and/or evangelical Christianity[1] has a heritage that encompasses ancient Christian influences will surprise many who identify themselves with this kind of Protestantism.[2] For such believers the ages of the church which follow the apostles, but predate the Reformation, constitute a kind of ecclesiastical "lost world," shrouded in the mists of empty ritualism, works righteousness, strange saints, and offering little relevance for grasping a vital Christian faith. Nothing could be further from the truth.

The problem is not merely that many Christians tend to view their

---

1. Free church Christianity is not synonymous with modern evangelicalism, although a large number of the religious affiliations within the free church legacy also identify themselves as "evangelical."

2. Most historians speak of the "free church" as that nonmagisterial part of the Protestant Reformation which began as various (so-called) "Anabaptist" groups in the sixteenth century, eventually becoming variegated into scores of self-sustaining movements such as the Hutterites, Mennonites, Quakers, as well as those which stem from Pietist and Puritan roots, such as Baptists, Quakers, Congregationalists, Evangelical Free, Methodists, and later, the Holiness and Restorationist movements: Nazarene, Disciples of Christ (or the Christian Church), Brethren, Pentecostal, Church of God, Adventist, and of course, Independent or Bible Churches.

faith in an ahistorical manner, but there is also the working assumption that true believers need only uphold the complete authority of the Bible and the free working of the Holy Spirit in the life of each individual in order to preserve the "pattern of sound teaching" (2 Tim. 1:13).[3] Christian authenticity is judged more by one's personal encounter with God, usually the conversion experience, than by conscious participation in an historical and ecclesiological tradition. To be sure, one's faith is not worth having unless it has been personally appropriated as a vital part of one's identity. And yet this individualizing of the faith has often served to disconnect a large number of Christians from the rich and vibrant heritage of the church's common past because its value is completely overshadowed by the dominance of the immediacy of contemporary experience. The disconnection has become especially acute in our postdenominational age wherein the privatization of religious experience and practice has taken precedence over loyalty to a doctrinal position or a particular church communion.

Implicit (sometimes explicit) to free church background is a general suspicion toward the historical church as an institution. Too many Protestants think erroneously that by virtue of being Protestants, a reliance on one's conscience and the leading of the Spirit offer grounds for nullifying the authority of the church. At the heart of this suspicion is the long-standing view that the institutional church "fell" or became corrupted just after the New Testament era, replete with the rise of ecclesial authoritarian structures, such as tradition and the episcopacy ("hierarchicalism"), which supposedly challenged the supremacy of Scripture. It would seem that Jesus' promise to build his church is a promise that can be applied only to select ages of church history, or may be interpreted in only a spiritual way. Most of the church's history then is a history of something having gone wrong, at least until the sixteenth century, when the Reformation ushered in a kind of second Pentecost, based on a recovery of the New Testament church. Rejection, then, not reformation, of catholicism has been the prac-

---

3. Within this view one finds a rejection of any hierarchical form of church government, not only in the sense of eschewing an episcopal form of authority, and in some cases any clergy at all, but also "free" from dictates of the state or empire which, at different times of the church's history, has given its endorsement to a particular communion within the church. The believer is free, therefore, to follow the faith in accord with the leading of his/her conscience (and if pertinent, theological guidance offered by the denomination or church leadership), according to Scripture.

tical result of this proposed "return" to apostolic days. And because "catholicism" is usually translated "Roman Catholicism," the former is indicted with all the purported sins of the latter, including a mistrust of the early Fathers, who are perceived as the spiritual and ecclesiastical ancestors of Roman Catholicism (and Eastern Orthodoxy) and therefore not of Protestants.

Anticredalism, antihierarchicalism, antipapacy, "Constantinianism," and other suppositions of the free church legacy have created a generally negative understanding of the first six hundred years of the church's history after the apostles. Small wonder that too many Christians find church history irrelevant to the task of discipleship! The great irony of this position is that nearly all free church and evangelical communions draw upon a post-Nicene trinitarianism and a Chalcedonian christology for their understanding of how the Bible ought to be interpreted, revealing just how formative the patristic era was and is for Protestantism. There can be no question about how often sixteenth-century reformers, such as Luther and Calvin, made appeal in their writings to the major confessions and writings of the early church. In fact, careful studies of certain free church communions demonstrate that there was in their earlier days a greater awareness of just how indebted they were to the catholicism of the early church. For this reason did one of the earliest confessions of the English Baptists, the "Orthodox Creed" (1678), see fit to include the Apostles', Nicene, and "Athanasian" creeds. The historic impetus of free church Christianity, on the whole, was not anticredal and certainly not antichurch. The issue, rather, had to do with how much normative authority should be given to the major great creeds and to the patterns of ecclesiastical practice that had been enshrined within late antique and medieval traditions.

There is still much to be resolved before free church and evangelical denominations can look upon early church history as part of their history and as an important basis for formulating their identity as Christians. Such a project must go beyond introducing Protestants to important patristic texts, though this is an important step in its own right.[4] The problem is that simply placing the writings of Tertullian, Cyprian, Ambrose, or

---

4. Two major projects in the United States are devoted to presenting excerpts of patristic biblical commentaries and related texts: The Church's Bible, general editor, Robert Wilken, published by Eerdmans Publishing Company, and The Ancient Christian Commentary on Scripture, general editor, Thomas Oden, published by InterVarsity Press.

Chrysostom before the attention of readers whose religious education has marginalized the pertinence of the ancient sources, leaves the problems of relevance and integration unanswered. So minimalized have been the early Fathers that a pattern of circularity over the years has evolved such that free church worshiping communities and educational institutions rarely produce individuals who are equipped to address the patristic inheritance, with the result that it is rarely addressed in these contexts.[5]

Tensions over dramatic but shiftless worship, lack of ecclesiastical accountability among members, and weak theology have led numerous evangelical and free church Christians to leave their congregations for settings (Episcopalianism, Roman Catholicism, or Eastern Orthodoxy) where the historic "memory" of Christianity plays a more active role in the life of the community. But a case can be made that there exists among Protestant free churches today a rising interest in how the life and thought of the early church could and should inform our own. The problems of modernity and the frustrating lack of direction in contemporary theology have taken their toll, leading seekers for Christian renewal back to the rudimentary teaching of the early Fathers. Even the concept of "tradition," so often vilified as the antithesis of the sufficiency of Scripture, is finding a new hearing among conservative Protestants. Quite rightly did Henri de Lubac observe that every time a Christian renewal has blossomed in our West, whether in thought or in life, it has blossomed under the sign of the Fathers. As the prime informant of a uniquely Christian use of Scripture, the deep roots of our ancient Christian legacy can provide a faithful commonality for Protestant Christians, a recognition that the faith is far richer than one's own personal and "praise" experiences.

But there is more than this at stake. Appropriating such roots is essential if free church and evangelical Protestantism is going to preserve its identity in light of its present tendencies toward internal fragmentation and accommodation to Western culture. It must not be forgotten that we are related to Christ in a twofold way, in communion vertically through the Spirit in one's own context and horizontally across the centuries through the consensual deposit of the church.[6] Both are necessary for the

5. For example, advanced degrees in early Christian literature and thought are still offered almost solely in Roman Catholic institutions, though there is a growing number of scholars trained in patristics who teach in Protestant seminaries and colleges.

6. J. B. Torrance, "Authority, Scripture and Tradition," *Evangelical Quarterly* 87 (1987): 249.

achievement of biblical orthodoxy even if Christians have had a tendency to dwell on either one to an extreme. One can point to numerous instances in church history where the human distinctives of the faith have overshadowed the redemptive work of the divine, and vice versa. Nonetheless, Christian doctrine has usually taken the path of intersection between the horizontal and the vertical, following the pattern found in the theandric incarnation of our Lord.

We are brought then to the question: how are we, given the historical inclination of free church Christianity, able to appropriate the early church in the future task of spiritual and theological formation? There is no getting around the fact that such a process of rediscovery will entail serious reconsideration about what the church's history means for today's church. Before we can responsibly go into the future, we must go back. But simply encouraging readers to read more church history misses the point here. What this book collectively argues for is that if the aim of contemporary free churches and evangelicalism is to be doctrinally balanced and exegetically faithful to the apostolic teaching, it cannot be accomplished without recourse to and integration of the foundational life and faith of the early church.

Make no mistake, the early church was far from infallible, as the ancients themselves knew. None of the scholars in the pages that follow imagine that the patristic era was a kind of "golden age" to which we must return in a romanticized fashion. On the contrary, our search has been for those historically tangible and mutable conditions that generated a central core of faith around which our various church or denominational traditions have grown. While the patristic churches manifested the "wholeness" or catholicity of the apostolic faith, they did so only partially and imperfectly, experiencing their own share of doctrinal discord, compromise with the world, and moments of faulty biblical interpretation. But, as the late John Howard Yoder has rightfully observed of ancient church history, if apostasy from New Testament principles was real, faithfulness must also have been possible. Both certainly occurred in the patristic age, as in every age of the church since then.

The ancient tradition as found in the major confessions and creeds, the rules of faith, and the doctrinal theology of the Fathers provides truth about God — in fact, primal truth about God. To make a serious claim for orthodox Christianity means that Protestantism (of all stripes) has to go beyond itself to the formative eras of its faith — *apostolic and patristic* —

which are themselves the joint anchor of responsible biblical interpretation, theological imagination, and spiritual growth.[7] Even so, the rediscovery of early Christianity is not an "end" but a "means" of offering us a place to stand as we seek to address the current challenges facing Christian integrity. The ancient church offers resources as we seek to construct a uniquely Christian vision in our present day. Protestants will thus be enabled to more readily cross that historical and theological divide which has for too long separated many believers from their roots and each other.

This volume represents a joint effort of scholars who are seeking to define some of the problems and frame potential answers for what kinds of bridges can be built over the divide that has distanced free church Christianity from its patristic past. As this occurs, it is inevitable that certain questions about our ecumenical responsibility be raised. Wolfhart Pannenberg's insistence that all Christians have a commission to seek the unity of the church[8] is an implicit and corollary task of the present volume. Coming from a decidedly Protestant orientation, these essays are not glossing over the significance of the sixteenth-century Reformation and the important problems it confronted within the Christian faith. It is not doubted that a correction within the medieval Catholic Church was necessary. At the same time, these essays do represent critical steps in reinvestigating the exact nature of those historical and theological differences, with a view that the catholic character of free church Christianity must be acknowledged and reconsidered in light of its relation to other Christian traditions.

For by its very nature Protestantism[9] originally meant a declaration of or testimony to its self-avowed principles of catholicity — that is, of faith in Jesus Christ, the Word of God, who is revealed through the preaching of the gospel, proclaimed in Scripture and in the life of the church, and manifested in the church's tradition. If the protestation of the sixteenth century was convinced that another kind of churchmanship was possible other than the one under the papacy, it was no less motivated by the con-

---

7. D. H. Williams, *Retrieving the Tradition and Renewing Evangelicalism: A Primer for Suspicious Protestants* (Grand Rapids: Eerdmans, 1999), p. 13.

8. Lecture before the faculty of theology of Loyola University Chicago, 28 February 2001.

9. The primary meaning of the Latin word *protestari* is to declare formally, or publicly testify. As a secondary meaning the term refers to a protest against error. For a passionate and scholarly study of free church perspective of Protestantism, see *The Catholicity of Protestantism*, ed. R. Newton Flew and Rupert E. Davies (London: Lutterworth, 1950).

viction that both the apostolic and patristic inheritance belonged to it and had to be restored to its rightful place as the basis of church reform. It is fidelity to this whole inheritance, as we will argue below, that the present church must retrieve and critique as the wellspring of its unique identity.

This collection of articles does not represent the proceedings of a conference. The book is itself a collaborative project in which a common but loosely defined vision governed the final product. Each contributor was invited to participate on the basis of his/her scholarly expertise within church history and as one who worships within the free church tradition. It was not a simple task to find persons with this kind of working combination and commitment. But it is hoped that the reader will receive these original essays in the same spirit as they were intended, namely, as starting points for identifying the issues and solutions to those problems which have prevented free church Christians from inviting early church Christians as fellow partners in the pilgrimage of faith.

HISTORICAL INTERPRETATION

The Canon of Scripture in the Church

FREDERICK W. NORRIS

For many faithful servants of God, questions about the Bible do not include queries about the canon. If you want a Bible, you go to a bookstore and purchase one or get it on-line. There are a number of translations from which to choose, of course. But the sixty-six authentic books of Christian scripture surely were there not long after the death of Jesus. The inspired Old Testament is the Hebrew Bible we share with Jews, who had it before Jesus was born. The New Testament was written primarily by apostles and recognized as inspired by God; in fact, by the end of the first century it had taken its present form. Therefore, we are on solid grounds when we accept Holy Writ as the single foundation for Christian faith.

Thirty years ago those interested in the origins of the Christian Bible might have found a somewhat similar Protestant scholarly consensus. In that view the Jewish canon of scriptures was virtually closed before Jesus' lifetime, or at least within decades of his death, at the Council of Jamnia in 90 C.E. It served as the Old Testament for early Christians. Followers of Christ basically finished the collection of their sacred writings, called the New Testament, by the end of the second century. The criteria employed for canonization are relatively plain: inspiration and apostolic authorship. The implications of this early canonical decision leave firmly in place the strong Protestant position that the Bible is the only touchstone of Christian faith.[1]

---

1. A classic example of this position is Hans von Campenhausen, *The Formation of the Christian Bible*, trans. J. A. Baker (Philadelphia: Fortress, 1972). Some still hold similar

Today the scholarly consensus has shifted dramatically. It claims that: (1) The earliest Christians did not inherit a completely closed canon of Scripture from Judaism, but rather a shifting group of holy scriptures, some of which were clearly recognized as authoritative; (2) the first canonical list that included twenty-seven books in a New Testament like the one we now read appeared in 367 c.e.; (3) the criteria employed to discern whether or not a writing was authentic were and are difficult to define; (4) without a firm canon in place so early in the life of Christian congregations, the *sola Scriptura* principle of authority proves to be remarkably problematic. This is particularly true for conservative Protestants who often view the early developments of monepiscopacy, councils, creeds, and ethical canons as rather uninteresting because they lack significant force.

I

To insist that first-century Judaism did not bequeath a final sacred canon to Christianity, we must begin with a clear definition of the difference between "scriptures" and "canon." In this essay the first term, "scriptures" (always in the plural), refers to books that have been acknowledged as authoritative, sacred writings. Jews or Christians would take such writings with ultimate seriousness as offering insight into God's will, as laying down God's plan. The second term, "canon," describes a list of Holy Writ from which nothing could be taken away and to which nothing could be added.

First-century Jewish communities had a number of sacred scriptures, but they did not yet have a closed canon that Christians could inherit. The more important point, however, is that Second Temple Judaism was itself quite diverse. We should have expected that Jewish recognitions of various writings as holy books would be dissimilar, and thus that no universally accepted list of the Hebrew Bible would have yet appeared.[2] Even before the

---

views. Roger Beckwith, *The Old Testament Canon of the New Testament Church and Its Background in Early Judaism* (Grand Rapids: Eerdmans, 1985), says there was a closed Jewish canon inherited by the early church which later was misguidedly enlarged through the addition of the Apocrypha and Pseudepigrapha. In his view, the sixteenth-century Protestant Reformation corrected the error.

2. David M. Carr, "Canonization in the Context of Community: An Outline of the Formation of the Tanak and the Christian Bible," in *A Gift of God in Due Season: Essays on Scripture and Community in Honor of James A. Sanders,* ed. Richard D. Weis and David M.

4

fall of Jerusalem in 70 c.e., Jews had lived widely separated from each other during almost all the days of any year. Jerusalem and Alexandria were definitely in contact, as were some other centers, but it is difficult to prove that the collections of scriptures used throughout the Diaspora were exactly the same. After the destruction of the Jerusalem temple, Jews had to learn to do without that great center as any factor, let alone as a unifying one.

The Jewish historian and apologist Josephus (ca. 37–ca. 100) presented a view of the Hebrew Bible that stands in opposition to these understandings of pluralistic first-century Judaism. He knew not only that the different scriptural books had been divided into categories of Law, Prophets, and Writings, or as he calls the latter, "hymns to God and principles of living for men." He also claimed that Judaism possessed a closed catalogue of divine books rather than a "multitude of books that conflict with one another." Indeed, Josephus insisted that for many years "no [Jew] has ever dared to add to, or take away from, or change" the contents of that list.[3] Thus, at least one important figure of first-century Jewry who had grown up in Palestine and lived in Rome insisted that Judaism had stood under a complete canon long years before he was born.

The rather ambiguous decisions of a Jewish conference at Jamnia in Palestine during 90 c.e., however, offer counterevidence. Leaders assembled there apparently wanted to make some sense of which Jewish scriptures were genuine. After the Romans demolished the temple twenty years earlier, Jews needed some carefully constructed "rule" that would help them grasp their identity in this new situation. The books sometimes called "the writings" seem to have been those most in flux. The assembled sages discussed which volumes "defile the hands," notably Ecclesiastes and the Song of Solomon. Their attempt to close the canon or at least to limit it more carefully may itself have been one reaction to the growing success of the Jewish sect of Christianity.[4]

Carr, *Journal for the Study of the Old Testament* — Supplement Series 225 (Sheffield: Sheffield Academic Press, 1996), pp. 22-29, warns that too many still think of canonization as a "unilinear process" within a single Judaism.

3. Josephus, *Against Apion* 1.8. Eusebius, *Ecclesiastical History* (= *HE*) 3.10.1-5.

4. Jack Lightstone, "The Formation of the Biblical Canon in Judaism of Late Antiquity: Prolegomena to a Reassessment," *Studies in Religion* 8, no. 2 (1979): 135-42, argues that no firm conclusions were reached about canon at Jamnia. Lee Martin McDonald, *The Formation of the Christian Biblical Canon* (Nashville: Abingdon, 1988), pp. 60-66, helpfully describes Jamnia in a similar way.

At the beginning of the fourth century Eusebius of Caesarea (ca. 260–ca. 339) was constructing his history of the church. Much interested in questions of both the Jewish and the Christian canon, he notices that in the last third of the second century Melito, Christian bishop of Sardis, journeyed to Palestine in order to discover what canon the Jews there used. Melito's *On the Pascha* is filled with such vitriolic polemic against the Jews[5] that we know his trip to Jerusalem most probably was intended to gain weapons for the fight. Perhaps his main concern was to see if the Jews of Sardis employed the same Hebrew Bible that those in Palestine did. He appears to be the first Christian writer to use the term "Old Testament" as the name for such Jewish scriptures. His catalogue was not the only collection of sacred books used by Jews at that time; he omits the book of Esther that Josephus included.[6] Eusebius also notes that Origen (185–ca. 251), in commenting on Scripture, offers a list of books rather similar to the catalogue from Josephus. But the books are ordered in a different way, perhaps influenced both by his Jewish teachers in Alexandria and Caesarea of Palestine and by his high regard for the Septuagint. He includes Ruth as part of Judges and Lamentations as a part of Jeremiah in the section including the prophets. In most other Jewish traditions, however, Ruth and Lamentations are considered part of the Writings, not the Prophets. He also refers positively to the books of Maccabees, evidently thinking them important enough to acknowledge, but he puts them outside the catalogue.[7] Thus Christians like Melito and Origen, who asked Jews about their scriptures, knew that Jewish communities apparently wanted a closed canon. In the second and third centuries, however, Jews were still working toward such a standard. For Josephus the claim that they had a closed canon formed a substantial part of a polemic used against the confused state of authentic literature among other religions. But there was no fully accepted canon of the Old Testament that Christianity could inherit in the first century, and beyond.

As Christians became more separated from daily intimate contact with Jews as members of their family, the Old Testament of the church was

---

5. Stuart Hall, *Melito of Sardis, On the Pascha and Fragments* (Oxford: Clarendon, 1979).

6. Eusebius, *HE* 4.26.13-14.

7. Eusebius, *HE* 6.25.1-2.

often the Septuagint Greek translation with its many books we call the Apocrypha and Pseudepigrapha. Various Jewish communities still found these latter books to be less than adequate, and eventually they often rejected these books which some Christians found sacred. While numbers of Jews questioned the so-called Apocrypha and Pseudepigrapha, writings in what became the Christian New Testament allude to or quote them more than 150 times.[8] Christian authors like Justin Martyr (ca. 100–ca. 165), Irenaeus (ca. 115–ca. 202), Tertullian (fl. 200), Clement of Alexandria (ca. 160-215), and Eusebius depended upon the Jewish Aristeas legend which insists that the Septuagint was totally inspired.[9]

The Septuagint was a translation made by Jews, but various manuscript witnesses to that translation do not always have the same text or the same books.[10] Some Jewish communities seem to have been offended enough by the Christian adoption of the Septuagint that Aquila, Theodotion, and Symmachus, second-century Jews, produced other, soon-preferred Greek translations of their holy books.[11] Thus Jews had no closed canon to offer Christians, and they also fought with Christians about which Jewish scriptures were the inspired ones.

II

The earliest canonical list of twenty-seven books in the New Testament appears in the last third of the fourth century.[12] It is quite possible that as early as the first century the authors of Matthew, Luke, and John saw what they were doing as the creation of more "scripture" similar to the holy books which Christians continually used, i.e., Jewish scriptures. The Gospels of Matthew and Luke employ the Gospel of Mark and evidently seek to adjust the overall picture of things. The Gospel of John has its own way of telling the story of Jesus. Mark appears to be the earliest attempt to cre-

---

8. Albert Sundberg, *The Old Testament of the Early Church*, Harvard Theological Studies, vol. 20 (Cambridge: Harvard University Press, 1964), pp. 54-55. McDonald, *Formation*, in Appendix A, lists the allusions and quotations.

9. The *Letter of Aristeas* appears in Josephus, *Jewish Antiquities* 12.2.118.

10. Karen Jobes and Moisés Silva, *Invitation to the Septuagint* (Grand Rapids: Baker, 2000), pp. 45-68.

11. McDonald, pp. 53-58, describes these developments.

12. Athanasius, *Epistle* 39.

ate a narrative, one far less interested in any possible dispute about whether or not it could claim to be "scripture."[13]

The conception of a closed "canon" that some Christians might have known was in the air in Jewish circles during the first century, and in the greater Greco-Roman world of which they were a part in the second century. Within the broader culture of the Hellenistic world around 200, Severian jurists were codifying Roman law and Jews were codifying the Mishnah.[14] During the reign of Diocletian near the turn of the fourth century, the Gregorian code of Roman law emerged.[15] When Theodosius ordered a new collection of that law in the fifth century,[16] Christians were still asking some significant questions about the limits of their scriptural canon.

The point is that Christian communities would have possessed recognized sacred writings called "scripture" by the end of the first century, the beginnings of our New Testament. They also might have had some sense of the need for a kind of closed "canon" late in the first century or during the second. The internal/external questions of which scriptures belonged in the entire Christian Bible were raised to a fever pitch by the teaching of second-century Gnostics and more particularly by Marcion (ca. 154). Some Gnostic teachings resisted any sense that the creator god was good. Thus the god referred to as the creator in what became both the Old and the New Testaments could not be the true deity. In that case there was no reason to refer to any "false" writings as genuine "scripture," unless some pieces of them spoke authentically.[17] Marcion, probably best put in a category other than the so-called Gnostics, shared something like their rejection of the Jewish god. What he wanted to do was make a clear distinc-

13. D. Moody Smith, "When Did the Gospels Become Scripture?" Presidential Address at the 1999 Annual Meeting of the Society of Biblical Literature, *Journal of Biblical Literature* 119 (2000): 3-20.

14. Dennis Groh, "Hans von Campenhausen on Canon: Positions and Problems," *Interpretation* 28 (July 1974): 331-43, makes the points about the Severian lawyers and the Talmud.

15. Michael Grant, *Constantine the Great: The Man and His Times* (New York: Charles Scribner's Sons, 1993), p. 184.

16. *The Theodosian Code and Novels and the Sirmondian Constitutions*, translation with commentary, glossary, and bibliography by Clyde Pharr with Theresa Sherrer Davidson and Mary Brown Pharr (New York: Greenwood Press, 1969).

17. Reading in *The Nag Hammadi Library in English*, ed. James M. Robinson, rev. ed. (San Francisco: Harper, 1990), makes that clear.

tion between law and gospel, between old and new. He dismissed all the scriptures of the Jews and worried about the interpolated Christian texts that various churches claimed to be holy writings about Jesus and the earliest church. He expurgated Luke and denied the purity of the other Gospels, edited Paul and compiled a canon of the New Covenant from what was left. As Tertullian says, he wrote with a knife rather than a pen.[18] Against these Gnostic and Marcionite challenges it became important for Christians to draw their own boundaries and defend what they viewed as genuine scriptures.

In terms of listing authoritative works,[19] Irenaeus of Lyons argued in about 180 that there were only four Gospels.[20] Origen, who labored in Alexandria and then in Caesarea of Palestine between 230 and 250, mentioned the four Gospels and other sacred writings. He did not, however, offer a complete list of which letters belong to Paul. Furthermore, he noted that 2 Peter as well as 2 and 3 John might not be genuine writings of the apostles Peter and John.[21]

Cyril of Jerusalem (ca. 315-86), in his *Catechical Lectures* given about 350, offered a list of Old Testament books and a twenty-six-book New Testament canon that did not include Revelation. Other writings were not of first rank; they should not be read in church or "even by yourself."[22] A synod in Laodicea of Phrygia about 363 decided that "no private psalms or uncanonical books should be read in church; only the canonical ones of

---

18. Tertullian, *Prescription against Heretics* 38.7; *Against Marcion* 1.19.4.2-3; 5.16-18. Ulrich Schmid, *Marcion und sein Apostolos: Rekonstruktion und historische Einordnung der Marcionitischen Paulusbriefausgabe* (Berlin: Walter de Gruyter, 1995), shows the passages that Marcion carved out of the Pauline epistles.

19. The best discussion of these canonical lists is in Bruce Metzger, *The Canon of the New Testament: Its Origin, Development, and Significance* (Oxford: Clarendon, 1987), pp. 201-47.

20. Irenaeus of Lyon, *Against Heresies* 3.11.8.

21. In his *Commentary on John* 1.6 and 5.3, Origen speaks of four Gospels and notes that 2 Peter as well as 2 and 3 John were not always considered genuine. (See Eusebius, *HE* 6.25.) In his *Against Celsus* 3.19-20, Origen mentions some of the Pauline letters, beginning the list with Ephesians, but refers to 1 Corinthians in 3.19 and Ephesians, Colossians, Thessalonians, Philippians, and Romans in 3.20. R. P. C. Hanson, *Origen's Doctrine of Tradition* (London: SPCK, 1954), pp. 133-45, argued that Origen had no list and probably no conception of canon. In Hanson's view, Eusebius in his history put small paragraphs from Origen together and thus gives the impression that Origen had a canon.

22. Cyril of Jerusalem, *Catechetical Orations* 4.33-36.

the New and Old Testament." But the list of genuine books, which is included in some manuscripts, is actually a later addition. We do not know what their catalogue was.

There has been significant argument in the last forty years about the dating of another important list, the Muratorian Canon. Is it more likely to have appeared in the second century or the fourth century? Whatever its date, it does not include the twenty-seven-book New Testament that Christians generally employ. Although mutilated and probably translated from Greek rather clumsily into Latin, it does not mention Hebrews, James, 1 and 2 Peter, or possibly 3 John. It rejects writings from Marcionites, Gnostics, and Montanists but includes the *Apocalypse of Peter* and the *Wisdom of Solomon*. Of those two inclusions, the latter may be a scribal mistake; the former is noted as not being accepted by all.[23]

In what appears to be a rather odd delay, the earliest known catalogue of precisely the twenty-seven books within our New Testament comes from a festal letter in 367 written by Athanasius of Alexandria (ca. 300-373). Yet even Athanasius's discussion mentions a group of books not numbered in his catalogue that he sees as suitable for private devotion and reading in worship. His Old Testament did not include the so-called Deuterocanonical Books, although in other places he referred to some of them as "inspired."[24] Strikingly Didymus the Blind (313-98), leader of the catechetical school of Alexandria and sixty years old when Athanasius died, offers no list. He appears not to use 2 and 3 John, although he refers to 1 John as "the epistle of John." He boldly says 2 Peter is a forgery, still read in church but not part of the canon, and quotes from a number of the Apostolic Fathers as authoritative.[25] Two other lists indicate not only variations but also a sense of uncertainty. Gregory Nazianzen (ca. 330-90) numbered the Old Testament in his roll, as did Athanasius, but he put the

---

23. The Muratorian Canon, an eighty-five-line fragment found in the Ambrosian Library in Milan (Codex 101, folios 10-11) during the eighteenth century, lists books of Scripture. The case for a later date is well argued by A. C. Sundberg, Jr., "Canon Muratori: A Fourth-Century Document," *Harvard Theological Review* 66 (1973): 1-41, and now by Geoffrey Hahneman, *The Muratorian Fragment and the Development of the Canon* (Oxford: Clarendon, 1992). The second-century date is defended by Everett Ferguson, "Canon Muratori: Date and Provenance," *Studia Patristica* 18 (1982): 677-83.

24. Athanasius, *Epistle* 39.

25. Didymus the Blind, *Patrologia Latina* 39:1742. Bart Ehrman, "The New Testament Canon of Didymus the Blind," *Vigiliae Christianae* 37 (1983): 1-21.

New Testament Catholic Epistles after the Pauline Epistles and omitted Revelation. He claimed that anything else "is not among the genuine [ones]."[26] Amphilochius of Iconium (ca. 350–d. after 394) seems to deny the authenticity of 2 Peter, 2 and 3 John, Jude, and Revelation. He knows he lives in the midst of ambiguity because all he will assert is that his catalogue is "perhaps the most unfalsified canon of inspired scriptures."[27]

It is clear from the evidence available to us, therefore, that a number of Greek Christian communities had not come to accept a closed twenty-seven-book canon of the New Testament by the end of the fourth century. The creation of the canon may have taken even longer than that. The Trullan Synod of 690 meant to close the Eastern New Testament canon, but contradictory opinions were recognized when the council laid out a list of which persons and groups of documents represented authentic church law. That decision mentioned authority figures who included the minor Catholic Epistles and Revelation and ones that left them out. The Trullan canon law itself contained two letters of Clement.[28] Even in the tenth century, there were at least six different lists of canonical scripture accepted in the Greek Church.[29]

I have noted that among Greek-speaking churches a compilation of four Gospels and collection(s) of Pauline letters was probably recognized in many churches by the end of the second century. But the battle in the Syriac-speaking Eastern Church between Tatian's single Gospel, the *Diatessaron,* and what we know today as our four Gospels had just begun in the second century. It was only settled in favor of the four during the fifth century when Rabbula of Ephesus (d. 435) insisted that the four Gospels supplant the *Diatessaron.* Theodoret of Cyrrhus (393-460?) collected 200 copies of the *Diatessaron,* put them away, and replaced them with copies of the four Gospels.[30] The Peshitta version of the Syriac New Testament appeared no later than the early fifth century; it excluded 2 Peter, 2 and 3 John, Jude, and Revelation. The East Syrian (Nestorian) Church used

---

26. Gregory Nazianzen, *Poems* 1.12.5ff.

27. Amphilochius of Iconium in Gregory Nazianzen, *Poems* 2.2.7, 8, under the name "For Seleucus."

28. Metzger, p. 230, describes the Trullan Council's decisions.

29. B. F. Westcott, *The Bible in the Church* (London: Macmillan, 1866), p. 227.

30. See William Petersen, *Tatian's Diatessaron: Its Creation, Dissemination, Significance, and History in Scholarship* (Leiden: E. J. Brill, 1994). Theodoret, *Treatise on Heresies* 1.20.

that version throughout its history. It remains the authoritative New Testament, not only of the church of the East (Nestorian), sometimes known as the Chaldean Syrian Church, but also of the Syrian Orthodox Church, whose center is in Kottayam, India.

The Georgian church puzzled over Revelation until the tenth century, the Armenian church until the twelfth. But the Ethiopic church has a larger New Testament canon that contains the twenty-seven, including Revelation. It also adds four sections of its *Sinodos,* a church order; *Clement,* a writing not like the one of a similar name well known in the West; two sections of *The Book of the Covenant,* also mostly concerned with church order; and the *Didascalia.*[31]

In the West a fourth-century list that appears in a tenth-century Cheltenham manuscript omits Hebrews, Jude, and James. The manuscript also appears to acknowledge only one genuine letter from both John and Peter, while the list its scribe copied includes three epistles from John and two from Peter. Yet, by the fourth and fifth centuries, strong figures like Rufinus (ca. 345-410), Jerome (ca. 347–419/20), and Augustine (354-430), as well as one synod in Hippo during 393 and two in Carthage, 397 and 419, found the twenty-seven-book New Testament canon to be the norm. But over one hundred medieval manuscripts of Jerome's Vulgate and various translations of the Vulgate biblical text include Paul's *Epistle to the Laodiceans.*[32]

It is clear, then, that there was no closed twenty-seven-book New Testament accepted by Christian churches at the end of the first century. Moves to close it were strong in the fourth century, but even then questions were still being asked about some books in various regions: most often Hebrews and Revelation as well as 2 Peter, 2 and 3 John, and Jude. Occasionally writings like the *Epistle to the Laodiceans,* attributed to Paul, two epistles of Clement, and some other pieces from the Apostolic Fathers were included.

III

The characteristics that mark a writing as an authentic biblical book are more difficult to establish than we sometimes think. Luke 1:1-4 says other

---

31. Metzger, pp. 218-28.
32. Metzger, pp. 229-39.

descriptions were in circulation, ones that the author of Luke considered in need of correction. He might have been thinking of our Gospel of Mark or he may have been referring to something like the Gnostic gospels that, as a rule, have come down to us primarily in fragmentary form.[33] Indeed, we would have to move the fragmentary Gnostic gospels back about a century from their usual dating if they are to be Luke's referent.[34] While that might provide an understandable context for his introduction, we cannot be certain what he meant.

How did the second-century churches recognize which Christian books were genuine scripture? Apostolic authorship certainly is an appropriate response, but that presents further difficulties. Our oldest manuscripts of the four Gospels only have the names of Matthew, Mark, Luke, and John on them as added features. We cannot tell if any of the eleven apostles actually wrote a Gospel. The case that Papias presents for an apostolic connection with at least one Gospel has merit. He thought that Mark had Peter's reminiscences as a source, but his views are uttered no earlier than the last third of the second century. Irenaeus, at about the same time, shared a similar view.[35] If accepted as true, their claims do not connect Mark's Gospel with an apostolic author but with an author who knew Peter and was his student. In their view, the Gospel of Mark was not written by an apostle but was used as an apostolic source.

Other New Testament books also may have only secondhand connection with an apostle. We do not know who wrote Hebrews. Origen thought it sounded like Paul and might have been written by a student of Paul, but in his view God alone knows.[36] We cannot identify the author of Jude because we do not know which James was his brother. We also must guess which James was responsible for the work under that name. Dionysius of Alexandria, a Greek-speaking bishop in the third century, noted that a single John wrote the Gospel and the epistles. In his opinion, however, a different author composed Revelation. Striking distinctions

33. John Dominic Crossan, *Four Other Gospels: Shadows on the Contours of Canon* (San Francisco: Harper and Row, 1985), p. 183, suggests that the *Gospel of Thomas, Egerton Papyrus 2, The Secret Gospel of Mark,* and the *Gospel of Peter* "relate in almost all ways possible to the intracanonical four."

34. See Bentley Layton, *The Gnostic Scriptures* (Garden City, N.Y.: Doubleday, 1987), pp. 12-16.

35. Papias in Eusebius, *HE* 3.39.15; Irenaeus, *Against Heresies* 3.1.2.

36. Origen in Eusebius, *HE* 6.25.11-14.

mark its word choice and Greek style.[37] Thus, in Dionysius's view, the writer of Revelation was not the apostle John.

Furthermore, a number of Gnostic gospels have an apostolic author attached to them.[38] The *Gospel of Peter* circulated and was first praised by Serapion the bishop of Antioch in the late second century, but after the church in Rhossus sent him a copy, he insisted that they should not read it.[39] Origen refused what was probably a Gnostic writing with Peter's name; he refers to it as "The Teaching of Peter." His terse comment insists that neither Peter nor any other inspired person was responsible for such a work.[40] Thus it is not possible to use apostolic authorship as the firm and final aspect for authenticating a writing as "scripture," and thus as a potential candidate for the "canon."

Inspiration as a criterion for knowing if a treatise were "scripture" and thus to be included in a "canon" is also problematic. The epistle sent by the Roman church to the Corinthians about 90, called *1 Clement,* urges the Corinthians to obey the words written in it because they are inspired by God.[41] One of the letters that Ignatius of Antioch wrote near the beginning of the second century to Asia Minor churches has a similar claim. In his instructions to the church in Philadelphia, he insists that his call for them to obey their bishop is not uttered in his words but in the words of God uttered by the Spirit.[42] Various leaders of the early church understood that in their time the Spirit had been poured out on all flesh. The question that had to be settled during the debates about Montanus and his prophetesses was the nature of Christian prophecy, not whether it had ceased. The so-called orthodox were concerned about the ecstatic character of Montanist prophetic speech.[43] Indeed, up through at least the fourth century, Christian writers rather commonly spoke of themselves

37. Dionysius of Alexandria in Eusebius, *HE* 7.25.6-27.

38. Among such titles are the *Gospel of Philip, Gospel of Thomas, Gospel of Judas, Gospel of Bartholomew, Gospel of Matthias,* and a series of gospels attributed to the twelve apostles.

39. Eusebius, *HE* 6.12.2-6.

40. Origen, *On First Principles* 1.8.

41. *1 Clement* 63.2.

42. Ignatius, *Letter to the Philadelphians* 7.1-2.

43. *The Montanist Oracles and Testimonia,* ed. Ronald Heine, Patristic Monograph Series, vol. 14 (Macon, Ga.: Mercer University Press, 1989), and *Montanist Inscriptions and Testimonia,* ed. William Tabbernee, Patristic Monograph Series, vol. 16 (Macon, Ga.: Mercer University Press, 1997).

and their own writings as inspired by God.[44] Therefore, although no Christian "scripture" would be looked upon as uninspired, many other writings claimed to be inspired. Thus it was impossible then, as it is now, to view inspiration as the sole factor for acknowledging what was "scripture" and what was not.

IV

The import of the information gathered to this point is not always clear. Many conservative Protestants seek to sift through these historical materials again and look for definitive ways in which very early Christians recognized the inspired, apostolic "scriptures" and saw in them a "canon." My suggestion is that reworking these investigations reaps few benefits. What we need to grasp is how much this new scholarly consensus about the development of the canon should more beneficially lead us to change the ways in which we describe the development of the church. The earliest list of a twenty-seven-book New Testament appears in 367, and there were still rather striking variations into the Middle Ages. In light of that, what is the force of some conservative Protestant arguments that whatever is not in the Bible should not be a part of the church? By the later fourth century when Athanasius made his list of New Testament books, many features of the church that evangelical, particularly free church, Protestants find questionable are already functioning. Does it make much sense to say that the fourth-century church was making very good decisions about the Bible but mostly poor ones about everything else?

For example, monepiscopacy had appeared no later than the beginning of the second century. Ignatius of Antioch was one such bishop. In his letters he refers to a series of other bishops in Asia Minor and may have introduced the conception to Rome during the time he was there awaiting his martyrdom.[45] By the third century, a single bishop for each large

---

44. Everett R. Kalin, "Argument from Inspiration in the Canonization of the New Testament" (Ph.D. diss., Harvard University, 1967), noticed how often early Christian writers claimed inspiration for themselves. In his article, "The Inspired Community: A Glance at Canon History," *Concordia Theological Monthly* 42 (1971): 541-49, Kalin also indicates that only false prophets in the Old Testament, pagan oracles, and philosophers were with some regularity viewed by Christians as uninspired.

45. Ignatius names himself the bishop of Syria in his *Letter to the Romans* 2.2 and

church was a common feature of ecclesiastical organization. By the fourth, a number of ambitious, talented, sometimes overbearing bishops assumed responsibility for whole regions, even though their roles were dependent as much on dignity and honor as established and sanctioned power.

Papal claims for the singular place of Rome's bishop had begun at least by the second century during heated debates about the proper date of Easter. Victor insisted that the Roman calculations were the correct ones, not only for Italy but also for the whole Mediterranean. Irenaeus, a friend of Rome, warned Victor that he claimed too much. Asia Minor and other regions of the eastern Mediterranean had used the Jewish dating of Easter since their beginnings.[46] Thus early papal claims were not unopposed, but after Constantine moved his capital to the East in the fourth century and Rome was sacked in the fifth, the papacy was the strongest religious and political institution in the West.

The point here is that monepiscopacy preceded a closed scriptural canon. Important bishops, sometimes alone, sometimes in concert, made judgments about many things, including which writings were to be accepted as inspired scripture. Canonical lists have come down to us from theologians like Origen who never entered the episcopacy. But most of the catalogues come from bishops like Athanasius, Cyril of Jerusalem, Gregory of Nazianzus, Amphilochius of Iconium, and others who served in such posts. Bishops shaped the canon.

The Niceno-Constantinopolitan Creed of 381, so often confessed in various churches' worship, appeared a bit later than Athanasius's canonical list of Scripture from 367, but it has a precursor in the 325 Nicene Creed. The Apostles' Creed is difficult to date, but it seems to have emerged by the mid–fourth century. The so-called rules of faith found in Irenaeus, Tertullian, and Origen have much of the content and structure of the later creeds; they represent late second- and early third-century efforts to describe the core of Christian faith in Asia Minor, France, North Africa, Egypt, and Palestine.[47] It well may be that there was a reciprocal relation-

---

speaks of Onesimus in *Letter to the Ephesians* 1.3, Damas in *Letter to the Magnesians* 2.1, Polybius in *Letter to the Trallians* 1.1, an unnamed bishop in *Letter to the Philadelphians* 1.1 and *Letter to the Smyrnaeans* 8.1-2, the latter named in *Letter to Polycarp*. Strangely, neither the title "bishop" for a particular person in Rome nor the name of such a bishop is mentioned in his *Letter to the Romans*.

46. Victor, bishop of Rome, and Irenaeus in Eusebius, *HE* 5.23-25.

47. Rules of faith can be found in Irenaeus, *Against Heresies* 1.10.1; 1.22.1; 3.4.2; Ter-

ship between these rules or creeds and the emerging canon. Christians whose confessions had to have a scriptural ring would only officially canonize books that resonated with their rules of faith and their creeds. The simple confession that Jesus is Lord preceded any closed canon and well might have been one criterion for recognizing which texts were inspired. Confessions expanded on the basis of scriptural verses could themselves function as tests for whether books were genuinely inspired or not.

Councils, modeled on the Jerusalem conference held by the first Christians (Acts 15), were used as regional gatherings for making important decisions as early as the Montanist controversy in the late second century. By the third century they functioned as accepted ways for reaching communal, ecumenical judgments. Constantine's call for the 325 Nicene Council only ratified such structures. Of course, it was this emperor who not only underwrote such a council but also had the wealth to arrange for the creation of fifty copies of the Bible as he knew it. And it was councils like those at Hippo, Carthage, and elsewhere that have left us lists of the books in the canon.

Ethical canons (not the biblical canon) became a rather expected procedure for councils to use as assembled leaders attempted to legislate the life of the church universal. In the third century, Paul of Samosata, bishop of Antioch, was removed from his see not so much because of his doctrinal views as for his bold demands that he be treated as the Roman official he was. He had a bodyguard, amassed a fortune, and redesigned the worship space to include a prominent throne for himself and a rather secluded spot where he and his cronies could make undisturbed decisions. He was dethroned because "disciples of Christ do not act like that."[48] Ethical rules were made that the bishops in councils thought were in line with what Jesus taught and the disciples practiced. These councils tended to see the true gospel of Christ in books that stood against some of the unethical practices they observed in their colleagues.

The Great Church that had employed these ways of regulating its life is the one that offered the significant decisions about the Christian canon. We must confess that the church recognized what the Spirit did; it is always

---

tullian, *Prescription against Heretics* 13.1-6 and *Against Praxeas* 2.1-2; and Origen, *On First Principles* 1. pref. 2-8. For their significance see Paul Blowers, "The *Regulae Fidei* and the Narrative Character of Early Christian Faith," *Pro Ecclesia* 6 (1997): 199-228.

48. See my "Paul of Samosata: *Procurator Ducenarius,*" *Journal of Theological Studies,* n.s., 35 (1984): 50-70.

too much to say that the New Testament is a construction of the church. But the canon does not appear outside the church; it emerges within it. When we accept the Bible as the Word of God, we are already standing within that Great Church as we operate with its definition, its recognition of Scripture. We can and should offer arguments for and against practices of the church in any era, but we cannot do it with the resounding "final answer" that such things are not in the New Testament. Our queries must focus on the usefulness of these developments for the life of the church. The earliest Christians lived without a twenty-seven-book New Testament just as much as they operated without monepiscopacy, papacy, government-supported councils, ecumenical creeds, and sanctioned ethical canons. Conservative Protestants need to learn to pose serious questions about these characteristics of the Great Church in terms of their efficacy and their corruptibility, rather than insisting that such features are not in the Bible and thus are always to be viewed with the utmost suspicion for that reason alone. Such thinking is not sufficient. The wonderful Latin wordplay *esse* as opposed to *bene esse,* what is "essential" to the church and what is a part of its "well-being," might prove a good arena in which to raise questions about and debate these issues. We must not fall into the trap of taking any description of "essence" as *the* category for looking at such queries. Perhaps the word "nature" is a bit more lively and helpful. But "well-being" seems appropriate.

Monepiscopacy and papacy have proved their worth to the well-being of the church at various times. Strong leaders with ecclesiastical power have been helpful. Ignatius's attempts to offer his coming martyr's witness through his letters to a series of Asia Minor churches include a number of wise sayings. He worries about the church at Antioch and prays that others will help them survive the persecution.[49] But churches have survived in times of persecution without their bishops. Pagan Rome tried to kill Christianity by attacking its bishops, only to find that congregations could live on without those leaders. Gregory the Great (d. 604), who called himself the servant of others, was a force for good. Even Hans Küng, who had numerous difficulties with the papacy, referred to Gregory as an inspiring example.[50] Much earlier, the great Celtic leader Columbanus (d.

49. Ignatius, *Letter to the Ephesians* 21; *Letter to the Trallians* 13; *Letter to Polycarp* 7-8.
50. Hans Küng, *The Church,* trans. Ray Okenden and Rosaleen Okenden (New York: Sheed and Ward, 1967), pp. 470-71.

615) had insisted that all popes should display sound principles of conduct and humility before God. They should be held accountable.[51]

Councils can provide a wide spectrum of viewpoints and opinions. When the church tries to express its unity through a council, it is making the attempt to describe its very nature. There is much to be learned by looking at the seven ecumenical councils received by Eastern Orthodoxy as guidelines of Christian life and thought. But Greek and Latin are not the church's only tongues; even in the early period there were others. Indian and Chinese Christians were not well represented at those seven councils. Christians living along the Silk Road had little or no influence in those bodies. Neither did the closer Armenian and Georgian churches. The decisions of those councils are less universal than they might have been.

Furthermore, councils can be horrendous examples of unchristian behavior. The "Robber Synod" of 449 included murder and was eventually adjudged to be anything but an inspired Christian gathering. Ecumenical councils have received their place of honor; they did not create it by themselves. Sometimes they have been supported by economic and political forces that represented neither the best intentions nor the best results that Christians could muster. Indeed, any council depends upon its reception by the faithful for its ultimate force. That does not mean that each new generation of Christians may vote on which councils it deems relevant. It means that the recognized ecumenical councils are what they are because they have been received by generations of faithful Christians.

Early on the church found that its doctrine might best be set out in creeds. There are small credal formulae within the books of the New Testament.[52] Councils and other arenas of gathered wisdom have given us summaries of our faith that often help us find our way in our time. When they are treated as contextualized statements for a particular era that have made their way into continuing church life, they can be sources of remarkable strength. But there is a certain sadness in knowing that what were at one time baptismal confessions to help believers internalize their faith have become, in the wrong hands, sources of exclusion and terror. Creeds need to be nestled within pastoral care that is mature and loving. When trinitarian

---

51. See James P. Mackey, "The Theology of Columbanus," in *Irland und Europa: Bildung und Literatur,* ed. Próinséas Ní Catháin and Michael Richter (Stuttgart: Klett-Cotta, 1996), pp. 228-39.

52. J. N. D. Kelly, *Early Christian Creeds,* 3rd ed. (London: Longmans, 1972), pp. 1-29.

and christological phrases uttered by Christians seem to be offensive, they must be viewed from within their own cultures and studied thoroughly before judgments are made. Theologians of good life and thought like Origen were declared heretics long after their deaths because they did not seem to fit later formulations. Thomas Aquinas was nearly adjudged heretical, and there have been others. These kinds of historical examples suggest that reaching such decisions about contemporary Christians should be less hastily and harshly finalized.

Ethical canons from the councils also offer help. We can see within them the life of Christians in various periods; surely if we did not have these conciliar rules, our information about daily life among those in the church would be much more limited. When the fourth-century Council of Laodicea insisted that women presbyters were not to be appointed in the church, we may be sure that there were some. Laws are not made against situations that do not exist.[53] Whether or not we agree with Laodicea's decision poses other questions. In any case, there is merit in remembering that doctrine and ethics, creeds and canons, should be viewed as parts of a whole. One of the things that emerges from the study of canon law is not that it is always universal and thus totally applicable, but that it is context-dependent and must be critically studied historically in order for its significance to be grasped.[54]

V

We must also understand that no single church earlier than the fourth century provided us with a list of our accepted New Testament canon. Indeed, only a healthy plurality of churches into the sixth or seventh century and an overwhelming majority by the medieval period had approved what we view as the New Testament canon. As noted above, both Ethiopian and Syrian churches use a different New Testament even today. And Roman Catholics regularly read a different Old Testament. Acknowledging that, we can begin to grasp that the simplistic propensity of some Protestants or Roman Catholics for setting the Bible over against the church fails to give us significant assistance for being Christians in the twenty-first century.

53. Council of Laodicea, canon 11.
54. The brilliant Orthodox canon lawyer, John Erickson, makes that case in his *The Challenge of Our Past* (Crestwood, N.Y.: St. Vladimir's Seminary Press, 1991).

The Bible alone or the tradition alone will not do. The Bible is deeply situated in various aspects of the tradition, and the best of the tradition is warranted by the Bible.

Early Christians tended to know this even as they struggled to recognize their scriptures and define their canon. One earlier use of the Greek *kanon* described "the rule of faith": what Christians believe. Irenaeus, Origen, and Tertullian have given us such "canons." When Christians began to make lists of the canonical scriptures, those catalogues appeared at various places in the outlines of their treatises. Up into the fifth century differing lists of canonical books did not begin every serious theological work. It did not occur to these ancient Christians that the first thing to settle was the limits of Holy Writ and then all else would fall into place. The first thing to settle was the content of the faith.

It is primarily in sixteenth-century European struggles between Protestants and Catholics that the character of the canon took first place. There it stands in the first paragraph of the Second Helvetic Confession (1566) and in the first decree from the Council of Trent (1546).[55] The unbearable need for one final authority had earlier caused Martin Luther to grope for help. During a debate with Johann Eck in 1519, he dabbled with the possibility of appealing to Eastern Church tradition as a counterweight, but Eck, who had bested Karlstadt and pushed Luther to jump into the fray, insisted that only a few feeble Eastern monks made any sense at all. Thus Luther seldom if ever returned to that possibility.[56] He did not find Eastern Christian tradition to be the weighty balance to the problems he had discovered in Western Christian tradition. For him *sola fide* had a doublet in *sola Scriptura;* together they formed the one authority on which all should stand against the Roman rabble.

---

55. The Second Helvetic Confession of 1566 begins with a chapter on Scripture, a second on its intrepretation, and then moves to its discussion of the doctrines of God and Trinity. *Creeds of the Churches,* ed. John Leith, rev. ed. (Atlanta: John Knox, 1977), pp. 193-96. At Trent, after discussing the procedures for dealing with dogma and reform and affirming their acceptance of the Niceno-Constantinopolitan Creed, the fourth session, held in 1546, offered the first decree, one that dealt with the sacred books and the apostolic tradition. *Decrees of the Ecumenical Councils,* vol. 2, *Trent to Vatican II,* ed. Norman P. Tanner (New York: Sheed and Ward, 1990), pp. 660-64.

56. Tuomo Mannermaa, "Theosis as a Subject of Finnish Luther Research," *Pro Ecclesia* 4 (1995): 37-48, claims that Luther used the concept of deification often, perhaps more than he spoke of the cross. If that contested claim holds, we will need to recognize a more significant influence of Eastern Orthodoxy in Luther's thought.

The sixteenth-century magisterial and "left-wing" reformers' appeals to the scriptural canon as ways to move through the morass of late medieval Western Christianity with its indulgences, simony, domineering power, and other cancers were indeed inventive and arguably needed. In that age much could be stripped away from the church that would improve her health. An abundance of misadventures had to be overcome for the church to survive. But Protestant and Anabaptist theologians were by no means the first people dedicated to changing the church. Every Roman Catholic monastic order had the improvement of the church as its goal. Medieval Catholic reformers, so-called forerunners of the Reformation, had already worked for substantial changes in theology and practice.[57] Centrist Catholics like Erasmus, who provided a critical Greek New Testament for Catholics, Protestants, and Anabaptists alike, had deep commitments to renewal, but they were squeezed out of the decision-making process by both the concerns of rising Protestant reformers and the growing influence of Roman hard-liners. The pressure put on them was not as severe as that meted out to the Anabaptists, but strict Protestants and Catholics found them to be untrustworthy.

A major difficulty that emerged in the remarkable sixteenth-century debate was the need to find one authority, one foundation to which all could appeal. As Christians have struggled to find such a place to stand during the modern era, they have found it imperative to put discussions of the canon first in the outlines of various theologies. Often they bring to the fore a sense of inspiration that would authenticate Scripture in ways that nothing else could. The perilous search for the solid rock that could not waver paralleled Descartes's foundationalism. In one of those strange reversals that occasionally take place in Christian theology, outsiders set the agenda. In order to struggle with the developments of modern thought from the seventeenth century on, theologians too often have accepted the field of combat laid down by their opponents and insisted that one and only one final substructure of Christian faith must be established. That, however, is Descartes's project, not the most important Christian one.

Such a search would have seemed decidedly odd in earlier eras. John Chrysostom suggested that Christians should not worry about the differences in the Gospels; most of the time they were in agreement about the

---

57. Heiko Oberman, *Forerunners of the Reformation: The Shape of Late Medieval Thought,* trans. Paul Nyhus (New York: Holt, Rinehart and Winston, 1966).

most important things. And their differences protected Christians against their enemies. Had all the texts said the same things without any inconsistencies, opponents would have known that the books were cooked up.[58] In other words, an inerrant, unified text would demonstrate clearly that the record had been falsified. Christians believe for many reasons rather than because we have one impregnable foundation.

Justly put, the church worshiped and served before it could discern what the books of a closed New Testament canon were; when it was true to its message, the church was led by the Spirit that inspired scripture. The Holy Spirit called the church to put itself under the judgment of writings it recognized as scripture. Church and scripture do not represent the two parts of a chicken-egg argument. We need not establish which is first nor live in agony because we cannot find the answer. They have existed in close intertwining with each other. Giving proper attention to either church or New Testament means that both must be taken seriously in conjunction with each other.[59]

The truth is simpler than that ambiguity. Jesus and his gospel both preceded the church and the New Testament. Jesus walked the earth as the incarnate Son of God. Those who believed in him at first told stories about his teachings and his deeds. Most scholars agree that Paul wrote his letters prior to the writing of our four Gospels. Nearly four decades passed after Jesus' death before written narratives of his life and ministry appeared. And it took the church nearly two centuries to recognize that only the four canonical Gospels were the authentic witnesses to who Jesus was and what he did. So too, we read the twenty-seven books and not others because the church by the sixth or seventh century widely agreed that these books were authoritative.

VI

After nearly forty years of struggles with these queries, I find rather comforting relief in the conclusion that biblical statements cannot by them-

---

58. John Chrysostom, *Commentary on Matthew*, homily 1.5-6.

59. See Thomas Hopko, "The Church, the Bible, and Dogmatic Theology," in *Reclaiming the Bible for the Church*, ed. Carl Braaten and Robert Jenson (Grand Rapids: Eerdmans, 1995), pp. 107-18.

selves provide a singular foundation for church reform because the canon is in the church. As a doctoral student at Yale, I had been formed by a Celtic heritage and an Anabaptist restorationist tradition focused through the nineteenth-century lens of Christian Churches/Churches of Christ. Thus I was somewhat shocked when I found that Roman Catholic priests and nuns as well as committed Orthodox laypeople were those who most strongly embodied much of my vision for the church. It was partly because they read Scripture devotionally, prayed continually, and witnessed humbly to their need for deep spirituality and virtuous living. All my weakening anti-Catholic arguments and my near total ignorance of Eastern Orthodoxy were being overcome in just a few months when I found that these folk were very close to any people recognized by my tradition as saintly. We all were a part of the church universal. They had well-worn Bibles and were part of Bible study movements within their communions. They posed significant questions to their own traditions.

Many of those Catholic students who were already ordained were willing to accept any position of ministry that their churches asked them to undertake. One priest, who graduated as an expert on Gnosticism through his study of the recently discovered Nag Hammadi documents, went straight back to the parish and thus to leadership at the local congregational level. I must confess that his life emerged in vivid contrasting color to a number of the mainline Protestants I met who were enthralled with "religious studies" and the possibility of teaching "religion" in a state university where being faithfully committed to any religion other than "objective scholarship" was passé.

It is good to know that the church has a Bible, or put another way, that the church's Scripture guides its life. I find the deepest understanding of Holy Writ neither in a closet reading by myself, nor in public meditation with only those of my heritage, but in conversation with the saints of the church in every era and region. Listening to the theologians of the Great Church struggle with Scripture in their commentaries or hearing Aquinas wrestle with the Gospels by quoting earlier theologians provides a kind of conversation that does not appear elsewhere. Knowing the church's interpretations of Scripture in each age deepens our sense of biblical truth.

The bright future for Christian communities is the recognition that the canon stands within the church. Yet we must remember that we do not read from within a neutral public square where all of us know the internationally accepted terms of a single logic or sense of persuasion, where we all accept the proper assumptions that every human makes. We read the New Testament from within the church — too often from only a particular denominational view — and try to live in the world so that people will ask us about our hope. Christians in my heritage have often been moved by the modern tales in which Bible translations were left behind when missionaries were killed. By reading them in their languages, the natives converted. The more common story, however, is that we must embody Scripture in the church within the world. To do that we need to critically study the resources of the Great Church: many bishops, councils, creeds, and ethical canons.

The Bible in use is what we seek, not preliminary senses of how it must be defended to the point of making it almost impossible to decipher except within our own narrow traditions. The precious reality is the canon in the church, studied by common folk and scholars alike, but understood best by believing Christians from any country or denomination who in the Spirit attempt to live out its truth. We worship and serve Jesus. And we read the Bible from within the community of faith.

Evangelicals, Irenaeus, and the Bible

D. JEFFREY BINGHAM

My title for this essay is prompted by the Augustinian notion of the two cities, the earthly and heavenly. As a teacher of patristics within the evangelical and free church tradition, however, a simple dualism, such as we see in Augustine's idea of the loves characteristic of each city, does not avail itself to me. The relationship I perceive between the two "churches," the early and the free, is more complex. Each is an expression of Christianity, informed by both culture and the Bible, at different moments in the epoch of Christ's bride, the church. Each has elements of purity. Each has shamed the groom. Each has read portions of the Bible correctly. Each has supplanted the Bible with culture. My purpose here is not to recount specifics of the assets and liabilities of each expression. Rather, I intend to focus on ways in which selected aspects of the early church's experience can inform and improve the free church. If I did not believe the reverse were also true, that the free church has assets of its own, I would not be a participating member of that community. But I assume, as does the institution where I teach, that benefit comes to my tradition from outside it.

My particular interest is how patristic exegesis may speak to contemporary evangelicals within the free church tradition. More specifically, I

This essay is offered in celebration of the inauguration of Mark L. Bailey as the fifth president of Dallas Theological Seminary, 19 October 2001. I wish to thank Douglas K. Blount, Glenn R. Kreider, and Rick Serina for their assistance in reviewing portions of this essay.

wish to provide some idea of how the study of Bible reading in the early church can be appropriated into the training of contemporary evangelical graduate students. The need for exposure to such Bible reading arises from a peculiar feature currently prominent within American evangelicalism.

The Free Church: Solipsism in Evangelicalism

Locating self-awareness of solipsism or individualism among evangelical thinkers and writers is not as difficult today as it was a quarter century ago. It is almost commonplace to critique it in lecture and literature. Whether such self-awareness has made its way into the mainstream of evangelical culture is another matter. In what follows I briefly survey such criticism from both within and without the tradition.

David Wells, for instance, in a discussion of "self-piety," sees American individualism as a threat to theology's very nature.[1] This individualism, stemming from the Enlightenment and endemic to modernity, dismisses theology outright as irrelevant because the individual has become self-absorbed and has located final authority in the self. The individual within this structure has dismissed all significant, authoritative connections outside of self.[2] For Wells, theology is replaced by individual consciousness and experience. Theology loses its authority in the light of the autonomous self.

For Michael Horton, American evangelical individualism not surprisingly ends in loss of community.[3] An emphasis on salvation as a personal, individual experience or relationship with Christ leads to a collapse of the church as covenant community. Soteriology is no longer centered around a common faith, creed, or experience. Sanctification concerns personal rather than communal growth. Worship becomes an individual spectator event rather than an event of common participation. Regrettably, corrective often comes in the form of a fragmented part of the community, a small fellowship group. The purpose of the group is to provide the "fellowship" missing in corporate worship.

1. David F. Wells, *No Place for Truth; or, Whatever Happened to Evangelical Theology?* (Grand Rapids: Eerdmans, 1993), p. 137.

2. Wells, pp. 141-43.

3. Michael Scott Horton, *Made in America: The Shaping of Modern American Evangelicalism* (Grand Rapids: Baker, 1991), pp. 166-71.

Stanley Grenz's summation is quite pointed:

> Piety among evangelicals has tended to be highly individualistic. "Bible reading" means private Bible reading; "prayer" means private prayer; "Salvation" means being saved as an individual; "being in Christ" means having a personal relationship with Jesus; "the empowerment of the Spirit" means being capable as an individual to act. As Daniel Stevick notes, "The Christian pilgrimage is made alone. God's salvation is individually directed. His help is in an individual companionship. The way is the lonely route of personal sanctification, personally attained. And the goal is a mansion built for one."[4]

Grenz notes that evangelical individualism derives in part from the Protestant notions of the priesthood of the believer and soul competency.[5] He affirms the principles in their meaning that redemption is not determined by any other person or by the church. Evangelicalism "exchanges the priority of the church for the priority of the believer," sees spirituality as "an individual matter," and pitches its preaching to the "individual listener."[6] For Grenz, although spirituality is predominantly an individual matter and responsibility, it is also a "corporate project." The individual "remains dependent on the group." The individual needs the group's resources of instruction, admonition, and encouragement, but does not require the community as a means of grace.[7] In his own systematic theology, Grenz faults classic individualism for its "truncated soteriology" and "inadequate ecclesiology." The program of God has community as its direction and experience.[8]

For Simon Chan, individualism that accompanies "christological spirituality" can produce negative results. Infatuation with one's personal relationship with Christ can diminish one's other relationships, and within the free church, he notes, this leads to schism.[9] Individualism also can lead

---

4. Stanley J. Grenz, *Revisioning Evangelical Theology: A Fresh Agenda for the Twenty-first Century* (Downers Grove, Ill.: InterVarsity, 1993), p. 50.

5. Grenz, *Revisioning Evangelical Theology,* p. 50.

6. Grenz, *Revisioning Evangelical Theology,* pp. 50-53.

7. Grenz, *Revisioning Evangelical Theology,* pp. 53-54.

8. Stanley J. Grenz, *Theology for the Community of God* (Nashville: Broadman and Holman, 1994), pp. 626-27.

9. Simon Chan, *Spiritual Theology: A Systematic Study of the Christian Life* (Downers Grove, Ill.: InterVarsity, 1998), p. 47.

to a preoccupation with feeling over what Chan calls "Fact."[10] The reality of the triune God's ministry within the life of the community is Fact. It exists whether an individual feels, internalizes, or accepts it. Protestantism, in its proclivity toward privatism in spirituality, puts the objective, "factuality," into the shadow of the subjective. Fact answers to private existence and concerns. Chan believes such a tendency "is one reason Protestantism did not develop a viable theology of the visible church."[11]

James Davison Hunter speaks also of "the subjectivism that pervades the private sphere" within evangelicalism.[12] It has a pressing effect upon the evangelical's view of God. The emphasis is frequently upon God's immanence. God is seen informally, familiarly, as a tolerant "daddy" with psychiatric talents: "The imagery of the immanence of God has translated from Divine Protector to Best Friend."[13] The evangelical accommodation to privatization and subjectivism has other results for Hunter. The self has become a fascinating frontier to be explored, charted, healed, admired, and pleased. At the same time, this generates a "psychological Christocentrism," which also produces an evangelical "narcissism and hedonism, the latter an extension of the former."[14] The hedonism frequently results in a duplicity between public expression and private experience. Rarely do evangelicals experience the exciting, rich, adventurous, happy, victorious life. But to admit this contradicts the message. He finds three areas from which narcissism detracts: "The narcissistic quality of this perception of the individual is in sharp contrast to the relative inattention of Evangelicalism to the common welfare of disadvantaged social groups and politically oppressed societies or even to the spiritual well-being of the church as a whole."[15]

Important elements of soteriology, and trinitarianism, are endangered by individualism, according to Peter Toon.[16] The notion and language of "a personal relationship with Jesus" reveals the influence of Western culture upon evangelicalism. Toon does not deny that faith and the

---

10. Chan, pp. 108-9.

11. Chan, p. 109.

12. James Davison Hunter, *American Evangelicalism: Conservative Religion and the Quandary of Modernity* (New Brunswick, N.J.: Rutgers University Press, 1983), p. 125.

13. Hunter, p. 124.

14. Hunter, p. 97.

15. Hunter, p. 98.

16. Peter Toon, "Is a Personal Relationship with Jesus What I Really Want?" *Touchstone* (September-October 1998): 13-14.

blessings of salvation are personal and matters of experience. But salvation is not individualistic. The Holy Spirit unites the believer to the Father through Christ within the context of the body of Christ. "Therefore," Toon writes, "there is never an individualistic union of a believer with God. The fellowship, union, and communion are truly personal and very real (as the saints testify), but are always also together with all others who are in Christ Jesus by faith and love with the Holy Spirit."[17] Any salvific relation to the trinitarian God is both personal and corporate through Jesus Christ.

Some of those writing on behalf of the free church construct paradigms for ecclesiology. Miroslav Volf argues for the "ecclesiality of salvation" and clarifies the question of an individualism of faith. "One cannot, however," he writes, "have a self-enclosed communion with the triune God — a 'foursome,' as it were — for the Christian God is not a private deity."[18] Volf aims his project at countering Protestant individualism. He offers a model of the church as image of the triune God where both "person and community are given their proper due."[19]

Others critique free church individualism by clarifying Protestant principles gone awry. Paul Galbreath and Timothy George, for example, bemoan the priority of community that has been supplanted by misunderstanding of the priesthood of believers. Galbreath argues that for Luther there was a new privilege for the Christian, but this "occurred within the context of community."[20] Likewise in Calvin, the individual's authority is subordinate to the labor of Christ within his body. George similarly writes that the isolated Christian is never in view for the Reformers. The idea was always of "a band of faithful believers united in common confession as a local, visible *congregatio sanctorum*."[21] He announces that individualism is suspect within Christianity and is related to a departure from both Bible and tradition.[22]

---

17. Toon, p. 14.

18. Miroslav Volf, *After Our Likeness: The Church as the Image of the Trinity*, Sacra Doctrina (Grand Rapids: Eerdmans, 1998), p. 173.

19. Volf, p. 2.

20. Paul Galbreath, "Protestant Principles in Need of Reformation," *Perspectives* 7-8 (October 1992): 15.

21. Timothy George, "The Priesthood of All Believers and the Quest for Theological Integrity," *Criswell Theological Review* 3 (1989): 291. Cf. Timothy George, "An Evangelical Reflection on Scripture and Tradition," *Pro Ecclesia* 9 (2000): 184-207.

22. George, "Priesthood of All Believers," p. 292.

Within discussions of individualism in evangelicalism, it is common to see the vice being related to the Enlightenment and modernism. A classic treatment of this connection is found in Karl Barth's *Protestant Theology in the Nineteenth Century* (1946). The eighteenth-century person is the one "who no longer has an emperor."[23] And that century begins Christian individualization, an attempt "to make Christianity a more *individual,* more *inward* matter."[24] Such individualization means many things: (1) the enthronement of the individual over every other authority; (2) the transformation of the external, objective into the internal, subjective; (3) the domination of the object; and (4) the original pietist who "knows no object which is not in the first place really within him."[25] This last one, for Barth, raises five challenges.[26] It jeopardizes the centrality of the temporal distance of the incarnation by emphasizing the "real birth in our hearts," "his real death . . . accomplished in ourselves," "his real resurrection" of triumph in us. It also threatens the centrality of community, "the man in the church who is related to his fellow man." Third, it substitutes authority from church, dogma, and Bible with "the inner personal authority of the man." Fourth, it jeopardizes the command by stressing its internalization, interpretation, or application rather than simply obedience. It also minimizes mystery and sacrament by finding mystery and invisible grace within the inner sanctum of self.

The type of individualism I have been discussing thus far is what I wish to call "individualistic solipsism." This type fixates upon the self as the fundamental reality in the spiritual journey and emphasizes the private and the personal. Inaccurate visions of Christian egalitarianism, expressed through inappropriate understandings of the priesthood of all believers or *sola Scriptura,* characterize it. The greater reality of the self opposes the reality of the community.

But individualistic solipsism is characterized not only by a relation to the private. It is also marked by a fixation upon the present. It is not only private experience which is sought after, but private experience informed by the contemporary moment. Such privatism cuts the believer off from *all* communities. He or she is separated from the body of Christ in the contemporary age as well as that of the past. *It is me, now.* This essential con-

23. Karl Barth, *Protestant Theology in the Nineteenth Century: Its Background and History* (Valley Forge, Pa.: Judson, 1973), p. 41.

24. Barth, p. 113.

25. Barth, pp. 113-14.

26. Barth, pp. 114-23.

nection between the individual and the present and the consequent disregard for the past is enunciated by British historian G. R. Elton. He compares self-centeredness to adolescence and growing up to a communal-historical awareness.[27] Adults function in company and have come to learn that prejudices which once seemed like eternal truths have powerful correctives in the complexities of history. World history is a study of the human community. Likewise, church history and Christian tradition reflect the community of the bride of Christ.

Such modern fixation upon the present, a twin of individualism, has been characteristic of modern optimism since the rise of natural science in the seventeenth century. Those engaged in that enterprise believed they were seeing things as they are for the first time with accurate understanding. God's natural order was *finally,* only now, being interpreted properly. Recall here Kepler's understanding of his own findings and calculations in *Harmonies of the World* (1619): "The die is cast and I am writing the book — whether to be read by my contemporaries or by my posterity it matters not. Let it await its reader for a hundred years, *if God Himself has been ready for His contemplator for six thousand years.*"[28]

But an overwhelming optimism in present insight is not peculiar to the seventeenth century. The twentieth century's fascination with technologies which would solve society's woes also figures here. History lost its place among the pragmatic disciplines like physical sciences. History could not cure cancer, alter human behavior, or build a faster computer. The physical sciences seemed daily to be dismissing past interpretations. Historians, however, found it difficult to share such timeless optimism. They knew the complexity of human existence and its essential relation to time: "Historians could not join in celebrating the triumph of technique over fundamental interpretations because their study of the past made them not only recognize how much more complex human life was than social science models assumed but above all how illusory was the denial of fundamental change [within contemporary models viewed as final or ultimate]."[29]

27. G. R. Elton, "Putting the Past before Us," in *The Vital Past: Writings on the Uses of History,* ed. Stephen Vaughn (Athens: University of Georgia Press, 1985), pp. 41-42.

28. Johannes Kepler, *Harmonies of the World* 5. "Proem.," trans. Charles Glenn Wallis, in *Epitome of Copernican Astronomy and Harmonies of the World/Johannes Kepler,* Great Minds Series (Amherst, N.Y.: Prometheus Books, 1995), p. 170.

29. Ernst Breisach, *Historiography: Ancient, Medieval, and Modern,* 2nd ed. (Chicago and London: University of Chicago Press, 1994), p. 406.

Legion are the causes of unhistorical attitudes in contemporary society. One can look at such convenient summaries as Stephen Vaughn's and still, by his own admission, they lack comprehensiveness. Whether the particular American pride in its freedom from the Old World; the emphasis in modernity upon nature and personal experience; the artificiality of urban rather than rural life; the rapidity and persistence of change in a technological society; the speedy growth of scientific data; an evolutionary, chance-oriented bias; or Einstein's theory of relativity, the conclusion is the same: the present is the most important part of history.[30]

But for evangelicals one element emerges as primary. Mark Noll points to it in his treatment of the role of populist revivalism. He sees a relationship between evangelicals, the life of the mind, and tradition which produces a union of individualism and immediatism. The revivals of the Second Great Awakening called upon individuals to immediately exercise faith themselves, to make a choice themselves without recourse to knowledge mediated by others from the past. "Revivals," says Noll, "called people to Christ as a way of escaping tradition, including traditional learning. . . . Everything of value in the Christian life had to come from the individual's own choice — not just personal faith but every scrap of wisdom, understanding, and conviction about the faith."[31] What matters, according to the revivalists, is that the individual make a choice immediately, *now*, based upon the immediate. This is not unlike the immediatism in eighteenth-century pietism as Barth had shown us. That perspective minimized the first-century event of the incarnation in favor of the individual's subjective experience of Christ's birth in his or her heart. The event, the past, the voice of others from the church, is supplanted by the immediate. Ambivalence toward the community in evangelicalism's individualistic solipsism is a product of both the private and the present.

Having presented the commonplace recognition of the problem of individualism within modernity and particularly within the evangelicalism of the free church, I wish to move now to one specific facet of that problem: individualistic solipsism in reading the Bible. We begin with Barth. He worried that the biblicism produced by individualism involves a

---

30. Stephen Vaughn, "History: Is It Relevant?" in *The Vital Past*, pp. 1-14.

31. Mark A. Noll, *The Scandal of the Evangelical Mind* (Grand Rapids: Eerdmans, 1994), p. 63. Cf. Martin E. Marty, *The Pro and Con Book of Religious America: A Bicentennial Argument* (Waco, Tex.: Word, 1975), pp. 43-44.

demand for the Bible to produce a set of expected answers, solutions, powers, and benefits. Such biblicism, interested more in gaining solutions and having curiosities satisfied than in submitting to the text, imposes one's sovereignty upon the Bible. Such approaches to Bible reading still persist in the free church. So Chan, who mourns the loss of the communal activity of reading: "Reading the Scripture has become a private, information-gathering exercise assisted by key charts, study Bibles and guide books."[32]

Here my particular interest differs. Because of the perceived unity between the private and the present, I wish to discuss the devaluation of tradition in evangelical Bible reading.

In the free church, not only is there the emphasis upon private Bible study, as Grenz and others have shown, but there is also emphasis upon study without consideration for how the church has read the text before now. There is, then, another type of solipsism, perhaps more common than the individualistic type, and just as troubling.[33] Many evangelicals read the Bible in groups, in community. They do so, for instance, in Sunday schools and midweek Bible study groups. Even a book with the individualistic title *The Bible: What's in It for Me?* has a section entitled "Why You Shouldn't Fly Solo."[34]

Such communal Bible study, nevertheless, is still consumed with present insights and usually ignores tradition. We will label it "communitarian solipsism." Communitarian solipsism attempts Bible reading with attention only to the present community and usually with great optimism about current methods of study, which are naively viewed as "scientific." This type of solipsism, separated from the Christian communities of the past, shows itself in both the evangelical congregation and scholarly community. It is an *us* and *now* solipsism, one founded entirely in *our* community. The average believer is taught modern Bible study methods which promise objective certainty under the guarantee that the method is inductive.[35] Biblical schol-

---

32. Chan, p. 116.

33. Cf. John Goldingay, *Models for Interpretation of Scripture* (Grand Rapids: Eerdmans, 1995), p. 242: "Interpretation is an inherently catholic enterprise. . . . The limitations of individual study are paralleled by the limitations of study of scripture within homogenous groups."

34. J. Stephen Lang, *The Bible: What's in It for Me?* (Colorado Springs: ChariotVictor, 1997), pp. 144-45.

35. By its nature, of course, induction does not guarantee certainty. But this seems lost on many evangelicals.

ars frequently share this same conviction. Historians of evangelicalism have usually connected a naive optimism, present in both congregation and study, to the tradition's debt of Baconianism and Scottish commonsense realism. The believer approaches the Bible systematically, without bias, and with an inductive method that will yield precise, correct meaning, because Bible reading is an issue of "scientific" method and common sense. The student apprehends the facts of Scripture directly and needs only to organize them. As Martin Marty summarizes the view, "The biblical scholar was something like the botanist, geologist, or museum keeper."[36] And of course, the view presupposes the pure objectivity of such scientific disciplines. Such claims reveal a lack of sensitivity to historical and hermeneutical factors in the art of biblical interpretation as well as nurture an unguarded optimism in one's own contemporary reading.

In recent years, however, in addition to making remarkable advances in learning and applying the historical-critical method, evangelicals also have become more hermeneutically reflective. For example, Kevin Vanhoozer interacts with the complexities of modern hermeneutical theory to provide helpful perspective for evangelicals. Rather than advocating the naive hermeneutical realism of Bacon which gives "pride of place to induction," reads texts with an "optimistic faith in the powers of observations," and is "oblivious to the problems of interpretation," Vanhoozer prefers the approach of critical realism.[37] Yet D. G. Hart, in a recent essay, sees evangelical biblical scholars still emphasizing the objectivity of their work against a larger culture which recognizes the role of prejudice and subjectivity in interpretation. Hart may overstate his case, but he recognizes the "old scientific optimism" still at work within some practitioners of the historical-grammatical method.[38] There remain remnants of the attitude of the nineteenth century reported by George Marsden: Bible study "was essentially a scientific question — a job for the philologist who studied closely the history of language. Once the original meaning was determined, it seemed to

---

36. Martin E. Marty, *Modern American Religion*, vol. 1, *The Irony of It All, 1893-1919* (Chicago and London: University of Chicago Press, 1986), p. 233.

37. Kevin J. Vanhoozer, *Is There a Meaning in This Text? The Bible, the Reader, and the Morality of Literary Knowledge* (Grand Rapids: Zondervan, 1998), pp. 48, 300-302.

38. D. G. Hart, "Evangelicals, Biblical Scholarship, and the Politics of the Modern American Academy," in *Evangelicals and Science in Historical Perspective*, ed. David N. Livingston, D. G. Hart, and Mark A. Noll (New York and Oxford: Oxford University Press, 1999), p. 318.

follow on Common Sense principles that the meaning of a Scripture should be settled once and for all."[39] Hart also notes the danger which that optimism poses to the importance of reading Scripture with the consciousness that it always takes place within a tradition. Such optimism often nurtures an ambivalence toward tradition. Why consult the past if the current method is superior and free from troublesome encumbrances of older biases? Nevertheless, Gerald Bray, in recognizing the persistent diversity in interpretations that result from the method, identifies an evangelical "unwillingness to take church tradition seriously" as a probable culprit.[40] The historical-grammatical method provides criteria for discovering meaning. But the criteria are not completely determinative.

Noll links the evangelical distance from tradition in Bible study to nonacademics as well. For the latter, principles, systems, expectations, and guidelines become authoritative traditions among people who have formally disowned traditions. Evangelicalism continues to share many features with fundamentalism on this score. If not a method, it is frequently a leader, a study Bible, or a handbook functioning as authority. Ironically, in the history of fundamentalism and evangelicalism, the very teachers who tout the objectivity of the inductive method have often been the ones to emphasize the necessity of intricate schemas — theirs, of course — for understanding the Bible. Timothy Weber has pointed out the incongruity between the hailing of the method and the need of the student to refer to notes in a study Bible.[41] Vanhoozer minces no words: "Fundamentalism thus preaches the authority of the text but practices the authority of the interpretive community."[42] Some evangelicals remain under that umbrella. The realism of Bacon ends up producing traditions that it sought to avoid.

So, even when evangelicals read the Bible within their contemporary communities, academic or ecclesiological, the concept of community is

---

39. George M. Marsden, "Everyone One's Own Interpreter: The Bible, Science, and Authority in Mid-Nineteenth-Century America," in *The Bible in America: Essays in Cultural History*, ed. Nathan O. Hatch and Mark A. Noll (New York and Oxford: Oxford University Press, 1982), p. 92.

40. Gerald Bray, *Biblical Interpretation: Past and Present* (Downers Grove, Ill.: InterVarsity, 1996), p. 562.

41. Timothy P. Weber, "The Two-Edged Sword: The Fundamentalist Use of the Bible," in *The Bible in America*, p. 114.

42. Vanhoozer, p. 425.

limited by an optimism surrounding the possibilities of the present. Though individualistic solipsism may be more readily acknowledged, communitarian solipsism is no less problematic. And even within a scholarly community that confesses a critical, rational realism, a functional optimism in contemporary assessments of meaning persists.

Neither solipsism, individualistic or communitarian, necessarily destroys the aptitude for accurate interpretations. They each contribute hypotheses for testing. But in order to avoid an uncritical naïveté about the superiority of any one community, an evangelical approach *must* include a communal concept of interpretation which eclipses both types of solipsism. If not, we are numbered with Kepler: has God waited two thousand years for someone to gaze upon his revelation with understanding? As Horton says, "A return to community must, therefore, entail a return to Christian tradition."[43]

Alister McGrath has usefully sounded this note. Acknowledging the criticism of tradition within the Reformation, McGrath goes on to encourage evangelical sensitivity to tradition by highlighting its communal essence.

> Yet the idea of "tradition" is of importance to modern evangelicalism. Evangelicals have always been prone to read Scripture as if they were the first to do so. We need to be reminded that others have been there before us, and have read it before us. . . . "Tradition" is thus rightly understood (for example, by the Reformers such as Luther) as a history of discipleship — of reading, interpreting and wrestling with Scripture. *Tradition is a willingness to read Scripture, taking into account the ways in which it has been read in the past. It is an awareness of the communal dimension of Christian faith, over an extended period of time, which calls the shallow individualism of many evangelicals into question. There is more to the interpretation of Scripture than any one individual can discern.*[44]

Attentiveness to tradition in Bible reading, then, is submission to the essentially communal nature of Christianity. It is a refusal to be infatuated with oneself as a Bible reader. But it is also another thing. It is the refusal to be infatuated with one's own time and methods.

43. Horton, p. 177.

44. Alister McGrath, *A Passion for Truth: The Intellectual Coherence of Evangelicalism* (Downers Grove, Ill.: InterVarsity, 1996), pp. 95-96, emphasis added.

The Early Church: Irenaeus, the Church, and the Spirit

In the latter part of the second century we find a thoughtful model for Bible reading which may speak helpfully to contemporary concerns within the free church. Irenaeus, bishop of Lyons, in his confrontation with the Gnostics and Marcionites, set forth an emphasis upon the gifts of the Spirit manifested in persons within the church as the environment within which true understanding takes place. A thoroughly biblical model, it was developed from 1 Corinthians 12:28 and Ephesians 4:15, 16.

The first text comes in *Against Heresies* 4.26.5, but he builds toward it strategically in the previous four paragraphs.[45] In 4.26.1 he argues on the basis of Matthew 13:38, 44, 52; Daniel 12:3, 4, 7; Jeremiah 23:20; and Luke 24:26, 46, 47 that the Old Testament Scriptures, read appropriately in light of the incarnation, show forth Christ and the blessings he brings. Although the heretics and the Jews miss the treasure of Christ-incarnate in the Scriptures, it is due to their lack of the proper christological prejudice, not the failure of the prophetic typology. Irenaeus introduces the necessary prerequisite for proper reading of Scripture: the occurrence of the passion and glory of the incarnate Christ. This is the interpretive paradigm the disciples of Jesus received from the Master in Luke 24:26, 27, 47.

The second paragraph, 4.26.2, builds from the first. The disciples of Jesus, the apostles, were succeeded by their disciples, the presbyters. These presbyters or elders (πρεσβύτερος) have a teaching and interpretive authority which provides the church with proper understanding of theological matters. These presbyters, for Irenaeus, are to be obeyed on the ground that they, with their succession in the line of bishops, have "received the certain gift of the truth according to the good pleasure of the Father."[46]

Discussion of the meaning of "the certain gift of the truth" *(charisma veritatis certum)* has revolved around two questions.[47] Is the *charisma*

---

45. The critical editions referenced are: *Irénée de Lyon: Contre les hérésies, Livres 3, 4, 5,* edited, translated, and annotated by A. Rousseau, L. Deutreleau, B. Hammerdinger, and C. Mercier, 6 vols., Sources chrétiennes (hereafter SC), nos. 210, 211, 100.1, 100.2, 152, 153 (Paris: Cerf, 1974, 1965, 1969). A convenient English translation is *Against Heresies, Books 1-5 and Fragments* (hereafter *AH*) in Ante-Nicene Fathers (hereafter ANF) 1.

46. *AH* 4.26.2 (SC 100.2:218.46-47; ANF 1:497).

47. See, e.g., K. Müller, "Das *Charisma Veritatis* und der Episkopat bei Irenaeus," *Zeitschrift für die neutestamentliche Wissenschaft und die Kunde der älteren Kirche* 23 (1924): 216-22; D. van den Eynde, *Les normes de l'enseignement chrétien dans la littérature patristique*

veritatis a spiritual, supernatural gift received in ordination which placed one within the prophetic order of those who truthfully transmit and teach divine revelation? Or is *charisma veritatis* a term which signifies the true doctrine, the deposit of faith, received according to tradition, which is maintained and passed on through purity of life and faithfulness of teaching? Put another way, is the gift a special *charisma* which imparts to the presbyter accuracy in teaching, or is it the doctrine of the apostles which God has given to the church through the succession of bishops?

In my mind, to differentiate between the two options is a movement in the wrong direction. To emphasize a spiritual gift to the neglect of the content of faith or to stress the doctrine of the apostles without acknowledging the gift brought by the Spirit to the presbyter is to misread Irenaeus. The concept of spiritual gifts is certainly on his mind within the context (we will see it again in 4.26.5), and so is the idea of the apostles' doctrine. The *charisma veritatis* is to be understood as a pneumatic gift which relates the individual presbyter to the church for the service of pastoral teaching in continuity with the apostles' doctrine. The presbyter, as gifted, teaches in fidelity to that message. But he receives this gift along with his inclusion into the line of succession leading back to the apostles. And this carries with it a necessary relationship between the gift and his guarding of the apostolic tradition. In accordance with 1 Timothy 3:2 and 2 Timothy 2:2, his teaching and purity of life are a measure of his relationship to the episcopacy.[48]

In 3.3.1 Irenaeus clearly states that bishops were appointed successors to the apostles in their *teaching*,[49] and in that ministry were to be beyond reproach. There is an inherent unity between the gift and the presbyter's teaching of the faith. The first does not exist apart from the second. Those

---

des trois premiers siècles (Paris: Gabalda & Fils, 1933), pp. 186-87; E. Molland, "Irenaeus of Lugdunum and the Apostolic Succession," *Journal of Ecclesiastical History* 1 (1950): 12-28; A. Ehrhardt, *The Apostolic Succession in the First Two Centuries of the Church* (London: Lutterworth, 1953), pp. 107-31; J. D. Quinn, "*Charisma Veritatis Certum:* Irenaeus, *Adversus Haereses* 4.26.2," *Theological Studies* 39 (1978): 520-25; L. Ligier, "La charisma veritatis certum des évêques," in *L'homme devant Dieu: Mélanges Offerts au Pére Henri de Lubac* (Paris: Aubien, 1963), pp. 247-68; N. Brox, "*Charisma veritatis certum* (Zu Irenäus *Adv. Haer.* IV, 26.2)," *Zeitschrift für Kirchengeschichte* 75 (1964): 327-31.

48. Cf. Jacques Fantino, *La théologie d'Irénée* (Paris: Cerf, 1994), p. 36.

49. The translation of A. Roberts and W. H. Rambaut (ANF 1:415) failed to capture this meaning with "government." But see Rousseau, SC 210:222-23.

who teach imperfectly, departing from the rule of faith, are not true gifted successors. For Irenaeus there are those who pass on the apostles' teaching with accuracy and humility through giftedness within the line of those who succeed the apostles. These are presbyters. Those who gather outside that succession or cause schisms are imposters who will be dealt with severely by God after the manner of Old Testament evildoers (Lev. 10:1-2; Num. 16:33; 1 Kings 14:10-16).

The third and fourth sections continue this line of thought by making explicit the differences between true and false presbyters. There are those whom many believe to be presbyters but are not. These are selfish, contemptuous, prideful, and evil in secret. The Lord who judges the heart, not appearance, will bring condemnation upon them after the words of Daniel (Hist. Sus. 13:56, 52-53) and his own words (Matt. 24:48-51; Luke 12:45-46). The true presbyters, however, stand apart. They "guard the succession of the apostles and with the presbyterial order[50] provide a sound word and unimpeachable conduct (Titus 2:8) for the example and correction of others."[51] He goes on to compare such presbyters to Moses, Samuel, and Paul (Num. 16:15; 1 Sam. 12:2-5; 2 Cor. 7:2).

Helpful to our understanding of Irenaeus's notion of gift is the parallelism between sound teaching and character. For Irenaeus the *charisma veritatis* is a grace for truth in doctrine and conduct. They form an indivisible unity.

Finally, he concludes that presbyters of the type described in 4.26.4 are the ones brought forth by the church in accordance with Scripture's teaching (Isa. 60:17; Matt. 24:45-46; Luke 12:42-43). The emphasis for him is upon *where* such presbyters can be found. Of course, they are located in *the church* where the *gifts* are dispensed by the Lord, and it is from within the church, from the presbyters of truth, that one should learn what is true: "Paul, teaching the place where one finds them, says, 'God has appointed in the church first apostles, second prophets, third teachers [1 Cor. 12:28].' Consequently, where the gifts of the Lord have been placed [1 Cor. 12:4], in that place it is necessary to learn the truth, that is, from those who

---

50. *Ordo presbyterii* is interchangeable with *episcopatus successio* (Douglas Powell, "Ordo Presbyterii," *Journal of Theological Studies* 26 [1974]: 290-328). Contra J. G. Sobosan, "The Role of the Presbyter: An Investigation into the *Adversus Haereses* of Saint Irenaeus," *Scottish Journal of Theology* 27 (1974): 129-46, who sees it as a college of presbyters.

51. *AH* 4.26.4. The Armenian has *successionem* for *doctrinam*. This is Rousseau's preference and is followed here (cf. SC 100.1:262-63).

have the succession of the church from the apostles and among whom abides sound and irreproachable conduct and purity and incorruption in word (Titus 2:8)."[52]

Such gifted presbyters preserve the church's faith in the one God, increase its love for the Son of God, and honor the Spirit who inspired the patriarchs and prophets, by correctly explaining the Scriptures.[53] For Irenaeus, the gifted presbyters fulfill the mandate of apostles, prophets, and teachers in the sense that they: (1) hold and preserve the apostles' doctrine, the church's faith; (2) proclaim that doctrine founded upon the prophets; and (3) explain the Scriptures.[54] The *charisma veritatis*, this grace of the Spirit upon presbyters within the church, enables them to proclaim and explain from the Scriptures that which is apostolic. In this way they are within the line of continuity with the prophets and apostles, but they are teachers. Or, as we see in our next passage, disciples.

In 3.24.1 Irenaeus contrasts, again, the heretics and the church in their different teachings on God, Christ, and redemptive history. The church's faith, in his view, has received harmonious testimony from the "prophets, apostles, and all the disciples," those who have preserved the faith "through the beginning, the middle, and the end." The three divisions refer in his mind to the three divisions of the progressive impartation of truth to the church. The prophets of the beginning indicate the Old Testament. The apostles of the middle period indicate those of the New Testament. The disciples of the end are the presbyters and those who follow the apostles' teaching by following the presbyters.[55] The true faith does not

52. *AH* 4.26.5 (SC 100.2:278.115-22; ANF 1:498). Cf. Thomas F. Torrance, "Early Patristic Interpretation of the Holy Scriptures," in *Divine Meaning: Studies in Patristic Hermeneutics* (Edinburgh: T. & T. Clark, 1995), p. 129.

53. For the trinitarian structure, cf. van den Eynde, pp. 185-86.

54. J. Bentivegna, "The Charismatic Dossier of Saint Irenaeus," *Studia Patristica* 18, no. 3 (1989): 46-47.

55. "Disciples" of the apostles, for Irenaeus, has four references: (1) Luke and Mark, who wrote Gospels as followers of Paul and Peter but were not apostles (*AH* 3.3.1; 3.9.1; 3.10.1; 3.10.6; 3.11.1; 3.12.1); (2) others (presbyters) who had seen and heard the apostles but were not evangelists (cf. 4.32.1; 5.5.1; 5.33.1; 5.36.2); (3) followers of the apostles, also named presbyters, who learned from those who had seen and heard the apostles (cf. 4.27.1); (4) the spiritual disciples, those who read Scripture along with the presbyters but are not presbyters (cf. 4.32.1–33.1). In 3.24.1 Irenaeus has (2), (3), and (4) in mind, contra Rousseau, SC 210:388, who sees them as (1). Irenaeus goes on to cite 1 Cor. 12:28 in support of postapostolic, i.e., post–New Testament, continuity within the church.

stall with the apostles. It continues to prosper through the apostles' disciples. He cites 1 Corinthians 12:28 in order to support this thesis. *In the church, by the vivifying, gifting presence of the Spirit, itself a gift from God* (John 4:10), the faith of the prophets, apostles, and disciples is preserved and renewed.[56] The reason is that there are those within the church, presbyters and others, who have been gifted in all appropriate ways: "For 'in the church,' it is said, 'God has appointed apostles, prophets, teachers' (1 Cor. 12:28) and all the other working of the Spirit (1 Cor. 12:11), of which all those who do not unite with the church, but deprive themselves of life by their evil doctrines and their depraved conduct, are not partakers. For where the church is, there is the Spirit of God, and where the Spirit of God is, there is the church and all grace; and the Spirit is truth (1 John 5:6)."[57]

What is of paramount importance for our purposes here, is to recognize that ultimately for Irenaeus the certainty of truth in the church is a matter of succession, "yet his strongest conviction, however difficult it may be to describe, was that it was a succession in the Divine Spirit."[58] M. A. Donovan concurs. For her, in Irenaeus "the role of the Spirit must never be underestimated. In the Irenaean perspective the bishops succeed to the apostles through the gift of the Spirit."[59] While the church has its authoritative teaching presbyters, this order does not supplant the Spirit in Irenaeus. This order is the Holy Spirit implementing his own government: "The governance of the Holy Spirit, given by the risen Christ to His church, is implemented through the working that the Spirit of God demonstrates in those whom God has placed in the church, first apostles, secondly prophets, thirdly teachers."[60]

Ultimately, then, in the matters of ecclesiastical authority and truth, one must think pneumatologically. After providing a survey of the Irenaean images of the Spirit in the church in his discussion of *Against*

---

56. Cf. Rousseau, SC 210:390-93. This corrects E. Molland's interpretation that *Dei munus* in 3.24.1 (SC 211:472.17; ANF 1:458) is to be read as the "church's preaching" or "our faith." This interpretation contributed to his understanding of the *charisma veritatis* as the "deposit of faith" (Molland, p. 26). He was following Müller, p. 218. Bentivegna, p. 43, concurs.

57. *AH* 3.24.1 (SC 211:472.22–474.29; ANF 1:458).

58. Ehrhardt, p. 124.

59. Mary Ann Donovan, *One Right Reading? A Guide to Irenaeus* (Collegeville, Minn.: Liturgical Press, 1997), p. 65.

60. Bentivegna, p. 46.

Heresies 3.24.1, Bentivegna gives a pointed conclusion: "For all these reasons the Holy Spirit, that the Lord conferred upon the church, must be considered as the real governor of the church."[61]

Yet one cannot think pneumatologically for Irenaeus without thinking ecclesiologically. His reading of Ephesians 4:15-16 makes this clear in complement to his reading of 1 Corinthians 12:28. His quotation of the Pauline word occurs in 4.32.1 in definition of the "spiritual disciple," or the accurate Bible reader. In contrast to the heretics, the spiritual Bible reader reads with a prejudice of faith: there is one God who created all things through the agency of his Word as is announced by Moses, John's Gospel, and Paul (Gen. 1:3; John 1:3; Eph. 4:5-6). The reader with this faith confesses one head of the church, Christ, and the ultimate unity of the diverse testimonies to him. Such a disciple "holds to the head [of the body] from whom the whole body, joined and entwined by every joint with which it is furnished, according to the measure of each part, makes bodily growth for the edification of itself in love."[62]

For Irenaeus "each part" refers to the Old Testament prophets. "Each one" *(unusquisque)* of them gave partial testimony to the one and only Christ in a unique manner. Each testimony when taken together with the others forms a whole which proclaims Christ in type and anticipation.[63] But there is another referent for "each part": Irenaeus intends the various members of the church whose gifted testimonies are equally necessary to the unity and maturity of the church, namely, the apostles, presbyters, and spiritual disciples (cf. Eph. 4:11-12). The heretics divide the prophetic words and split and pervert the one God and the one Word. But the spiritual reader clings to the prejudice of unity, a prejudice delivered by the apostles to the presbyters. When such a person reads Scripture, all its parts will be understood as consistent with each other. Behind this confidence stands the framework of prophet, apostle, and ecclesiological presbyter, a framework of theological and christological unity. The true disciple reads the Bible with an eye to the words of the presbyters because they have the doctrine of the apostles, which is in accord with the prophetic announcement.

But what is it that provides confidence in each of these parts which

---

61. Bentivegna, p. 44.

62. *AH* 4.32.1 (SC 100.2:798.24-27; ANF 1:506).

63. *AH* 4.33.10 (SC 100.2:822.170–824.189; ANF 1:509). See especially SC 100.2:824.178, 186.

the head uses to nurture his body? Once again we are back to the Spirit. The Spirit has been superintending the prophet, the apostle, and the presbyter; the prophecies of the future, the explanations of the present, and the interpretations of the past: "Such a disciple who is truly spiritual, because he has received the Spirit of God who was with humanity from the beginning in all the economies of God, predicted the future, declared the present and fully explained the past, 'Judges all and himself is judged by no one' [1 Cor. 2:15]."[64] The disciple who reads the Bible in accordance with the church's reading, that of the presbyters, reads it in a manner continuous with the apostles (and prophets). Both have been given to the church as parts, which, within their measure, contribute to bodily growth. The spiritual disciple also makes a contribution and is preserved from judgment, for his interpretation is true.

In this way the spiritual disciple "holds to the head" by viewing things as the Lord himself did. The Lord, the Word, "united the beginning to the end, being the Lord of both."[65] The continuity of revelatory history is a *sine qua non* of Christianity for the bishop of Lyons. The church must imitate Christ, "the body following the head."[66]

Irenaeus is reading Ephesians 4:15-16 within the context of the chapter, particularly 4:5-6, 4:11, and 4:14, and in light of 1 Corinthians 2:15. The theological and christological bias of unity is informed by Ephesians 4:5, 6, which he cites. When he thinks of the prophets, apostles, and disciples as the parts which contribute to the body's growth, he is casting his eye upon Ephesians 4:11: "And his gifts were that some should be apostles, some prophets, some evangelists, some pastors and teachers." And we are to understand that his attraction to the passage in a context where he is opposing the false doctrine of the heretics is influenced by Ephesians 4:14. This verse speaks of the protection the church receives from deceitful doctrine by virtue of the maturity gained through the gifted members referred to in Ephesians 4:11.

In unity with many patristic interpretations, Irenaeus takes the prophets of Ephesians 4:11 as Old Testament prophets. This view is largely rejected today. Yet Irenaeus's main point is the importance of listening to the voice of the "gifted ones" within the church in one's own Bible reading.

---

64. *AH* 4.33.1 (SC 100.2:802.1-5; ANF 1:506).
65. *AH* 4.34.4 (SC 100.2:858.105-7; ANF 1:512).
66. *AH* 4.34.4 (SC 100.2:860.117; ANF 1:512).

Those attentive to the Spirit within the gifted community become spiritual themselves.

The Free Church and the Early Church

It is in the Irenaean vision of the Spirit's gift within the community led by the presbyters that I find a helpful and biblical corrective to both individualistic and communitarian solipsism. Evangelicals in their Bible reading need the influence of the community past and present because there the Spirit resides. Christ has gifted the community with teachers who by the Spirit's enablement see and proclaim the meaning of Scripture in continuity with the prophets and apostles. Members of the free church may not wish to identify with Irenaeus's episcopal or presbyterial confidence, but they must join him in his pneumatological-ecclesiological confidence. The evangelical's optimism must never be in a method, ancient or modern. Nor should the evangelical be overcome with an anthropological confidence or confidence in a milieu. Any suspicion directed toward the results of ancient exegesis must also be directed toward contemporary methods.[67] To be truly evangelical, to be truly free, is to be pneumatologically oriented. This means to recognize what the Spirit is bringing forth through gifted teachers in the present; it also means recognizing what the Spirit has brought forth in the past. The focus on the Spirit within such gifted teachers defeats any notion of solipsism, for it is an interest outside of either "me, now" or "us, now." Evangelicals within the free church must go to tradition in order to look for the gift within others. They must journey to the exegesis of the past in search of the Spirit's fruit. And where is the gift of the Spirit? In the church. In the community, both of today and yesterday. As Irenaeus wrote:

> For where the church is, there is the Spirit of God, and where the Spirit of God is, there is the church and all grace; and the Spirit is truth (1 John 5:6).

---

67. Cf. Goldingay, p. 239; Michael Cahill, "The History of Exegesis and Our Theological Future," *Theological Studies* 61 (2000): 344-45. Cahill relates the renewed interest in the history of exegesis to postmodernism. I would hope evangelicals would return to the history of interpretation because to do so is essentially Christian.

The Correction of the Augustinians:
A Case Study in the Critical Appropriation
of a Suspect Tradition

GERALD W. SCHLABACH

Accordingly, dear reader, whenever you are as certain about something as I am go forward with me; whenever you stick equally fast seek with me; whenever you notice that you have gone wrong come back to me; or that I have, call me back to you. In this way let us set out along the Way of Charity together, making for him of whom it is said, Seek his face always.

Augustine, *On the Trinity* 1.5

Corresponding in 408 with two dear friends who were renowned for having abandoned their aristocratic Roman wealth and privileges in order to live out Jesus' gospel imperatives, Augustine accepted their gentle correction. Paulinus of Nola and his wife Therasia had insisted that they discuss this life rather than speculate on the next. Yes, Augustine now agreed, this was the really difficult question. For surely "we must die, in a gospel sense, by a voluntary departure, withdrawing ourselves, not by death, but by deliberate resolution, from the life of this world." Yet his very duties as a bishop required him to enter judiciously into the very lifestyle he had tried to flee. Only by doing so might he help others to find their true welfare by learning "to live by dying" and to prosper by renouncing the passing attractions of this life. But his dilemma was that frivolous luxuries would tempt him if he participated too enthusiastically, though subtle pride would tempt him if he renounced too decisively.[1]

Another burden was even greater: his own exercise of fraternal correction. Simply to correct fellow Christian teachers was tricky enough. But the pastoral duty in applying church discipline was even more arduous. Bishops of the day spent much of their time arbitrating conflicts in their communities, often playing a role among their parishioners that was increasingly like that of a judge in civil cases.[2] When Augustine turned to Scripture for guidance, he found injunctions both to judge well and to judge not, to rebuke publicly and to meet with offenders in private. The biblical way itself seemed to involve unceasing tensions. And his greatest difficulty arose when it came time to apply sanctions. Even with no motive except the spiritual welfare of those he must judge, he could never be quite sure when harshness would embitter rather than sober them, nor when leniency would evoke grateful repentance rather than complacency.[3] How to adjust punishment rightly was a "deep and dark" question, and "I confess that I make mistakes daily in regard to this."[4]

Free church thinkers suspect much worse when it comes to disciplinary matters. Augustine's way of correcting and punishing fellow Christians, after all, came to include recourse to the sword of civil authority. At the root of free church dissent from mainstream branches of Western Christianity, which developed by claiming the mantle of Augustinianism, is the conviction that Augustine's way of correcting and punishing fellow Christians was not just a workaday mistake but a fundamental one. Unless his "correction" is itself correctable, then, his legacy must remain suspect. That legacy includes his robust witness to God's grace, his poignant cri-

---

1. Augustine, *Letter* 95.1-2.

2. Fredrick van der Meer, *Augustine the Bishop: Religion and Society at the Dawn of the Middle Ages*, trans. Brian Battershaw and G. R. Lamb (New York: Harper Torchbooks/The Cathedral Library, 1961), pp. 258-67. "Almost unnoticed, the bishop had become a city judge, and the powers which his predecessors had exercised during the persecution by virtue of Church law and apostolic tradition now had behind them the weight of a vastly increased authority, for the bishop's decisions were now binding under the civil law. . . . Perhaps this was the most burdensome part of his office." For a summary of the kinds of cases Augustine dealt with, see pp. 260-61.

3. For an example of Augustine's struggle to find the proper and redemptive balance, see *Letter* 209.

4. Augustine, *Letter* 95.3-4.

tique of human arrogance, and his supple doctrine of Christian love. If correction is not mutual, therefore, the loss will be mutual.

A Matter of Humility, Not Pride

To be sure, an Augustine pulled as he was between a desire for a holy life in a wholly Christian subculture and a call into relationship with the worldly for the sake of evangelism and pastoral care suddenly seems a fruitful conversation partner. Free church communities know well the continuing struggle to discern a faithful stance within the host societies where they live as resident aliens. Even if they should eventually part with him on some matters or many, to linger over his own struggles might prove instructive.

In fact, careful study of Augustine suggests that on a surprising number of points he may even turn out to be an ally and fellow pilgrim.[5] Augustine has deeply influenced Western Christian ways of relating church to society and state, for example, although he did more to frame the problem than resolve it. His most definitive word on the subject was that Christians must think of themselves as Jeremiah's exiles, living in Babylon, seeking the peace and well-being of their host society yet resisting its imperial claims upon their loyalty.[6] If some of Augustine's own policies and practices tended to collapse the critical tension in such a social stance, and if later developments within Western Christendom amount to a series of failed experiments at negotiating the tension, then the unfinished nature of his political ecclesiology leaves plenty of room for internal critique.

In many ways Augustinianism is not so much a settled doctrinal system as a field of tensions. Anyone who defines Augustinianism too neatly will probably get it wrong. Still, a working definition is possible if we accent rather than suppress the tensions it holds together. Augustine coupled a trenchant indictment of human responsibility for sin and evil with thor-

---

5. So I have argued, for example, in "Augustine's Hermeneutic of Humility: An Alternative to Moral Imperialism and Moral Relativism," *Journal of Religious Ethics* 22, no. 2 (1994): 299-330; "Deuteronomic or Constantinian: What Is the Most Basic Problem for Christian Social Ethics?" in *The Wisdom of the Cross: Essays in Honor of John Howard Yoder*, ed. Stanley Hauerwas, Chris K. Huebner, Harry Huebner, and Mark Thiessen Nation (Grand Rapids: Eerdmans, 1999), pp. 449-71.

6. Augustine, *City of God* 19.26.

oughgoing reliance on God to heal the human will through grace. He coupled the sovereignty of God's grace with confidence that moral transformation can begin in this life. He evoked a poignant vision of human beings restless to know and love the great and mysterious God of all creation, along with an unexpected vision of a God whose greatness appears most evocatively of all in the earthy, bloodied humility of Jesus Christ. In the Trinity itself — which as doctrine seems like a cluster of tensions all its own — he saw the revelation of God's own mutually self-giving love as the very secret of community at the core of all reality. And if the community called church remains a mass of still-sinful Christians, Augustine nonetheless held that view in eschatological tension with his faith that the church is already the body of Christ, participating in the very trinitarian life of God as member loves member in mutual love.

At least in the West, and at least indirectly, Augustine has probably influenced any Christian who wrestles with such convictions, for it is he who did so much to sharpen them. In some such sense, free church Christians sometimes are more Augustinian than they may know. By contrast, thinkers in mainstream churches of Western Christianity — Roman Catholic, Lutheran, and Calvinist, especially — recognize the authoritative role that Augustine's thought has played in the formation of their own theologies. These I will call traditional Augustinians. To grapple with their theologies is also to grapple with Augustine's legacy.

One reason for free church thinkers to enter self-consciously into contention over the Augustinian legacy is simply to appropriate his thought more carefully when they do, and to critique him more knowledgeably when they must. For pragmatic reasons if no other, going to the source and learning to grapple with Augustine himself may better prepare free church thinkers to make the case for their own theologies in ecumenical debate. But there is more. For those who linger over his texts, the poignancy of Augustine's vision of God and human beings longing mutually for community, amid the tragedies and sufferings of a good creation marred by sin, has a power of its own. Ultimately, reasons of heart rather than pragmatism may argue for them to consider the very substance of his thought.

Free church thinkers will not want to appropriate or ally themselves at every point, of course. For there remains the matter of correction. In much of his writing on fraternal correction, Augustine seems far less circumspect or humble than he did in his letter to Paulinus and Therasia. After all, he extended the logic of such correction beyond his own flock in hopes of drawing rival Donatist Christians into catholic unity. And for the sake of their correction he rationalized recourse to imperial sanctions that put the proud sword of the state in the service of the church. *On the Correction of the Donatists* is a name editors have applied to letter number 185 in the collected works of Augustine as though it were a formal treatise.[7] He wrote that letter in 417 to the Roman military official Boniface in order to overcome any scruples the nominal Christian might have about using his imperial power to "compel them [the Donatists] to come in." Augustine's use of Luke 14:22-23 to rationalize such compulsion was as forced as it was fateful for later centuries.[8] Perhaps Augustine was still overcoming his own scruples, not just those of Boniface. He had once opposed state sanctions, in part because he feared an influx of false catholics who would be a pastoral headache.[9]

On other matters, Christians in the free church tradition will assess Augustine in divergent ways. As they debate doctrines of free will and grace among themselves, free churches alternately move toward and away from Augustine. Certainly they differ markedly from one another in their assessment of Augustine's just war theory, and too many have been lured into harnessing the power of the state for Christian causes. But to be part of the free church tradition and to understand its ecclesiology is implicitly to agree on this much: when Augustine involved the imperial Roman state in "the correction of the Donatists" in hopes of healing the split between North African Christians, he was wrong — wrong enough that it has been necessary to form new and independent church communities in order to correct the legacy of his kind of "correction."

Nevertheless, there is deep Christian wisdom worth drawing from Augustine's theology. But the challenge inherent in any free church appropriation of patristic thought comes into especially stark focus with Augustine. Appropriating patristic thought fairly, charitably, yet selectively requires in Augustine's case that we read him against himself, yet not gratuitously or through forced readings. To take up such a challenge in the presence of one of the most complex and influential Christian thinkers ever, might in fact be altogether too formidable, or even arrogant.

---

7. Augustine, *The Correction of the Donatists*, Nicene and Post-Nicene Fathers, 1st. ser., 4:29-51.

8. See, for example, *Letters* 93.2.5; 173.10, and *Correction of the Donatists* (= *Letter* 185) 6.24.

9. Augustine, *Letter* 93.5.16-17 to Vicentius.

And yet Augustine himself was at his best when he exercised his own capacity for self-correction. Likewise, the ensuing tradition of Augustinianism has been at its best when it too has shown itself capable of self-correction. For free church interpreters to enter into Augustinian debate bearing their critique is not only possible but renders a needed service. Given the vast influence of Augustine upon many streams of Christian thought through the centuries, correcting every Augustinian theology one by one would obviously be a preposterous and presumptuous project, if that were what we meant by "the correction of the Augustinians." Rather, the intent is to examine what Augustine's approach to correction has sometimes meant, has too often meant, and could yet mean. Such a project is not triumphalistic, but rather a plea to renounce any kind of Augustinian triumphalism. For the humbler, mutually vulnerable mode of correcting fellow Christians that free churches have proposed as a corrective for Augustine's way may well nurture the greatest sustaining virtue of the Augustinian tradition.[10] Of course, this does require openness by free church thinkers to learn from Augustine and the Augustinians too.

Augustinianism as a Self-Correcting Tradition

Once one notices how seldom church historians, theologians, and philosophers stop to define what they mean by "Augustinianism," that very feature may become one of the most intriguing features of his legacy. Maybe they cannot do so, at least neatly. Augustine himself did not provide the well-ordered, finely outlined doctrinal account that some think necessary to

10. For sixteenth-century Anabaptist statements on fraternal correction, see Balthasar Hubmaier, "On Fraternal Admonition" (1527), in *Balthasar Hubmaier: Theologian of Anabaptism*, ed. H. Wayne Pipkin and John H. Yoder (Scottdale, Pa.: Herald, 1989), pp. 372-85; Pilgram Marpeck, "Judgment and Decision," in *The Writings of Pilgram Marpeck*, ed. and trans. William Klassen and Walter Klaassen (Kitchener, Ont., and Scottdale, Pa.: Herald, 1978), pp. 309-61; Menno Simons, "A Kind Admonition on Church Discipline," in *The Complete Writings of Menno Simons*, ed. John Christian Wenger, trans. Leonard Verduin (Scottdale, Pa.: Herald, 1956), pp. 407-18. For twentieth-century Mennonite treatments, see John Howard Yoder, "Binding and Loosing," in *The Royal Priesthood: Essays Ecclesiological and Ecumenical*, ed. Michael G. Cartwright (Grand Rapids: Eerdmans, 1994), pp. 323-58; Marlin Jeschke, *Disciplining in the Church: Recovering a Ministry of the Gospel*, 3rd ed. (Scottdale, Pa.: Herald, 1988); John Driver, *Community and Commitment* (Scottdale, Pa.: Herald, 1976), pp. 40-53.

have an adequate theology in the first place. To identify his system exactly has proven elusive. A restless searcher before he became an authoritative Christian teacher, he continued to search restlessly throughout his career. As his thought developed, many themes recurred, sometimes as abiding preoccupations and sometimes as stable convictions, but often in tension with each other. In the memorable image of one leading interpreter, James J. O'Donnell, the recurring themes in Augustine are jazzlike riffs, and the music of this theology holds together more through the studied improvisation of a Miles Davis than the architectonic design of a Mozart, or a Thomas Aquinas, or a John Calvin.[11] For every conviction in Augustine that was secure enough for some later interpreter to call it the essence of Augustinianism, careful readers will note a counterpoint.

Admittedly, to present Augustine's thought as a jazzlike interplay of riffs, or as a field of tensions, is a modern or even postmodern approach that departs from the tendency of influential Augustinians in the past to build or impose tight systems upon his thought. Yet our very hindsight allows us to notice that as rival Augustinianisms have attempted to build their own systems on select themes that he himself held in tension, their debate itself has tended to constitute a self-correcting tradition that has carried forward his jazzlike legacy. Different ages have chosen their own Augustines and formed variant Augustinianisms all along.[12] In the early medieval period, the monks who did so much to keep Christian learning alive valued Augustine above all as an interpreter of Scripture. Later, high medieval Scholasticism valued him as a source for metaphysics and ethics. Medieval mystics and theologians generally stressed with Augustine that the love of God must unify the loves and life of any human creature whom God's grace is transforming. Protestant Reformers, however, found in Augustine's refutation of his contemporary Pelagius a precedent for their own rejection of justification through works righteousness. Nineteenth-

---

11. James J. O'Donnell, "The Authority of Augustine," *Augustinian Studies* 22 (1991): 28-29.

12. Since Augustine himself did not provide a definitive, essential summary of Augustinianism, one at least might expect to find comparative studies of how different centuries and traditions have appropriated him. But that too is a surprisingly neglected question — and all the more so in light of Augustine's thoroughgoing influence. Thankfully, a surge of Augustine studies in the last decades has recently borne fruit in a new encyclopedia which at least allows for working comparisons: see Allan D. Fitzgerald, ed., *Augustine through the Ages: An Encyclopedia* (Grand Rapids: Eerdmans, 1999).

century Protestant thinkers took renewed interest in Augustinian piety and subjective interiority. The twentieth century saw a renewed interest in Augustine's political insights, though without reaching a consensus.

To be sure, there have been some constant themes within the various Augustinianisms. Throughout the centuries the priority that Augustine placed on grace has consistently obtained among all who have taken his thought seriously. Nonetheless, predestination, which he considered an inexorable implication of grace, has received a more mixed reception. And the priority that Augustine placed on God's grace has not always saved him from austere moralists who, by citing him for their own purposes, have helped exaggerate his reputation as the archetypical authority figure of Western Christianity. In reaction, many circles confirm Augustine's influence backhandedly by identifying him mainly with some particular teaching (on sexuality, original sin, predestination, coercion, or just war) and then blaming him for the perversion of Western Christianity as a whole, without always reading him as a whole.

Given the rich web of convictions that Augustine held in tension, no one can interpret or teach him without proposing some system to show how his thought coheres. Yet interpretation always risks imposing upon Augustine himself and muting many of his themes. Writing in 1902, Eugène Portalié placed Augustine's teachings into an order that followed the overarching structure of Aquinas's *Summa theologiae* with suspicious fidelity.[13] Meanwhile, Benjamin B. Warfield, the early twentieth-century defender of Calvinist orthodoxy, argued that Augustine's doctrine of grace stood in conflict with his doctrine of the church, which controlled the dispensation of grace through sacraments until the Reformation vanquished the latter doctrine in favor of the former.[14] The influential neo-orthodox Protestant thinker Reinhold Niebuhr sometimes portrayed his own work as a recovery of Augustine's orthodox doctrine of sin and human limitation in the face of misguided liberal optimism about human perfectibility.[15] But by his own admission, Niebuhr long neglected a doc-

13. Eugène Portalié, *A Guide to the Thought of Saint Augustine,* trans. Ralph J. Bastian (Chicago: H. Regnery Co., 1960).

14. Benjamin Breckinridge Warfield, *Calvin and Augustine* (Philadelphia: Presbyterian and Reformed, 1956), p. 322, cited by Jaroslav Pelikan, *The Mystery of Continuity: Time and History, Memory and Eternity in the Thought of Saint Augustine* (Charlottesville: University Press of Virginia, 1986), p. 148.

15. Reinhold Niebuhr, "Reply to Interpretation and Criticism" and "Intellectual Auto-

trine of grace that would correspond to his doctrine of sin.[16] And so it goes.

The diverse contrapuntal shape that Augustine's legacy has taken suggests that free church thinkers too can join in on the long debate that we might best think of as constituting "Augustinianism." Certainly when free church interpreters enter the arena, they can expect that any retrieval of his thought for the sake of constructive theology will need to be selective. But by now it should be clear that this has always been true, even when avowed Augustinians have written as though they were thinking Augustine's own thoughts.

Subtly or frankly, even the most respectful interpreters of Augustine have admitted the need to appropriate his thought selectively. Balanced and irenic toward Catholic and Protestant traditions alike, Jaroslav Pelikan agreed that Warfield was right, and that Christians must choose as the Reformation did between various ways of being in continuity with Augustine, depending on whether one emphasizes his doctrine of grace or his doctrines of sacrament and church.[17] Striving on the other hand to insist that Protestants have been wrong to see contradictions in Augustine's theology, Portalié nonetheless closed his presentation with a diplomatically worded admission that while Augustine's doctrine stands intact and eminently Catholic, this is thanks to later clarifications of its more subtle points by later theologians and church councils.[18] Recent interpreters are far bolder. In one chapter of a collection by philosophers entitled *The Augustinian Tradition*, William E. Mann noted that since Augustine has left us "a provocative framework of concepts and vivid examples" rather than "a tidy set of normative principles," his posterity has "some freedom to speculate about the ways in which the framework might be fleshed out; perhaps,

---

biography," in *Reinhold Niebuhr: His Religious, Social, and Political Thought*, ed. Charles W. Kegley and Robert W. Bretall (New York: Macmillan, 1956); Reinhold Niebuhr, *Human Nature*, vol. 1 of *The Nature and Destiny of Man* (1941) (New York: Scribner's, 1964), p. 49.

16. Against charges that he had been preoccupied with original sin, Niebuhr wrote: "I must plead guilty to this charge in the sense that it was a long time before I paid as much attention to the Christian conception of the cure as to the diagnosis, to 'grace' as well as to sin" ("Intellectual Autobiography," p. 10).

17. Pelikan, *The Mystery of Continuity*, pp. 146-48; Pelikan, *The Emergence of the Catholic Tradition (100-600)*, vol. 1 of *The Christian Tradition: A History of the Development of Doctrine* (Chicago: University of Chicago Press, 1971), pp. 330-31.

18. Portalié, pp. 93-94, 328-29.

with some caution, even about how the bones of the framework might be differently reconstructed."[19]

Far from distorting Augustine's thought, such candid willingness to contest him may be the most fitting way to appropriate his wisdom, for it invites the kind of self-correcting discourse that best reflects his own. Constant conversation and controversy shaped Augustine's theological development, after all. Trained as a professor of rhetoric, Augustine debated with friends, colleagues, opponents. One controversy or another occasioned most of his writings. Over the years, however, Augustine's most important interlocutor was himself. At his most critical juncture, he had even been his own most important opponent.

Doctrines, Puzzles, and Causing Love

As important as was controversy for shaping Augustine's thought, he was not simply torn by every wind of contrary doctrine. Nor was the resolution that unified his thought simply doctrinal. As a young man, Augustine had been torn above all by his own divided loves. The unity he sought was first of all integrity of person through the reorientation and healing of his love. Thus we will find the unity of his thought not so much in his doctrinal synthesis as in his narrative quest.

Augustine's was a lifelong quest to love rightly — to find and experience the fullness of salvation through a love of God that reoriented every other possible human love, and then to convince others to do the same. The doctrines in which he was most secure, the tensions by which he thrived, the puzzles he left unresolved, and even the temptations into which he arguably fell all responded in some way to this quest. The Thomistic philosopher Étienne Gilson recognized this when he admitted that the order to Augustine's thought was not the "synthetic, linear order displayed by doctrines which follow the process of the intellect"; rather Augustine's method of exposition was "necessarily different because it is suited to a doctrine whose center is grace and charity." Augustine's task therefore was "not so much to cause knowledge as to cause love."[20]

---

19. William E. Mann, "Inner-Life Ethics," in *The Augustinian Tradition,* ed. Gareth B. Matthews (Berkeley: University of California Press, 1998), p. 141.

20. If the order of Augustine's thought was not synthetic and linear, Gilson discerned

To stress the central place of *caritas* (charity or right Christian love) in Augustine's thought is not to impose an order but to apply a hermeneutical key that he himself supplied and invited. In *Confessions* 10.3.3 he noted that his readers would only understand what he was up to if they themselves read his confessions with charity. And in the closing pages of the first book of *On Christian Doctrine*, Augustine argued that to build up Christian love is the goal and sum of Scripture, and thus the key to understanding and teaching faithful Christian doctrine.[21] This conviction operated at every level of Augustine's thought — in his own narrative quest, in his interpretation of Scripture, in his most refined philosophical arguments, in his conceptions of both the cosmos and the human condition. No Augustinianism can claim to be in continuity with Augustine himself if it subordinates this one theme, line of inquiry, and teaching that arguably shaped all others.

Key to Augustine's very quest to love rightly was its very failure. It wound its way though the death of a best friend, the unreliability of most friendships, the problematics of sexuality, the fleeting satisfactions of ambition, and his thwarted pursuit of wisdom itself. What he began to learn was a lesson he could not live: every human love, to be right, must find its stability and orientation in love for God. Through his own efforts, however, he was unable to love God, except perhaps fleetingly and from across a distant abyss. Thwarting his love for God was opposition from the many competing loves that tore his heart in contrary directions, but for which he himself was responsible. He, least of all, could heal himself. For when the divided self exercises its disintegrated will, it can only will by reproducing its own fragmentation. And the very effort at self-correction through his own intellect and will confirmed his deepest human rebellion, the pride by which we seek to save or secure ourselves independently of God. This is the pride that God exposed and began to heal by coming to us in the jarring humility of Jesus Christ, "the Godhead at our feet," sharing our very clay in weakness.[22]

We will best understand, weigh, and order his most famously Augus-

---

something more like a wheel with a center: the natural order of an Augustinian doctrine is to branch out around one center, and this is precisely the order of charity. Étienne Gilson, *The Christian Philosophy of Saint Augustine* (New York: Random House, 1960), pp. 236-37.

21. Augustine, *On Christian Doctrine* 1.36.40.

22. Augustine, *Confessions* 7.18.24. Most of this paragraph summarizes arguments and analyses in book 8 of the *Confessions*.

tinian "doctrines" if we narrate their unfolding in continuity with this quest. If they seem to cohere, and if some systematic ordering is possible, that will be because Augustine was trying "not so much to cause knowledge as to cause love." If they sometimes seem puzzling, at odds, or in tension, that may be because the causes of love are always complex and often a mystery. If they seem at points to err, that may well be because the effort "to cause love" so easily goes awry when it departs from the gracious way of love that Augustine himself had encountered in the mystery of Christ's incarnation.

In particular, Augustine's own quest to love rightly provides an authentic way of ordering key Augustinian doctrines concerning (1) sin, (2) grace, (3) the order of love, (4) the mystery of the Trinity, (5) the church as the body of Christ, (6) the pilgrim life, and (7) free will and predestination. Such an ordering does not impose a system because it corresponds to the way that each developing conviction led Augustine existentially to new questions. But if questions remain hanging on (8) the political character of the church, it is precisely these that free church thinkers find themselves compelled to contest.

1. Sin

Human beings were responsible for evil, yet they should not be so proud as to imagine that they are able to free themselves of the consequences of their sin by themselves. Already quite early in Augustine's career, these two poles of tension begin to emerge in his conceptions of sin, evil, and the human condition. Augustine's early journey had passed through the secret society of Manichaeism, until a late version of Platonism removed him from the grip of their heresies and led him almost to Christian faith. Perhaps the Manichees had helped sensitize Augustine to suffering, but they had also given him ways to evade responsibility for evil by blaming it on material existence itself. The Platonists led him to see that the created world is good, while evil is simply the privation of good or a disorder among goods. They also deepened his love for the one God in whom all things might find unity, though even they could not teach him to do more than long for union with the divine. At best he might love God for a brief contemplative moment, only to fall back into his usual cacophony of competing loves. And so Augustine indicted Platonists too, for their greatest philosophical achievements only confirmed their deeper sin of pride, as they fantasized themselves able to ascend to God through their own will and intellect.

2. Grace

Thus Augustine's quest to love rightly is what exposed the problem of will, which cannot heal itself and come to love rightly. The problem of will in turn demonstrated the priority of God's grace in all human transformation. To fully grasp the lesson of his own conversion, Augustine needed some eight years, the crisis of finding himself a still-fallible bishop, and a fresh reading of Paul. But from then on God's grace was a stable reference point in all he wrote about the limits and possibilities for human transformation in the loves of any Christian, in the church, and in human society. Even so, his reflections on these themes proceeded as a series of developing questions more often than as a sequence of stable propositions. For example, is predestination the necessary corollary to a robust doctrine of grace? If so, what keeps it from undermining human responsibility? The doctrine of original sin provided one answer but opened up other problems, such as the meaning of God's justice and the status of sexuality. When push came to shove, Augustine always pursued whichever teaching seemed necessary to affirm the sovereign priority of God's grace, and yet he never entirely let go of untidy counterconvictions. He expected moral transformation to begin in this life even if life could not complete it, and he expected preacher and parishioner alike to participate in the process.

3. The Order of Love

Augustine had discovered that for any love of creatures to be right, it must find its orientation "in God," the source of every creature's life and goodness.[23] To love any creature rightly was to desire and help it recognize its good in relation to God, within the ecology of right relationships among all creatures that God created it to fulfill. Augustine's vision of love requires an eschatology that looks forward to the state in which "God will be

---

23. See book 4 of the *Confessions*, especially 4.10.15; 4.12.18-19.

all in all"[24] as all creatures love all others through the love of God. What is true in love for neighbor is true for the self on one hand and the enemy on the other: the good that we seek when we love neighbor, self, or enemy is not a private good of each one's willful and egocentric devising, but participation in the common good of right and mutual relationship with God and all other creatures in God. To know the details of any creature's good often remained a puzzle, however. Augustine's vision of a cosmic order of love provided a coherent framework for his moral arguments and exhortations on issues ranging from war to marriage to treatment of the poor to pastoral duty. Yet a framework for deliberation is not yet a decision. On case after case he must still ask what combination of respect and intervention, or forgiveness and discipline, would change a heart, stop an injustice, or restore mutually loving relationships. And he must "confess that I make mistakes daily in regard to this."[25]

4. Mystery of Trinity

Augustine's doctrine of love is finally his doctrine of the Trinity. Only through the incarnation of Jesus Christ the Mediator do we really know the love of the ungraspable God who created the universe. Only as Christ draws us into his own relationship of mutual love with his Father do we have the power to respond to God's love. The reality of their loving mutuality is for Augustine the very person of the Holy Spirit. Without the mystery of Christ incarnate, God would remain not just mystery but elusive, and God's will would remain sketchy. Without the mystery of the Holy Spirit, we might know of Christ but not participate in the empowering mutual love of Christ and his Father. By showing us what God loves, and how God loves, Jesus Christ fills up the content of love for God, and all other loves "in God." What Augustine recognized, but may not have let weigh heavily enough, is how christocentric his own trinitarian formulation needed to be to cohere, not just in speculative theory, but in loving practice. The humility and nonviolence of God in Jesus Christ had transformed his own life, but he did not always allow that narrative — the nar-

24. 1 Cor. 15:28; cf. Augustine's use of this phrase in *Homilies on the Gospel of John* 65.1; 67.2; 83.3.

25. Augustine, *Letter* 95.3.

rative of Jesus converging also with his own — to transform his reliance on prouder and more violent ways of attempting "to cause love." Reading Augustine's christology back through everything else in his narrative quest may be precisely what requires us to answer some of his questions differently, even while accepting those questions.

5. The Church as the Body of Christ

Further specification of the content of love for God should also continue where the firstfruits of a new creation begin to appear in the community of mutual love. For if believers are members of the body of Christ, and even enemies of Christ could yet become brothers and sisters in Christ,[26] then it would be impossible *not* to love Christ when we love the brother or sister, suffering and rejoicing together as each member suffers or rejoices.[27] In his loftiest preaching, therefore, Augustine could sometimes present the people of believers living as a community of mutual love as the eschatological appearing of God's own mutual, trinitarian love in history.[28] And yet Augustine recognized the gritty realities of church life all too well.

6. The Pilgrim Life

Part of what helped Augustine critique and move beyond Platonic ways of questing for the divine was the interior crisis that coincided with his ordination and early years as a bishop. Truthful teaching had been his passion for years, but was still a kind of avocation. Now it was his solemn responsibility, being charged with the care of other lives, not just his own soul, and with faithful transmission of the orthodox biblical teaching of the whole church, not just his own speculative Christian philosophy. Having felt awe in the presence of a bishop such as Saint Ambrose,[29] he knew himself to be unworthy. He could now confess a stable love of God, yet as he examined

26. Augustine, *Homilies on the Gospel of John* 8.10 and 9.3; cf. 1.11 and 8.4.

27. Augustine, *Ten Homilies on the First Epistle of St. John* 10.3.

28. Cf. Augustine, *Ten Homilies on the First Epistle of St. John* 10.4: to bear one another's burdens (Gal. 6:2) "is the consummation of all our works — love. There is the end, for which and unto which we run our course: when we reach it we shall have rest."

29. Augustine, *Confessions* 5.13.23; 6.3.3.

himself in what may be the most extraordinary part of his *Confessions,* in book 10, the imprint of old loves and habits lingered on. Even under grace, human transformation did not come easily. Recognizing the hidden struggles of his own heart, he could be charitable before the failings of his people. But the job of evoking greater love in them through preaching and adjudication confirmed how far Christians themselves had to go on their pilgrimage. Then when efforts at conciliation with rival Donatist bishops failed and wore him down, the Donatists only seemed to confirm Augustine's deepest objection to their teaching: their dream of a church already pure, unspotted, and unwrinkled was doomed because it was self-contradictory in its very pride.[30] For that sin Augustine had little patience, or so it seemed, for pride could trick him too.

7. Free Will and Predestination

When Augustine, as a mature baptized Christian and a bishop, prayed to God in *Confessions* 10 for the strength of will and self-control that others expected him already to have mastered, he inadvertently set off the most knotty and intractable controversy of his career. Augustine's debate with the monk Pelagius and those who took up his cause is the controversy that has probably interested Protestants most, for it defined many terms of their own debates over grace, free will, original sin, baptism, Christian holiness, predestination, and the relation between human works and God's work of salvation. Pelagius read Augustine's prayer for strength of will as a whining excuse for doing less than God had already given the baptized believer power to do. Augustine read Pelagius's objections as one more instance of the subtle but proud attempt at the self-determination he had already rejected in his own early Platonism and in the rival Donatists. Again we do well to stay oriented in Augustine's narrative in order to retrieve Augustinian thought judiciously. Augustine's convictions on the intransigence of human sin and the absolute human need for God's grace to heal the divided human will grew from his longing to love rightly, not vice versa.[31] Many have seen Augustine's theory of predestination as the flip

---

30. To sense how the Donatist controversy progressively wore Augustine down and tried his patience, compare *Letters* 33, 88, and 93.

31. See especially book 8 of the *Confessions.*

side of his doctrine of grace, but such a view abstracts the logic of his doctrine away from the logic of his narrative. Paradoxically, he as human agent recounted that narrative precisely to evoke love for God in his listeners by persuading them of their own debt to God.[32]

8. Imperial Church or Pilgrim Church?

What some Augustinian rivals have failed to notice is how many of these tensions converged, opened cracks, but could have cohered differently in Augustine's ecclesiastical politics. Ordered narratively and conjointly, Augustinian doctrines lead to continuing questions as often as they settle them. Sin, grace, and the need to unify our loves "in God" lead to more versions of the question of how "to cause love" both in any human will and in the body of Christ: how shall the doctor of grace fulfill his pastoral obligations as a preacher who exhorts moral improvement? If love of neighbor means carrying neighbors to God (*Confessions* 4.12.18) but internal habits and social pressures mire them in resistance to their own true good, what are the means by which Christian leaders ought "to compel them to come in"? Specifically, do these means include imperial sanctions? Augustine confessed that his own will had been healed through the humility of Christ, which had subjugated his stubborn will only in the most paradoxical of ways. So how then could paternalistic domination through human political power heal other wills? If God alone can dominate without pride (10.36.59), and pride is in fact the most fundamental human sin, should the church not renounce all recourse to imperial political domination and the pride by which it threatens and takes human life? Augustinian fields of tension threaten to open up fissures, giving way to contradiction rather than paradox, once we name the question that Augustine had many ways to formulate but never quite did: how can a pilgrim church possibly be an imperial church?

---

32. Even by the logic of Augustine's metaphysical speculations, one may embrace his robust doctrine of grace without committing to predestination, for his own exploration of time and eternity renders the "pre" in predestination wholly mysterious, even nonsensical. At the very least, there is room for a rich debate between rival Augustinianisms.

Augustine's Way of Correcting: A Critique

The exact influence of writings such as Augustine's *Correction of the Donatists* upon the inquisitorial practices and persecutions of later centuries is subject to dispute.[33] What should be indisputable is this: for Augustine to exercise his formidable intellectual and rhetorical skills in order to rationalize imperial involvement in ecclesiastical disputes would have been influential even if every one of his writings on the subject had been lost. For Augustine had many conceptual tools and the clout to take the church in another direction.

These were the very decades in which even a recently "Christianized" Roman Empire was turning out to be a poor investment for Christian hopes. Augustine more than any major Christian thinker since the Constantinian settlement drew back from celebrating the events of the previous century as some kind of fruition of the promised kingdom of God. Rather, he was concluding as he wrote his massive *City of God* following the sack of Rome in 410 that at its core, the earthly city of the Roman Empire remained proud and self-serving, and the church could only make use of the shadowy peace it offered if it was keen to keep its true loyalty elsewhere. In these very same years, however, Augustine's policy toward the rival Donatists was casting shadows on his own emerging sense of how the church might seek the peace of the earthly city even as it sustained undivided loyalty to the heavenly.[34]

Some free church Christians have championed the Donatists as spiritual predecessors.[35] The Donatists insisted that the true church must be

33. Emilien Lamirande, *Church, State, and Toleration: An Intriguing Change of Mind in Augustine* (Villanova, Pa.: Villanova University Press, 1975), pp. 70-73.

34. Arguably, the climax of book 19 of Augustine's *City of God* on the limits and possibilities of earthly peace comes in chapter 26, where Augustine cites Jeremiah's injunction that the Hebrew exiles in Babylon should seek the peace (well-being, *shalom*, or *bonum*) of the city in which they found themselves.

35. Two of the most forthright and prominent articulations of this view are that of Ludwig Keller, *Die Reformation und die älteren Reformparteien in ihrem Zusammenhange* (Leipzig: S. Hirzel, 1885), and Gottfried Arnold, *Unparteyische Kirchen- und Ketzer-Historie von Anfang des Neuen Testaments biss auff das Jahr Christi 1688* (Frankfurt am Main: Bey Thomas Fritsch, 1699), which placed the Donatists in a kind of alternative apostolic succession that included the Waldensians, Cathari, Anabaptists, and so on. Cf. the influential statement by Harold S. Bender, "The Anabaptist Vision," in *The Recovery of the Anabaptist Vision*, ed. Guy F. Hershberger (Scottdale, Pa.: Herald, 1957), p. 36. Bender noted Keller's thesis with-

pure, without spot or wrinkle (Eph. 5:27), as well as persecuted, necessarily small, and unaligned with the emperor. They contested Catholic claims to apostolic succession because some Catholic priests and bishops had offered incense to the emperor and turned over the Scriptures to his forces in order to avoid imprisonment. They contended that current imperial persecution was a sign that they, the persecuted, were the true church. They vehemently claimed North African martyr traditions as their own. They argued that Catholic recourse to the very sword that Jesus had refused in defense of his cause was a sign of apostasy. Valuing unambiguous boundary markers, they refused to recognize Catholic baptisms and required converts to be rebaptized if necessary. Much of this sounds especially familiar to Mennonites, who trace the modern origins of the free church movement through the sixteenth-century Radical Reformation. Interrogators from both Roman Catholic and magisterial Protestant churches accused the Radical Reformers of a renewed Donatism, in fact, and labeled them Anabaptists (Re-Baptizers).

Closer examination of the Donatists discloses that their own record was not quite so pure, however. They do not quite qualify as proto-Anabaptists. The purity they valued was ritual purity more than ethical purity. Their argument that nonalliance with the emperor was a sign of fidelity to the Lordship of Christ came late. Augustine could always object that such claims were disingenuous, for their bishops had been the ones who first asked the emperor Constantine for recognition as the church of North Africa. And when the anti-Christian emperor Julian briefly renewed imperial persecution in the middle of the fourth century, but favored them, they rejoiced. The Donatist leaders with whom Augustine debated did not contest these charges, and they do not seem to have opposed imperial sanctions against recently outlawed pagan temples, rituals, and priests.[36] Nor did they renounce ties to a violent wing of their own movement, the Circumcellions. This guerrilla-like group had apparently arisen to redress economic grievances, but was also known for brutal ambushes

out either approval or refutation, but cited certain Mennonites who accepted it entirely. Menno Simons himself, however, distanced himself from the Donatists and Circumcellions as strenuously as he could; see Menno Simons, "A Pathetic Supplication to All Magistrates," in *The Complete Writings of Menno Simons*, p. 525.

36. Neither did they renounce these actions by the predecessors. Perhaps they recognized that to do so would have undercut their case in another way, since their claim rested on untainted lines of apostolic succession.

upon traveling Catholic clergy as well as impetuous attacks in urban centers that seemed to invite reprisals they could then call martyrdoms.[37]

Augustine did not limit his rationale for sanctions against the Donatists to questions of civic order. Roman authorities clearly had reasons to suppress at least the Circumcellions for their attacks on public safety, and Augustine sometimes appealed to their responsibility in this regard. Few would begrudge him his lobbying efforts if that was their extent. But as Augustine once explained, he had joined other bishops in approving imperial sanctions against Donatism (not just Circumcellion violence) precisely because it seemed so useful for the church and the Christians it recovered. Former Donatists themselves professed gratitude for the sanctions they had once resented. Some might have come to the Catholic Church in fear of imperial laws, Augustine claimed, but now they loved the unity of the church ardently.[38]

Certainly much about Augustine's change of mind was consistent with his wider theological and ethical convictions. In his own life God's grace had, in a way, acted coercively to punish his sins, frustrate his habits, and then heal his will against his will or a part thereof. So when former Donatists now said that custom and habit rather than conviction had prevented them from becoming Catholics until fear jolted them into action, Augustine heard something he recognized, and took divine and human coercion to work in compatible ways.[39] Over the years Augustine had discerned God using all kinds of evils in order to correct erring human beings.[40] Augustine's very ethic of love made room for a paternalism by which one might love one's neighbors precisely by intervening to help them realize their truest good.[41]

---

37. Though much evidence here comes from Augustine's own letters, it finds corroboration in the existence of yet another offshoot. A small group of churches known as the Rogatists seems to have broken with Donatism in part because its leaders refused to cut ties to their violent fringe. See *Letter* 93.2.5 and 93.3.11 to the Rogatist bishop Vicentius.

38. Augustine, *Letter* 93.5.16-17. See *Letter* 61.1, 5 for Vicentius's argument and cf. *Correction of the Donatists* (= *Letter* 185) 2.7; 3.13. On Augustine's earlier worries about the pastoral difficulties from an influence of resentful ex-Donatists passing as Catholics, see also *Correction of the Donatists* 7.25.

39. "Who can love us more than God does?" Augustine asked rhetorically. "And yet [God] not only gives us sweet instruction, but also quickens us by salutary fear, and this unceasingly" (*Letter* 93.1.3–93.2.4).

40. Augustine, *Confessions* 5.8.14; *City of God* 1.1; *Sermon* 22.3.

41. To be sure, Augustine insisted that those who exercise disciplinary correction of

Nonetheless, Augustine's recourse to the sword of the state for the purposes of fraternal correction also stood in tension with some of his deepest theological convictions, a tension finally sharp enough to open a fissure in his thought. If Augustine was right that God's grace can in a way coerce, he should still have recognized that it coerces in a qualitatively and paradoxically different way than human domination. At a critical and revealing juncture in his *Confessions*, Augustine did begin to recognize this. In book 10 he was surveying the temptations with which he still struggled as a recently ordained bishop. Precisely at the point where he confessed his most abiding and perplexing temptations, he noted that God alone knows how to dominate others without pride (10.36.58). As he worried aloud that he would never be able to separate his legitimate duty to influence and discipline others from his lingering passion for self-vindication, he anticipated what would arguably be his most abiding temptation, to dominate others *with* pride. What he missed was the qualitative difference between God's domination and human domination. His explanation was that God cannot be proud because he has no overlord to rebel against. Yet his own experience of God's grace provided a more profound distinction. In converting Augustine and beginning to heal his will, God had if anything dominated him through humility.

Augustine's diagnosis of Platonic pride had in fact been a diagnosis of his own pride, in the months and years just prior to his conversion. The Platonists he described near the end of book 7 shunned the way of Christ's incarnate humility — the Godhead at our feet, bloody and in our clay — "like a torture" (7.18.24; 7.21.27; cf. 10.41.66–10.43.70). It was precisely the humility of Jesus Christ that Augustine confessed he had needed both to assent to God's truth and to gain "strength sufficient for me to have joy in you"; Christ's lowliness "would be my teacher" (7.18.24). Book 8 elaborates. Working at various levels, this book is in fact the story of the conversion of many people who mentored Augustine by embracing the humility of Christ. Some were famous, some lowly; some were recognized saints, oth-

---

any kind do so with moderation and without any desire for revenge (see *Letters* 93.12.50; 104.2.5; 104.2.7; 104.3.10; 133.2; *Sermon* 82.4). But these exhortations also drew upon an ethic of intentionality that helped him imagine ways it might be possible to persecute or wage war so long as one's interior disposition was right. See *Letters* 93.2.8; 93.5.16; 138.2.11. For a devastating critique of Augustine's teaching on warfare as breaking down because he called for motives that he knew finally to be inscrutable, see Robert L. Holmes, "St. Augustine and the Just War Theory," in *The Augustinian Tradition*, pp. 323-44.

ers anonymous believers. What all had evoked and should now evoke in the reader was not fear but love. Years later, in *City of God* 10.29, Augustine would summarize by describing Christ's incarnation as "the supreme instance of grace" which "could not be commended in a way more likely to evoke a grateful response, since through Christ's humility a love once far away had come near to mortals."

In the throes of his conversion, Augustine must learn from both a vision of a woman named Continence and a providential turn to a page in Saint Paul to relinquish the weak strength by which he had attempted to change himself and instead "put on the Lord Jesus Christ."[42] The lesson of Continence was that he could only have the integrated life he desired by not having or grasping at it through his own weak strength of human will, but only by putting on the strong weakness of Christ. This was itself a lesson in humility. Yet when Augustine sought to convert the Donatists through policies and sanctions that used the very human power of the sword to crimp their habits and hedge their wills, he seems to have succumbed to the pride and incontinence he had predicted would be his most abiding temptation. Short of eternal communion with God, the greatest good that Augustine could imagine was mutual love and unity in the body of Christ. But a great good can be the greatest occasion for sin, particularly when we seek to hurry what we can only receive from God as a gift. Augustine knew that true Christian charity must operate continently: trusting God to give the gift and refusing to manipulate others in a way that undermines respect for them as creatures of God. Attempting "to cause love" within the divided Christian community of North Africa through recourse to imperial tools of domination was an act of incontinence, not trust, of a pride that was surely subtle but hardly the Christlike humility that had converted him. Thus opened a fateful fissure rather than a creative tension in his legacy.

---

42. Augustine, *Confessions* 8.11.27; 8.12.29. The text that Augustine took up and read was Rom. 13:13-14. I have written at greater length of the role of humility and continence in Augustine's conversion in "Friendship as Adultery: Social Reality and Sexual Metaphor in Augustine's Doctrine of Original Sin," *Augustinian Studies* 23 (1992): 130-32; "'Love is the Hand of the Soul': The Grammar of Continence in Augustine's Doctrine of Christian Love," *Journal of Early Christian Studies* 6 (1998): 86-91.

Prospects for Mutual Correction

Augustine knew that he must stand correctable. One could only correct rightly, after all, who stood ready to be corrected.[43] Even the apostle Peter needed Paul's correction.[44] As he worked for a conciliatory solution in his first years of controversy with the Donatists, Augustine claimed to invite correction even from them.[45] Was some of this rhetorical convention or a negotiating pose? Undoubtedly so. Yet in other, more intimate and candid moments, Augustine seemed willing to put the doctrines that later centuries would consider characteristically "Augustinian" on the table for scrutiny.[46]

If Augustine has admitted his own need for correction, and if even the most loyal Augustinian would not dare assign him a status higher than Peter's, critics have not only the right but also the responsibility to enter into lively debate both within and with his thought. As one well-read Christian journalist has stated the matter, "Precisely because Augustine is so often spectacularly right, it is all the more damaging when he is wrong."[47] As we have seen, the well-working of any ongoing Augustinian tradition requires that we invite both possibilities, through continuing practices of mutual correction that begin with close readings, at once charitable and critical, of his own work. In the process traditional Augustinians and free church critics may in fact discover that they are needing one another's correction. Let me suggest one example in each direction.

43. For general remarks to this effect, see, for example, Augustine, *Our Lord's Sermon on the Mount* 2.19.64; *Sermon* 82.12.

44. Augustine, *On Baptism* 2.4.5; 2.14.19; also see *Letter* 82.2.5.

45. Augustine, *Letters* 33.3; 88.10-11.

46. Augustine, *Letter* 95.6, written in 408. Writing to Simplicianus at least a decade earlier, as his doctrine of grace and the predestination it apparently implied were just coalescing, Augustine was even less sure, understandably: "This only I ask, that on account of my weakness you intercede with God for me, and that whatever writings of mine come into your sacred hands, whether on the topics to which you have in a manner so kind and fatherly directed my attention, or on any others, you will not only take pains to read them, but also accept the charge of reviewing and correcting them; for I acknowledge the mistakes which I myself have made, as readily as the gifts which God has bestowed on me." *Letter* 37.3 (preface for the treatise entitled *To Simplicianus*).

47. Ivan Kauffman, personal E-mail correspondence, 6 February 1999.

Ecclesiology and Politics

Needless to repeat, free church Christians who find themselves engaging the Augustinian debate from within Mennonite communions will insist that they have much to say, exhort, and correct at the junction of ecclesiology and politics. I have made this case primarily in relation to Augustine's Donatist policy because an intra-Augustinian critique is possible almost entirely on Augustine's own terms. However, once we train ourselves to notice the necessary tensions in his thought, to accept the inevitability of multiple Augustinianisms, to welcome the mutual correction of their debate, and to relinquish (as he would want us to do) the nasty habit of trying to prove him right about everything, the possibility of an intra-Augustinian debate concerning Christian participation in warfare opens up as well.

Everyone "knows" that Augustine is the father of the just war tradition in Christianity — and that is precisely the problem.[48] Because everyone "knows" it, they too seldom subject the texts to close scrutiny in context, to see how much normative weight Augustine actually intended his comments on warfare to have. Closer scrutiny would suggest, in fact, that virtually every time Augustine addressed the issue of warfare, his comments were at the service of some other argument, or else were in letters to military officials that involve pastoral accommodation more than systematic reflection. Furthermore, in the latter case they sometimes relied on rhetorical moves that his more systematic work actually calls into question.[49]

Book 19 of the *City of God* is no doubt among Augustine's most systematic and important treatments of both ecclesiology and political theory. Read in context, however, little to nothing in this famous text amounts

---

48. For examples of Mennonite statements associating Augustine (sometimes together with Ambrose) with the beginnings of the just war tradition and Constantinian accommodation with the state, see John Howard Yoder, *The Priestly Kingdom: Social Ethics as Gospel* (Notre Dame, Ind.: University of Notre Dame Press, 1984), pp. 74-75; Yoder, *The Royal Priesthood*, pp. 57-58, 62, 89, 154; John Driver, *How Christians Made Peace with War: Early Christian Understandings of War* (Scottdale, Pa.: Herald, 1988), pp. 79-84.

49. For example, in *Letter* 189.6 to Boniface, Augustine exhorted the Christian general that peace should be his only intention even when waging war. Yet in *City of God* 19.12, Augustine observed that all creatures (even monsters) always seek peace anyway. Thus, in Augustine's exhortation to Boniface only the "only" carried normative weight, and amounted to little more than a platitude.

to a normative claim that Christians should participate in the military or governmental functions that "necessitate" torture, execution, or soldiery.[50] Such a normative conclusion is only possible if we import assumptions into the text: for example, that the "wise man" in book 19 is a Christian rather than the most moral of pagan philosophers, whose tragic dilemmas reveal not so much a model for emulation as the limitations of pagan philosophy. But that is exactly what either Augustine or Augustinian interpreters must prove; simply to assume this is question begging.

The point here is obviously not to make Augustine out to have been a covert pacifist. He certainly was not. Rather, it is to show that Augustine's support for Christian military participation fits into his larger body of thought far less securely than interpreters have historically assumed. Insofar as historic peace churches within the free church tradition turn out either to be heirs of Augustine in some way or to need Augustine's witness in other ways, they will have unexpected room to make their case within the long Augustinian debate over just how to answer the very fruitful question that Augustine left hanging: how is a pilgrim people in exile within the earthly city to seek the peace of that city?[51] Free church apologists will want to address that question primarily on biblical terms, of course, but they can also stand on Augustinian terrain and say that after all the centuries it is time to explore another kind of Augustinian answer to the challenge of being a pilgrim people, one that has been possible all along.

Faith and Practices

Some traditional Augustinians will worry that a selective, pacifist, free church reworking of Augustine's social ethics could lead to quietism or withdrawal from social responsibility. But we should notice that those who reject Augustinian theology often do so worrying about another kind of quietism. For to insist with him on the sovereignty of God's grace might seem to strip all human doing from the economy of salvation, and thus marginalize discipleship and ethics. Perhaps these positions are twins sep-

---

50. See *City of God* 19.6-7 for the passage thought to claim otherwise.

51. I have said more about the convergence of Augustinian problematics and the thought of free church theologian John Howard Yoder in "Deuteronomic or Constantinian."

arated at birth, however. Perhaps each will more easily discover the truth of its identity by searching with the other for their common roots. In other words, rereading Augustine together may yet help both Christian streams to find fresh insights into the otherwise tired problem of the relationship between faith and works.

By now we should suspect that any tension in Augustine's thought might prove to be a resource for continuing Augustinian self-correction. Many of the most characteristically Augustinian of Augustine's own practices as pastor, teacher, and preacher succeed precisely by failing![52] Augustine's philosophical contemplation had failed to grasp God, and he knew that ultimately his words could do no better. Yet their very emptiness opened both him and his reader to recognition and praise for what God alone can do and has done. As James Wetzel has explained, because we are creatures of time, we can only recognize the grace at work in human actions as we look back upon them confessionally. A sinful will cannot work itself forward into grace, it is true. For the pride that embeds itself in any such attempt will only confirm our sin. Yet grace can look back and trace how God has used even our sinful actions to lead us to God.[53]

The logic of grace-disclosing practices extends beyond language and rhetoric to the shape of the moral life itself, as Augustine understood it. If all right and loving action must work through continence, the paradox of continence is that it must recognize itself as God's gift. Otherwise it is at bottom incontinent after all. As he explained in his treatise On Patience, the virtue that Christians need to do all manner of loving acts must not take credit for itself. If it does, its source too is pride.[54] Such insights can help free churches keep their discipleship rooted in grace, particularly as they allow practices of worship to shape both.

---

52. See, for example, Confessions 10.6-27, climaxing in an indictment of proud seeking in 10.23. For analyses of this same pattern elsewhere in Augustine, see John Cavadini, "The Structure and Intention of Augustine's De Trinitate," Augustinian Studies 23 (1992): 103-23; "Time and Ascent in Confessions XI," in Collectanea Augustiniana: Augustine: Presbyter Factus Sum, ed. Joseph T. Lienhard, Earl C. Muller, and Roland J. Teske (New York: Peter Lang, 1993), pp. 171-85; "The Sweetness of the Word: Salvation and Rhetoric in Augustine's De Doctrina Christiana," in De Doctrina Christiana: A Classic of Western Culture, ed. Duane W. H. Arnold and Pamela Bright (Notre Dame, Ind.: University of Notre Dame Press, 1995), pp. 164-81.

53. James Wetzel, Augustine and the Limits of Virtue (Cambridge: Cambridge University Press, 1992), pp. 134-59.

54. Augustine, On Patience 12.15–19.22; 26.29.

Let us imagine an archetypical practice of discipleship. Jesus' disciples themselves are leaving on one of their first missionary journeys, two by two, following his instructions to travel without any money in their sacks. To go in faith they must in fact go, be on their way, act. Yet they cannot act by scheming or plotting how they will be provided for, else they will not go rightly, act in trust, or really obey their Lord and Teacher at all. Only at the end will they be able to look back and see how they have been brought to the telos of their journey, the fulfillment of their mission in trust. Imposter disciples, on the other hand, might take pride in their own faith, even after the completion of their journey, but thus reveal their faith to have been more like a savvy gamble. True disciples who have acted in faith, meanwhile, will find that their joy upon completing Jesus' mission issues not in self-satisfaction but in praise and gratitude to God. In retrospect, the practice that was an expression of their faith revealed faith itself to have been God's gracious gift.

Conclusion: Grace, *Voluntas,* and Voluntary Church

By gift, imposition, and the very contradiction between gift and imposition, Augustine became an unavoidable part of our histories. At his best, his practices revealed the mystery of God's grace. At his worst, his practices represented the manipulative managing of grace. The legacy of that fissure has played itself out in church histories that have tended to split grace from discipleship.

On one side of the split, therefore, the "voluntary church" has regularly been in danger of devolving into a blunt voluntarism that does not seem to need grace. This is voluntarism in that philosophical sense of the term wherein human beings are understood to determine themselves through the faculty of their own will or *voluntas.* Because free church ecclesiology requires voluntary in the sociological sense of freely chosen participation, the strength of these churches is a zeal, commitment, and intentionality among so many of their members. But the inherent danger of voluntarism has too often expressed itself in works righteousness, exclusivism, and other forms of pride.

Other churches have split grace from discipleship in the opposite direction, however. Augustinian Christianity as traditionally developed in mainstream churches has regularly been in danger of failing to trust in

God's grace after all. The strength of this tradition is its continuing stress upon the sovereignty of God's grace. But the danger that Augustine's example has made harder to avoid is that sovereignty itself may come to be seen as a means of God's grace — that domination and hierarchical control will be rationalized as proper tools for preparing other wills to welcome grace.

And so we may only open ourselves to the full mystery of God's transformative grace in human lives if we have it continently by not having it through either form of trust in human willpower — either the kind that tempts traditional free church Christians or the kind that tempts traditional Augustinian Christians. From the Augustinian side that will require a humility generous enough to embrace the corrective that the free church tradition embodies. From the free church side that will require a generosity humble enough to accept that, precisely as a corrective, their own tradition is not self-sufficient and must rediscover its place within a larger catholic whole.

Of course, none will sense a calling to do the hard and gentle work of mutual correction without love. Whatever part Augustine's thought has to play in the tasks of Christian discernment and reformation, his own expectation was that fellow Christians would only really hear him through charity.[55] If Augustine himself evokes such love, it is through the poignancy of his own vision of God's love, which captivates the imaginations and hearts of those who linger over his texts despite all their nettle. But if Augustine and something of the Augustinian legacy do evoke our love, it is worth noting that they do not "compel [us] to come in" by the sword of violence at all.

Still, we do confront something double-edged. To reenter the Augustinian tradition may seem counterintuitive and discomforting at first. Thankfully, that is but one edge of what is finally an opportunity. The other edge is this: to reenter on the strength of Augustine's sheer poignancy gives the lie to all other ways of attempting to compel divided Christians into unity. To reenter the debate that is Augustinianism, alternately to commune and correct as mutual love and fraternal correction in the body of Christ require, is to show what Augustinian correction should have been all along.

RE-READING THE LEGACY OF THE PROTESTANT REFORMATION

Sola Scriptura in Zürich?

PHYLLIS RODGERSON PLEASANTS

The sixteenth century was a time of massive change in western Europe, where everything that had been considered authoritative was challenged. Within the Christian tradition *sola Scriptura* became a hermeneutical principle for those who challenged the religious power structure. The baptismal controversy in Zürich in the 1520s can be a case study for examining this principle of Scripture alone as the ultimate authority for defining truth in the Christian tradition.

The writings of Conrad Grebel (1498-1526), Balthasar Hubmaier (1485?–1528), and Huldrych Zwingli (1484-1531), three leaders in the controversy, illuminate the influences in their struggle to be faithful to Scripture. Zwingli was the leader of reformation in Zürich (1519-31). Grebel was a lifelong citizen of Zürich whose father served on the governing body of the city. Hubmaier came to Zürich several times in the 1520s to learn about the reform and to participate in the debates concerning the reform, but he never lived in Zürich. He was a reformation leader first in Waldshut and then in Mikulov. Much of his writing against Zwingli was done from Mikulov.[1]

The conflict over baptism emerged between people of good will, all of whom claimed to be following the principle of *sola Scriptura* for defining truth. The consequences of the controversy, including the deaths of the

---

1. Czech name for the town in Moravia where Hubmaier ministered. Nikolsburg is the German name.

three leaders and the suffering of many more, were tragic. Studying the conflict from the perspective of the participants' reliance on Scripture reveals that Scripture is never alone. It is always understood within a specific historical context with all the limitations to understanding "appertaining thereunto." Other scholars have examined the sociocultural, political, and economic aspects of the context that contributed to the conflict.[2] This study will examine the factors within the discourse about reliance on Scripture that led to different constructions of how Scripture addressed the immediate context.

Scripture is not self-evident. Notwithstanding the protestations of the Reformers that they were presenting the plain meaning of Scripture, it was never plain enough that they agreed on what Scripture meant. Scripture must be interpreted in every context. The extant texts of Grebel, Hubmaier, and Zwingli preserve for us traces of the debate surrounding the reliance on Scripture interpreted for faith and practice in every aspect of life in sixteenth-century Zürich.[3] This study will demonstrate that in the discussion Scripture was not alone, but the following factors contributed to the development of the conflict: the actual availability of Scripture text, the focus on different parts of Scripture, the use of patristic biblical commentators, the timing for implementing interpretations of Scripture, and the development of authoritative groups for validating an interpretation of Scripture.

---

2. A few examples are: Ulrich Gäbler, *Huldrych Zwingli: His Life and Work,* trans. Ruth C. L. Gritsch (Edinburgh: T. & T. Clark, 1986, 1983); Werner O. Packull, *Hutterite Beginnings: Communitarian Experiments during the Reformation* (Baltimore and London: Johns Hopkins University Press, 1995), where he also refers to Claus-Peter Clasen, *Anabaptism: A Social History* (1972); James Stayer, *The Anabaptists and the Sword* (1975); James Stayer, Klaus Deppermann, and Werner O. Packull, *From Monogenesis to Polygenesis: The Historical Discussion of Anabaptist Origins* (1975); and James Stayer and Werner O. Packull, eds., *The Anabaptists and Thomas Müntzer* (1980); Arnold Snyder, "Biblical Text and Social Context: Anabaptist Anticlericalism in Reformation Zurich," *Mennonite Quarterly Review* 65, no. 1 (1991): 34-53; George Hunston Williams, *The Radical Reformation* (London: Weidenfeld and Nicholson, 1962).

3. Robert Hodge and Gunther Kress, *Social Semiotics* (Cambridge: Polity Press, 1995, 1988), p. 12; cf. Packull, p. 16.

Beliefs in Common

Grebel, Hubmaier, and Zwingli had some significant beliefs in common. Each of them asserted that his understanding was based on Scripture. In sixteenth-century Zürich, Scripture functioned as the authoritative text in the intricately intertwined religious and political discourses. Zwingli had argued for practice being based on the Word of God from the very beginning, claiming that he "must rescue the sacred writings so wickedly tortured" in his conflict with the bishop of Constance. In his response to the bishop he said Scripture was to be the "touchstone" for every doctrine.[4] Following the First Zürich Disputation in 1523, Zwingli said, "But in those matters which pertain to divine wisdom and truth, I will accept no one as judge and witness except the scriptures, the Spirit of God speaking from the scriptures."[5]

Since 1522 Conrad Grebel had been working with Zwingli and expressed gratitude to him in a poem attached to Zwingli's reply to the bishop "for the gospel restored."[6] Grebel's enthusiasm was apparent in his letter to Vadian where he stated, "And would that by the grace of God all would pray for me, that I accept this ministry in earnest and triumph in it."[7] When Balthasar Hubmaier testified in the Second Zürich Disputation (1523), he said, "For Holy Scripture alone is the true light and lantern through which all human argument, darkness and resistance, can be recognized."[8] Even the Zürich Council, the governing body for the city and

---

4. Leland Harder, *The Sources of Swiss Anabaptism: The Grebel Letters and Related Documents* (Scottdale, Pa.: Herald, 1985), p. 181; cf. Fritz Buesser, "The Spirituality of Zwingli and Bullinger in the Reformation of Zurich," in *Christian Spirituality: High Middle Ages and Reformation*, ed. Jill Raitt in collaboration with Bernard McGinn and John Meyendorff (New York: Crossroad, 1987), pp. 301-5.

5. Harder, pp. 201-2.

6. Harder, p. 186; cf. Harold S. Bender, *Conrad Grebel c. 1498-1526: The Founder of the Swiss Brethren Sometimes Called Anabaptists* (Goshen, Ind.: Mennonite Historical Society, 1950), pp. 74-75, 101, 164.

7. Harder, p. 190.

8. Harder, p. 238; cf. Walter Klaassen, "Speaking in Simplicity: Balthasar Hubmaier," *Mennonite Quarterly Review* 40, no. 2 (1966): 139-44; Peder Martin Idsoe Liland, *Anabaptist Separatism: A Historical and Theological Study of the Contribution of Balthasar Hubmaier (ca. 1485-1528)* (Ann Arbor: University Microfilms International, 1983), pp. ix, 2, 35, 107, 109, 112, 119; Eddie Louis Mabry, *The Baptismal Theology of Balthasar Hubmaier* (Ann Arbor: University Microfilms International, 1985), pp. 92, 265.

canton, claimed to accept the authority of Scripture for their legal decisions. At the conclusion of the First Disputation the council accepted the authority of Scripture and ordered all preachers to follow Zwingli's example to "preach nothing but what can be proved by the holy gospel and the pure divine scriptures."[9]

The three reformers also had in common their understanding of the sacraments, which they believed to be based on Scripture. For them the sacraments were limited to baptism and the Lord's Supper. Furthermore, they shared the understanding that sacraments were signs pointing to a reality but not imparters of that reality. Baptism did not save, impart God's grace, forgive sins, instill faith, or do anything. It was a symbol to the congregation of either a faith promised or a faith confessed, but the act did not bestow faith. In fact, Zwingli conceded to the Anabaptists that there had been benefits to the dispute in the many areas where they had reached agreement on the abolition of certain practices in the baptizing as well as the meaning of baptism itself.[10] Zwingli recognized what they had in common when he said the Anabaptists saw "clearly that the sacraments cannot purify" even when he rejected their view that the sacraments "make a man sure of the thing that has been accomplished within him."[11] Even John Eck, former mentor of Balthasar Hubmaier, in his refutation of Zwingli said Zwingli and the Anabaptists had many views in common, especially concerning the sacraments. He even charged that Zwingli had shared the Anabaptist view on baptism.[12] Thus the baptismal controversy developed between people who in the beginning of the Zürich reformation shared the same belief about the authority of Scripture and the same understanding of the sacraments.[13]

---

9. Harder, p. 198.

10. Zwingli, "On Baptism," in *Zwingli and Bullinger*, Library of Christian Classics, vol. 24, trans. G. W. Bromiley (London: SCM Press, 1943), pp. 153ff.

11. Huldreich Zwingli, *Commentary on True and False Religion*, ed. Samuel Macauley Jackson and Clarence Nevin Heller (Durham, N.C.: Labyrinth Press, 1981), p. 184; Gäbler, p. 128.

12. John Eck, "Refutation of the Articles of Zwingli," in *On Providence and Other Essays*, ed. William John Hinke (Durham, N.C.: Labyrinth Press, 1922, 1983), pp. 79-83.

13. Cf. Willard M. Swartley, ed., *Essays on Biblical Interpretation: Anabaptist-Mennonite Perspectives*, Text-Reader Series, vol. 1 (Elkhart, Ind.: Institute of Mennonite Studies, 1984), pp. 15, 19, 33, 48, 327; Torsten Bergsten, *Balthasar Hubmaier: Anabaptist Theologian and Martyr*, ed. W. R. Estep (Valley Forge, Pa.: Judson, 1978), pp. 287-89.

Text Editions and Passages of Emphasis

Sharing the belief in the authority of Scripture for faith and practice, however, did not ensure uniformity of interpretation. Zwingli and the Anabaptists were not using the same Scripture passages or even the same version of the Scripture. The time of the conflict over believer's baptism versus infant baptism was also the time when the Scripture was still a "work in progress" in terms of its availability to more people than priests trained in the Latin text. The Anabaptists relied on the Scriptures that had been translated into the vernacular, the language of the people, which until 1529 meant only the New Testament. Grebel and Hubmaier emphasized the New Testament, arguing that Christ's words were commands.[14] Hubmaier would counter Zwingli's arguments about baptism and circumcision by using the Old Testament far more than his Zürich colleagues, but he insisted on the primacy of the New Testament passages.[15]

Grebel and Hubmaier were not involved in the translations of Scripture appearing in Zürich, even though they had the linguistic ability to provide their own translations. However, Zwingli was intensely involved in translating Scripture into the vernacular. He had Latin, Greek, and Hebrew editions of the entire canonical Scripture at his disposal.[16] Zwingli's contribution to this conflict was to use both Testaments, saying it was not a case of one Testament superseding the other, as his opponents argued. God's covenant spanned the entire biblical record, and there were types of rites in the Old Testament which preceded what would appear in the New Testament, but all the rites expressed God's covenant.

Through this covenant methodology, Zwingli linked Passover and Lord's Supper, circumcision and baptism. He argued that as the children of the Hebrews were included in the covenant signified by circumcision, so too are the children of Christians included in the covenant now signified by baptism. In a personal letter written in 1524, Zwingli used New Testa-

---

14. H. Wayne Pipkin and John H. Yoder, eds. and trans., *Balthasar Hubmaier: Theologian of Anabaptism* (Scottdale, Pa., and Kitchener, Ont.: Herald, 1989), p. 53; cf. William R. Estep, *The Anabaptist Story* (Grand Rapids: Eerdmans, 1975), pp. 15, 17, 140-45; Packull, pp. 28-29, where he says "Zwingli's own public preoccupation with the New Testament from 1522-1525" influenced the Anabaptists' concentration on the New Testament; Swartley, p. 34.

15. Pipkin and Yoder, pp. 123ff., 129, 135, 179-80; cf. Swartley, pp. 5, 6-10, 26; Williams, pp. 828, 832, 834.

16. Packull, pp. 19, 27-29.

ment verses, especially from Romans, to link circumcision and baptism.[17] In his treatise on baptism written a year later, Zwingli described baptism as a covenant and pledge, but he also focused on refuting the interpretation of the Anabaptists concerning specific passages of Scripture such as Matthew 28.[18] While Grebel and Hubmaier argued that Christ instituted baptism during his resurrection appearance recorded in the twenty-eighth chapter of Matthew, Zwingli declared that Jesus was baptized by John, so that baptism was instituted earlier than the Anabaptists claimed and before people came to faith in Christ.

The third part of Zwingli's "Refutation of the Tricks of the Baptists" (1527) was the extensive development of his defense of infant baptism on the basis of covenant and election. Also in this section Zwingli used a probability argument as the logic for believing that infants were baptized in the New Testament references to households.[19] Zwingli's later writings repeated many of these ideas, but he did not develop them further.[20]

Charges and countercharges of who was correctly interpreting the Scripture litter the conflict between the former colleagues who were now becoming opponents. Conrad Grebel's colleague Felix Mantz in his petition of 1524 said Zwingli proclaimed a Scripture principle which he did not follow. In fact, he said, Zwingli and his colleagues believed the same about baptism as those who supported believer's baptism, but would not declare

17. Harder, pp. 306, 309; cf. Euan Cameron, *The European Reformation* (Oxford: Clarendon, 1991), pp. 138-39, 140.

18. Zwingli, "On Baptism," pp. 141-45.

19. Zwingli, "Refutation of the Tricks of the Baptists," in *Ulrich Zwingli (1484-1531): Selected Works,* ed. Samuel Macauley Jackson (Philadelphia: University of Pennsylvania Press, 1972; originally published 1901), pp. 219ff.

20. Zwingli, *On Providence and Other Essays,* pp. 21-22; "An Account of the Faith of Huldreich Zwingli Submitted to the German Emperor Charles V," pp. 45-46, and "Letter of Huldreich Zwingli to the Most Illustrious Princes of Germany," pp. 194-95, in Zwingli, *On Providence and Other Essays;* Jackson and Heller, *True and False Religion,* pp. 121-22, 132-34, 184, 197; cf. Gäbler, pp. 128-29; Timothy George, "The Presuppositions of Zwingli's Baptismal Theology," in *Prophet, Pastor, Protestant: The Work of Huldrych Zwingli after Five Hundred Years,* ed. E. J. Furcha and H. Wayne Pipkin (Allison Park, Pa.: Pickwick, 1984), p. 80; R. Gerald Hobbs, "Zwingli and the Study of the Old Testament," in *Huldrych Zwingli, 1484-1531: A Legacy of Radical Reform,* ed. E. J. Furcha, ARC Supplement #2, Faculty of Religious Studies (Montreal: McGill University Press, 1985), pp. 148-49; Gottfried W. Locher, *Zwingli's Thought: New Perspectives* (Leiden: E. J. Brill, 1981), p. 114; Edward Furcha, review of *Tauflehre und Taufliturgie bei Huldrych Zwingli,* by Adolf Fugel, *Mennonite Quarterly Review* 44, no. 4 (January 1990): 442; Packull, p. 22.

it. Mantz was confident that believer's baptism would prevail if only "the Word be allowed to speak for itself freely and simply."[21] During the 1525 trial in Zürich of Grebel, Mantz, and Blaurock, Mantz said nothing had compelled them to challenge infant baptism "but the clear and true scriptures" which had convinced them that infant baptism was no baptism and that believer's baptism was the true, Scripture baptism.[22] In his dialogue with Zwingli's book on infant baptism, Hubmaier argued that Zwingli was not being true to his own principles about Scripture which he enunciated in the First Zürich Disputation. Hubmaier demanded that Zwingli prove infant baptism on the basis of Scripture with precise verses to support his argument. Furthermore, he insisted that Zwingli had preached, written, and taught early in his reformation movement that there was no Scripture foundation for infant baptism.[23]

While the Anabaptists were vehement in their denunciation of Zwingli for being less than honest about what he believed about Scripture, Zwingli was no less vehement in his claim that they had lied about him. By 1530 Zwingli stated, "Moreover that I was ever averse to infant baptism or was tinged with Catabaptism, no lover of the truth and right ever said of me. . . . If Balthasar had that writing of mine, no doubt his executioners found it upon him, or he left it to the Catabaptists. Let, therefore, those who have it show it, and convict me of treachery or high treason."[24] Zwingli had not always been so adamant. Five years earlier he had written, in his discussion of circumcision and baptism as signs of the covenant instead of confirmation of faith, that he had once been deceived by the error and "thought it better not to baptize children until they came to years of discretion. But I was not so dogmatically of this opinion as to take the course of many today."[25] The years of conflict had intensified Zwingli's conviction that he had been deceived earlier and that his expansive vision of baptism was the true scriptural understanding of baptism.

Zwingli was no less intent in denying that the Anabaptists truly un-

21. Harder, pp. 312, 314; cf. Abraham Friesen, "Acts 10: The Baptism of Cornelius as Interpreted by Thomas Muentzer and Felix Mantz," *Mennonite Quarterly Review* 44, no. 1 (January 1990): 5-22.

22. Harder, p. 441.

23. Hubmaier, "Dialogue," in *Balthasar Hubmaier: Theologian of Anabaptism*, pp. 177-87, 194-95; cf. Bergsten, pp. 275-80.

24. Zwingli, "Letter of Huldreich Zwingli," in *On Providence and Other Essays*, p. 126.

25. Zwingli, "On Baptism," p. 139.

derstood Scripture. He denounced their apparent rejection of the Old Testament by saying it was the scripture Christ used. Therefore, the Old Testament applied to Christians of all times, and to reject the Old Testament was to reject Christ. Zwingli claimed that he and his supporters were held accountable to the entire Scripture while the Anabaptists only held themselves accountable to their own spirit. Zwingli always believed that he bested the Anabaptists with superior arguments because they were from Scripture.[26]

Although Zwingli, Grebel, and Hubmaier claimed that their beliefs about baptism were based on Scripture alone, they were not reading the same text. Grebel and Hubmaier relied on the New Testament while Zwingli used both the Old and New Testaments. These three reformers emphasized different Scripture passages to support their positions. Using different texts and emphasizing different passages within the texts contributed to the argument about true scriptural baptism.

Biblical Commentary Resources

Another factor that influenced the discourse about reliance on Scripture was the biblical commentary resources the leaders were using in their study of Scripture. Humanism, the study of the humanities which had revived interest in Greek and Latin literature, also had renewed interest in the early biblical commentators like Origen, Chrysostom, Jerome, and Augustine. Reading ancient sources sparked zeal for the patristic vision that the correct understanding of Scripture could change communities, not only individuals.[27] Zwingli, Grebel, and Hubmaier had been influenced by the humanist vision. Worship in Zürich demonstrated the influence by including linguistic studies on the biblical text, patristic source commentary, and finally the sermon which explained the text and applied it to daily life.[28] All three leaders in this controversy provide evidence of their familiarity with patristic sources.

Grebel was enthusiastic about Tertullian and even helped secure a

26. Zwingli, "Refutation," pp. 126, 146, 152, 156, 179.

27. James D. Tracy, "*Ad Fontes:* The Humanist Understanding of Scripture as Nourishment for the Soul," in *Christian Spirituality*, pp. 257, 263.

28. Roland H. Bainton, *The Reformation of the Sixteenth Century* (Boston: Beacon Press, 1952), pp. 86-87.

new translation of his works for Vadian, reformer in St. Gallen and Grebel's brother-in-law.[29] How much Tertullian influenced Grebel's contributions to the debate over Scripture cannot be proven from Grebel's writings. Indeed, Harold Bender said it could not be proven whether or not Grebel even read Tertullian. Kenneth Davis, on the other hand, contended that because Tertullian stressed themes which were "vital to the Swiss Anabaptist synthesis," Tertullian was an important influence from the beginning.[30] What is proven by the extant texts is that none of the ancient commentators carried definitive authority for Grebel. He willingly dismissed their arguments that baptism saves, saying that Augustine, Tertullian, Theophylact, and Cyprian taught this and dishonored both the faith and the suffering of Christ by their teaching.[31] For Grebel such authorities were included in "human opinion" and carried no authority over the "clear Word and rites of God."[32]

Zwingli and Hubmaier were far more familiar with the patristic sources than Grebel and used them more often in their writings and sermons. Both turned to patristic sources to prove that their views could be found in the ancient church. However, neither held that patristic understanding was normative for understanding Scripture and freely disagreed with patristic authors, especially about the meaning of baptism. Ancient sources were valuable to them chiefly for buttressing the truth they believed to be revealed in Scripture.

Hubmaier, early in the controversy, set out his goal to "Search in scripture, not in papal law, not councils, not fathers, not schools," in order to know the truth. He remained consistent with this goal by disagreeing with the patristic sources when they did not support what he believed was the scriptural understanding of baptism. In his work on the baptism of believers published in 1525, Hubmaier said that even if the church had baptized children since apostolic times, it would "still not be right, because a wrong is always a wrong." Then he claimed that Pope Gratian, Cyprian, and Augustine proved that baptism had not always been the way it was in

29. Harder, p. 162; cf. Kenneth R. Davis, "Anabaptism as a Charismatic Movement," *Mennonite Quarterly Review* 53, no. 3 (1979): 221, 223; Williams, p. 127; Bender, pp. 73, 193.

30. Bender, p. 193; Davis, p. 223.

31. Bender, p. 290.

32. Bender, p. 293; cf. p. 180; Geoffrey L. Dipple, "Humanists, Reformers, and Anabaptists on Scholasticism and the Deterioration of the Church," *Mennonite Quarterly Review* 68, no. 4 (1994): 473.

his own day. In his writing against Zwingli's book on infant baptism, Hubmaier claimed that by relying on patristic sources, papal law, and the theological schools, "we have wholly and completely fallen so far from the Word that nothing any longer remains with us which looks like a Christian church or a devout way of life."[33] While he cited Augustine sometimes in support of his beliefs, Hubmaier condemned Augustine's view about original sin, the guilt of children, and the salvific function of baptism.

Throughout his writing against Zwingli's book on infant baptism, Hubmaier either refuted the latter's interpretation of the ancient sources or challenged Zwingli's sources with others Hubmaier believed confirmed his own interpretation of Scripture.[34] His most extensive writing on patristic sources, *The Opinion of the Ancient and New Teachers*, stacked source upon source on every point which the baptismal controversy covered in order to provide support for his position. Hubmaier believed the ancient sources proved that those who practiced believer's baptism were safely within the tradition of the ancient church. It never deterred Hubmaier from his argument that some of the sources he quoted supported infant baptism. Because he was writing in the heat of crisis, Hubmaier did not have the luxury of time to develop a thoughtful, systematic, scholarly exposition. In haste he took passages out of context and did not fully explain how he understood them. Hubmaier was not engaged in a study of the development of the beliefs of his sources, but only in affirming in every way he knew what he believed Scripture taught.[35]

Regardless of his familiarity with the patristic sources, Hubmaier only relied on them as far as they could illuminate what he believed to be the truth in Scripture. All the ancient authorities were tested by Scripture, not the other way around. Hubmaier accused the supporters of infant baptism of reversing the order and relying on the ancient sources when they lacked Scripture. In his discussion with Oecolampadius, Hubmaier accused him of relying on the Fathers because he lacked scriptural basis: "You speak to me much of Tertullian, Origen, Cyprian, Augustine, councils, histories, and old customs. I must somehow think that you lack the

---

33. Hubmaier, "Eck," in *Balthasar Hubmaier: Theologian of Anabaptism*, p. 53; Hubmaier, "Christian Baptism," p. 137; "Dialogue," p. 176, both also in same volume.

34. Hubmaier, "Dialogue," pp. 180, 197, 210, 216, 221-22, 224-25, 227.

35. Hubmaier, "Ancient and New," in *Balthasar Hubmaier: Theologian of Anabaptism*, pp. 245ff.; cf. H. Wayne Pipkin, "The Baptismal Theology of Balthasar Hubmaier," *Mennonite Quarterly Review* 45, no. 1 (1991): 48; Bergsten, pp. 280-81, 284; Liland, p. 38.

scriptures, which do not want to come out of the quiver." He repeated that charge against other preachers in Basel who also challenged his understanding of baptism: "In summary, to conclude, Dear friends, you cry so strongly and so much about custom, old practices, holy fathers, councils, and the long traditions of the mother, the Christian church, that everyone must note how you are lacking in scriptures. And there is, however, no Christian church or mother, other than the one conceived in the Word of Christ, born out of the Word of Christ, and married through the Word to Christ."[36]

Early in his reform Zwingli had stated his exegetical principle that Scripture interpreted Scripture. "Further, the meaning of scripture must be verified, not from the writings of the Fathers, but from scripture itself. I, in turn, offer to clarify the dark passage of scripture, not from the top of my head and through useless prattle; the meaning I elicit from scripture, I shall also support from scripture. Scripture must be my judge as well as the judge of everyone else; but no person must ever be the judge of the word of God."[37] However, this exegetical principle never stopped Zwingli from consulting patristic sources. He used patristic sources to bolster what he believed was the truth revealed in Scripture, using ancient interpretations of the text to challenge his own thinking about the text. Scholars have noted that Zwingli used patristic sources in his arguments without always attributing his arguments to them because he believed they were proven true by Scripture, not the reverse. Irena Backus argued that Augustine's exegesis of John informed Zwingli's own choice of Scripture and argument in the Baden disputation. And George H. Williams wrote that Tertullian and Lactantius influenced Zwingli's linking of the Old and New Testaments after Bullinger introduced him to their arguments about covenant.[38]

While Zwingli did not often refer to patristic sources in his writings on baptism, he appeared to delight in pointing out that both Origen and Augustine traced infant baptism back to apostolic origins, although he

---

36. Hubmaier, "Infant Baptism," in *Balthasar Hubmaier: Theologian of Anabaptism,* pp. 290-91, 293.

37. Zwingli, "Exposition and Basis of the Conclusions or Articles Published by Huldrych Zwingli, Zurich, 29 January, 1523," in *Huldrych Zwingli Writings: The Defense of the Reformed Faith,* trans. E. J. Furcha, vol. 1 (Allison Park, Pa.: Pickwick, 1984), p. 373.

38. Irena Backus, "Ulrich Zwingli, Martin Bucer and the Church Fathers," in *The Reception of the Church Fathers in the West: From the Carolingians to the Maurists,* ed. Irena Backus, vol. 2 (Leiden: Brill, 1997), pp. 628, 639, 641, 643-44; Williams, p. 131.

quickly asserted that he was not granting them "the authority of scripture," merely proving the "antiquity of infant baptism."[39] He repeatedly used Augustine's understanding of signs as externals and not the eternal reality they represent in his own interpretation of sacraments as signs.[40]

Like Grebel and Hubmaier, though, Zwingli had no hesitation in disagreeing with patristic sources, even Augustine. For example, at the beginning of his writing on baptism, Zwingli wrote: "In this matter of baptism — if I may be pardoned for saying it — I can only conclude that all the doctors have been in error from the time of the apostles . . . for all the doctors have ascribed to the water a power which it does not have and the holy apostles did not teach. . . . At many points we shall have to tread a different path from that taken either by ancient or more modern writers or by our own contemporaries. We shall be guided not by our own caprice, but by the Word of God."[41] Later in the same treatise Zwingli singled out Augustine's teachings on original sin and guilt as erroneous even though he acknowledged his appreciation for Augustine. The reformer also distinguished between where Augustine was wrong and where he had been misinterpreted.[42] Nevertheless, Zwingli was consistent in using patristic sources to affirm that his understanding of Scripture was within the Christian tradition instead of trying to establish a consensus of the sources to serve as the normative interpretation of Scripture.

Hubmaier and Zwingli shared a similar approach of using ancient sources to prove that one's interpretation of Scripture was a part of the Christian tradition since ancient times. All three of the reformers affirmed that ancient sources were not more authoritative than Scripture, but were only authoritative insofar as they conformed to Scripture. Nevertheless, their similarities did not lead to a consensus on interpretation. The diversity of understandings, sometimes within the writings of the same early Father, fueled the conflict in Zürich. Just as the opponents could hurl different Scripture texts at each other, so they could support their interpretations of those texts with ancient sources. While all three reformers affirmed Scripture as the sole definer of truth for faith and practice, their differing interpretations of Scripture concerning baptism were becoming

39. Zwingli, "Refutation," pp. 184, 251.
40. Zwingli, "Declaration," p. 29; "An Account," p. 48; "Letter of Huldreich Zwingli," p. 113, all in *On Providence and Other Essays.*
41. Zwingli, "On Baptism," p. 130.
42. Zwingli, "On Baptism," pp. 153-54.

entrenched because they were shored up by biblical and patristic texts that affirmed contradictory interpretations.

Timing of Reform

A third factor found within the discourse about reliance on Scripture was the timing of when one should put into practice what was learned from Scripture. Each of the three reformers recognized that this time of tremendous change was a moment of crisis for the entire society, "an eschatological time of decision for the church, for the nations and for the individual."[43] However, their responses reflected variations in the haste with which they felt they needed to establish biblical understanding. That timing was a factor in the conflict can be seen in Vadian's 1524 letter to Grebel:

> My wish concerning you would be and always has been that you conduct yourself with humble propriety toward Zwingli and Leo and not be so demanding or contentious, in the awareness that they are the ones who are engaged to promote the Word of truth and yet who are not totally able to throw out and abruptly abolish everything that came into misuse through so many years. That is practically what the conflict over baptism is all about. With time it will undoubtedly be regulated according to the witness of the Word of truth as will other things. For this cause I would always be especially glad to see peace between you and a healing understanding.[44]

Grebel never accepted Vadian's rationale. He had a sense of urgency about the need to effect reform as quickly as possible. At the very least, Grebel wanted to speed up the process for reform and took seriously the responsibility to live in such a way as to challenge self-satisfied religious people. Whether or not he believed he was living in a new age is not directly stated in Grebel's writings. However, Zwingli once accused him of saying that their actions were "just as if the Messiah were already at hand."[45]

43. Locher, p. 155.
44. Harder, p. 322.
45. Bender, p. 157; Packull, p. 7; cf. Timothy George, "The Spirituality of the Radical Reformation," in *Christian Spirituality*, pp. 356-58, and Williams, pp. 857-63, for discussions of the end-times expectations of the Radical Reformers in general.

Grebel's disillusionment with Zwingli and the Zürich government in their pace of reform began in 1523 when they decided to delay implementing changes to the Mass. Grebel wrote to Vadian, "They have disregarded the divine will on not celebrating the Mass, and have prescribed a middle ground with diabolical (I know) prudence." As 1524 unfolded, his frustration with the lack of progress in implementing reform based directly on Scripture was palpable. In a September letter to Vadian, Grebel said he believed Zwingli had turned from God to the Zürich Council and he refused to sit idly by and accept this. Urgency was reflected in this letter. "For I do not know how long I shall tarry or if after a short while my Maker will raise me up." In fact, Grebel compared what happened to the church in Zürich with Daniel's prophecy. "And as Daniel prophesies, there will be in the temple an abomination of desolation, and the desolation will persist until the consummation and end."

Writing to Thomas Müntzer, the German reformer antagonized by Luther's pace of reform, Grebel argued that slow reform was worse for people. He said that through the study of Scripture on his own he had learned the shortcomings of the leadership in Zürich and now he believed that "a false forbearance is what leads to the suppression of God's Word and its mixture with the human. Indeed, we say it brings harm to all and does disservice to all the things of God." In fact, Grebel, urging Müntzer to act only according to Scripture, wrote, "[A]nd proclaim and establish the practices of the apostle with the Word. If that cannot be done it would be better to leave everything in Latin, unchanged and uncompromised." Grebel told Müntzer that "It is far better that a few be correctly instructed through the Word of God and believe and live right in virtues and practices than that many believe deceitfully out of adulterated false doctrine."

Grebel feared that the pace of reform was slowed because the people of Zürich depended on Zwingli instead of reading Scripture for themselves, and that lack of firsthand knowledge of Scripture directly impacted their willingness to conform themselves to God's Word. Such unwillingness to conform to God's Word, Grebel believed, would result in suffering for those who did conform. After all, the conflict over baptism did bring about the persecution Grebel had predicted. Grebel's sense of urgency was fueled by what he told Vadian was the need to "warn about the coming sword," the judgment of God. In fact, he wrote that if not warning about the "coming sword . . . is to have believed and loved and forborne in a Christian way, then the truth of God is the most untrue untruth."[46]

While sharing Grebel's belief about believer's baptism, Hubmaier did not share Grebel's intensity of disillusionment or his urgency. Hubmaier was as clear as Grebel about the need to institute reform based on Scripture as soon as possible. However, he was still willing to work with Zwingli and the Zürich Council long after Grebel had given up. Hubmaier's concern was to defend the truth and act according to conscience. That Hubmaier had a different sense of timing can be seen in his 1525 letter to Oecolampadius. He had not yet been baptized himself, but had begun to question infant baptism as true baptism. He noted in this letter that he was corresponding with Zwingli. Then he described for Oecolampadius an infant dedication service that he performed in lieu of baptism. However, he wrote: "If there are parents of a sick child at a given time, who most earnestly wish the child to be baptized, I baptize it. In this matter, I take on sickness myself along with the sickly little ones, but only for a time, until better instructed. But as for interpreting the Word, I do not give ground in the least respect."[47] Clearly pastoral concerns influenced Hubmaier's timing for accomplishing reform.

Nevertheless, Hubmaier did not believe pastoral concerns should stop one from speaking the truth. In a letter to the Zürich Council about baptism (1525), he spoke positively of both Zwingli and the council. In fact, he wrote that the conflict over baptism was bringing much offense, doing harm to the church. "Still one cannot for that reason let the truth be so coarsely trampled in the mud. I and every Christian must say something according to his conscience." For Hubmaier everything should be submitted to the Word of God; people should be willing to admit their mistakes and work together because "truth will ultimately win out."[48] Finally, in his dialogue against Zwingli's book on infant baptism wherein Zwingli had accused the Anabaptists of destroying "Christian peace," Hubmaier defended the strife on the grounds of defending the order of God. "Where now a Christian sees that these outward things, which Christ himself insti-

46. All of the above information about Grebel is from Harder, pp. 276, 283, 286, 288, 293, 302.

47. Hubmaier, "Oecolampad," in *Balthasar Hubmaier: Theologian of Anabaptism*, pp. 71-72.

48. Hubmaier, "Zurich Council," in *Balthasar Hubmaier: Theologian of Anabaptism*, pp. 90-92.

tuted, are being thrown to the ground, he is obligated to cry out without ceasing about that and not stop, even though the outward worldly peace among the godless is thereby shaken. For the order of God should always go upright and be confessed, even though the entire world thereby fall back." Hubmaier had no qualms about accusing Zwingli of dissembling concerning his understanding of the truth about baptism revealed in the Scripture.[49] Although Hubmaier struggled himself to defend the truth since he recanted more than once under interrogation, his ideal was that a Christian leader would implement the truth as soon as that leader understood the truth of Scripture without operating on the basis of fear.

Zwingli's sense of timing for implementing reform was distinctly different from those advocating believer's baptism. Consistent in every document was Zwingli's concern for public order. He was willing to wait to bring more people to support reform through preaching and education.[50] It is almost a caricature of this period that Luther's focus was on how he could be saved while Zwingli's was on how his people could be saved. In a 1526 letter to Vadian, Zwingli expressed his concern: "The incorrigibly impetuous audacity of these people first pains and then irks me. I could wish that the newly reviving Christianity would not be inaugurated with a rumble of this sort."[51]

Like Hubmaier, Zwingli's implementation of reform had a pastoral dimension. He had a genuine concern for those who were upset and struggling with the radical changes that were occurring. After the Second Disputation about the Mass, when it had been decided not to proceed without further study, Zwingli wrote: "[A]ll men should do their utmost to have such misuse abolished, in which one person claims to be sacrificing himself for another, but it should be done with such moderation and prudence that uproars do not occur in the process. Appropriate ways will be found to abolish it."[52] Zwingli's response to Grebel and Stumpf when they came to him and begged him to lead in the beginning of a "pure" church, one separated from the established church, clearly revealed a fear of disorder and the consequences of such disorder for the believers: "I feared that in

---

49. Pipkin and Yoder, pp. 177-87, 194-95.

50. Furcha, "Zwingli's Early Reforms," in Furcha, ed., *Huldrych Zwingli, 1484-1531*, p. 88; Jackson and Heller, *True and False Religion*, p. 39; cf. Buesser, p. 310; D. Jonathan Grieser, "Anabaptism, Anticlericalism and the Creation of a Protestant Clergy," *Mennonite Quarterly Review* 71, no. 4 (1997): 520.

51. Harder, p. 449.

52. Harder, p. 266.

that state of affairs a separation would cause some confusion. . . . I did not doubt that without disorder, the number of the believing would ever grow larger by the unremitting administration of the Word, not by the disruption of the body into many parts."[53] In his tract on baptism Zwingli reiterated his concern: "Therefore, good Christians, do not try to push ahead too quickly: for to press on regardless of the weak is the mark not of a strong but a restless spirit which cannot wait until the poor sheep can catch up behind."[54] Zwingli urged that some practices which were not impious could be tolerated for "love of the weak."

Baptism was among those practices.[55] Zwingli did not think baptism was of immediate concern. He had mentioned the need to examine the Scripture about baptism in his "67 Theses" presented in the First Disputation. However, the issue about baptism was not treated until the last thesis, so it did not attract any attention. In a personal letter Zwingli wrote, "[I]f man's salvation is dependent on the grace of God . . . I say we then have no reason to argue so violently about the outward sign. Such quarrels result only in offense and injury." He concluded the letter by begging Christ to "instill the spirit of peace into the hearts of contentious people" and to "preserve his church."[56] Zwingli consistently referred to the arguments over baptism as contention over externals which he did not perceive as essential because neither the honor of God nor purity of conscience depended on externals.[57]

In addition to the use of different Scriptures and ancient church sources, the argument over timing for implementing scriptural-based reform increased the conflict and pushed the leaders further apart. The result was that the Anabaptists increasingly saw Zwingli not as a leader because they believed he compromised the gospel. Zwingli viewed the Anabaptists as seditious, using the issue of baptism to cover their "real" in-

---

53. Zwingli, "Refutation," p. 133; Zwingli, "On the Preaching Office," in *Huldrych Zwingli Writings: In Search of True Religion: Reformation, Pastoral, and Eucharistic Writings,* trans. H. Wayne Pipkin, vol. 2 (Allison Park, Pa.: Pickwick, 1984), pp. 151-52, where Zwingli says what he feared has happened.

54. Zwingli, "On Baptism," p. 158.

55. Zwingli, "Refutation," p. 142; cf. Furcha, "Zwingli's Early Reforms," p. 88.

56. Harder, p. 310.

57. Zwingli, "On Baptism," pp. 130, 154; Harder, pp. 318, 320; Jackson and Heller, *True and False Religion,* p. 197; Zwingli, "Refutation," p. 186; Zwingli, "On the Preaching Office," pp. 153, 182.

tention of overthrowing the government.[58] Scripture was not alone in how these three leaders understood baptism.

Magisterium

The final factor in this conflict over Scripture and how to implement its authority in every aspect of life was that the conflict pushed each leader to establish his own "magisterium." Grebel, Hubmaier, and Zwingli agreed in rejecting the magisterium of the papacy. In the conflict with the papacy, though, there was the need for protection and validation, and the Zürich Council had begun acting in that role when it protected its pastor Zwingli. However, when Grebel, Hubmaier, and Zwingli could find no reconciliation about what Scripture said and how to implement it, the hope of a unifying magisterium collapsed as each of them turned to a group of people they deemed authoritative for validating their interpretation of Scripture and how to put it into practice. Each leader believed these groups derived their authority from the leadership of the Holy Spirit and that together they and their followers would be guided by God to the truth. Even so, Grebel, Hubmaier, and Zwingli did not accept as authoritative the magisterium adopted by the others.

Zwingli's partnership with the Zürich Council is obvious. He did not so much submit to the council as he continued developing a relationship of mutual interest that had begun with his arrival in Zürich in 1519. Before Zwingli ever set foot on Zürich soil, the council had already established the precedent of being the regulative body for church affairs. From the beginning Zwingli affirmed the council as the instrument for orderly change in society.[59] Had the council not protected him in his early years of reform, Zwingli might not have viewed them as essential to a reform of society in head and member. However, they did protect him against the bishop of Konstanz (Constance) and were willing to work with him to achieve reform. Zwingli used Scripture to defend its government as one established by God.[60] He supported the council in its attempts to establish local control

---

58. Harder, pp. 340, 375; Zwingli, "Refutation," pp. 134, 178, 187-88, 190-93, 208; Zwingli, "On the Preaching Office," p. 151; Heinz Noflatscher, "Heresy and Revolt: The Early Anabaptists in the Tyrol and Zurich," *Mennonite Quarterly Review* 68, no. 3 (1994): 317.

59. Gäbler, pp. 14-18. Gäbler makes very clear that the council is an inclusive term referring to both the Large Council and the Small Council, representative bodies governing the city.

60. Cf. Snyder, "Biblical Text and Social Context."

over life wrested from the abbots, abbesses, and the bishop of Konstanz. The council shared Zwingli's concern for public order as they faced opposition from other cantons and beyond. While Zwingli's interests and the council's were not always the same, they were mutually beneficial to each other for what they hoped would be a providentially ordered society.

Zwingli's vision was for the entire society to embrace reform where all of life would be governed by the authority of Scripture. He believed this would happen as the people were led to greater understanding of Scripture by their representative leaders in government and the church.[61] For Zwingli the entire community was the church, which he expressed in the biblical (and patristic) imagery of wheat and tares growing up together,[62] though he denied the council authority to determine the truth of Scripture. In the Second Disputation, when challenged that he would act according to the Zürich government rather than the Word of God, Zwingli asserted that he did not give the council authority to determine his actions or to decide what Scripture said: "I shall also preach and act against it if they decide otherwise. I do not give the decision into their hands. They shall also certainly not decide about God's Word — not only they but the whole world should not. This convocation is not being held so that they might decide about that, but to ascertain and learn from the Scripture whether or not the mass is a sacrifice. Then they will counsel together as to the most appropriate way for this to be done without an uproar."[63]

At the same time, Zwingli did accept the council's authority to determine how scriptural findings would be implemented "without an uproar."[64] Zwingli criticized the Anabaptists for what he believed was acting on their own initiative. He accused them of refusing to recognize the authority of the "whole church," the council, church leaders and ordinary people, in determining the course of life in Zürich society.[65] According to Zwingli, disputes about Scripture needed a judge: "Although many goods

61. Buesser, pp. 311-12; Cameron, p. 153; Ulrich Gaebler, "Zwingli the Loser," in Furcha, ed., *Huldrych Zwingli, 1484-1531,* p. 4; Gäbler, pp. 128, 130-31; Harder, pp. 707-8 n. 18; Locher, pp. 154-55, 218-19; Williams, pp. 89-90, 193-94.

62. Zwingli, "Refutation," p. 133.

63. Harder, p. 242; cf. Packull, p. 16.

64. John H. Yoder, "The Believer's Church Conferences in Historical Perspective," *Mennonite Quarterly Review* 65, no. 1 (1991): 16.

65. Zwingli, "On Baptism," pp. 158-59; Zwingli, "Refutation," pp. 177-79, 187-93, 197-98, 208; Zwingli, "On the Preaching Office," pp. 150-51.

are abused, chief among them the spiritual ones, the matter must, none-theless, be decided by a judge, i.e. the magistrate. . . . For to start removing the magistrate which acts in a Christian manner is just like pushing the sheep out into the wilderness without a shepherd."[66] Zwingli feared that his entire reformation would be undermined if the council did not serve a regulatory role in church affairs.

> See what a door they are trying to open to all vices under pretence of religion, persisting as they do in these devices of their own invention and daring to defend all their presumption with the assertion, "We must obey God rather than you," even when manifestly they are acting against all love. If they carry their point, this defence of the Apostles will become a laughing-stock, for everybody will find somewhere in Scripture words that he can distort into an excuse for his irregularities, and then say: "God is to be obeyed rather than you."[67]

Zwingli's magisterium was modified from that of the medieval Catholic Church. Authority did not rest in the hands of one person. Instead, for Zwingli, God would rule as the Holy Spirit worked through the believers, the church leaders, and the government living under the authority of Scripture.

When the Zürich Council rejected Grebel's views on the Mass and believer's baptism, Grebel rejected the concept of a governing body as an appropriate body for dealing with Scripture. He increasingly turned to the group of like-minded believers for validation of the interpretation of Scripture for faith and practice, admitting to Müntzer that they were meeting in secret to "correctly" celebrate the Lord's Supper.[68] They continued to do so throughout the baptismal conflict, as is evident in the account of the first believer's baptism in the home of Anna Mantz: "They came to one mind in these things, and in the pure fear of God they recognized that a person must learn from the divine Word and preaching a true faith which manifests itself in love, and receive the true Christian baptism on the basis of the recognized and confessed faith."[69]

---

66. Zwingli, "On the Preaching Office," p. 154.

67. Jackson and Heller, *True and False Religion,* p. 299; cf. Zwingli, "On the Preaching Office," 152.

68. Harder, p. 288; cf. Packull, p. 21.

69. Clyde L. Manschreck, ed., *A History of Christianity: Readings in the History of the Church,* vol. 2 (Grand Rapids: Baker, 1981; originally published 1964), p. 73.

For Grebel the authoritative group for interpretation and implementation was the remnant community, the few who were willing to risk everything for the truth, as he had written to Müntzer.[70] Had the Zürich Council supported his views on immediately implementing the changes in the Mass and believer's baptism, Grebel probably would have recognized a different magisterium. When they did not, he turned to the group of like-minded believers he believed were guided by the Holy Spirit in their earnest searching of the Scriptures for validation of what was the true interpretation.[71] He recognized that the smaller group could implement its understanding of the truth much more quickly and argued for the freedom to be able to do so. Of course, such an approach flew in the face of Zwingli's concern for order and for the reform of the entire society according to the truth of Scripture.

Hubmaier's magisterium was a blend of the other two. Like Grebel, Hubmaier believed that the voluntarily gathered congregation was the magisterium for determining the truth of Scripture and working to enact the truth in every aspect of life. He believed the whole society could be included, but it would be by individuals choosing to join. "After the person has now committed himself inwardly and in faith to a new life, he then professes this also outwardly and publicly before the Christian church, into whose communion he lets himself be registered and counted according to the order and institution of Christ."[72]

However, like Zwingli, he believed that what was done should be blessed by the local authorities. Unlike Grebel, Hubmaier supported the government as ordained by God based on the same Scripture passages used by Zwingli. He believed Christians could be government officials and participate in reform. In his *Apologia* Hubmaier claimed "that no preacher in the areas where I have been has gone to more trouble and labor in writing and preaching than I in order that people should be obedient to the

---

70. Harder, p. 288.

71. Cf. George, "Spirituality," p. 346, Packull, pp. 9, 16-17; Swartley, pp. 21, 25, 37, 50, 51; Williams, p. 829.

72. Hubmaier, "Summa," in *Balthasar Hubmaier: Theologian of Anabaptism*, p. 85; cf. Bergsten, p. 275; Liland, p. 98; Mabry, p. 121; James W. McClendon, Jr., "Balthasar Hubmaier, Catholic Anabaptist," *Mennonite Quarterly Review* 65, no. 1 (1991): 25, 32; Packull, p. 7; John D. Rempel, *The Lord's Supper in Anabaptism: A Study in the Christology of Balthasar Hubmaier, Pilgram Marpeck, and Dirk Philips*, Studies in Anabaptist and Mennonite History, vol. 33 (Waterloo, Ont., and Scottdale, Pa.: Herald, 1993), pp. 36, 44; Yoder, pp. 13, 18.

government."[73] Hubmaier had achieved far-reaching reform in Waldshut and Mikulov, where the government legitimated the reforms adopted by the congregation and participated in those reforms, including support for believer's baptism. Because he was supported by the governing authorities, Hubmaier could work for reform within the voluntarily gathered group of like-minded believers and within the whole society. For Hubmaier, his magisterium included both the group of believers voluntarily gathered together by baptism and the government. The believers were authoritative under the leadership of the Holy Spirit in interpreting Scripture, and the government was authoritative under the leadership of the Holy Spirit for validating the interpretation by enacting it in daily life.

Conclusion

Studying texts does not mean one can recover the entire controversy. There is no guarantee that texts convey "the meanings and effects that their authors hope for."[74] Texts provide traces of the discourse. They do not re-create the situation with all the mixed motives of everyone involved. Grebel, Hubmaier, and Zwingli each claimed to be acting on the basis of Scripture alone. However, their own writings betray this claim and reveal other factors which influenced them.

In sixteenth-century Zürich Scripture was accepted as authoritative for faith and practice: how one lived and how one maintained a civic society. The ideal was that the Scripture would determine what was true instead of a hierarchy or accumulated tradition. However, Scripture is never alone because it must be interpreted within a context and is therefore affected by political, economic, sociocultural factors that contribute to the context. More narrowly, this study has demonstrated that within the discourse about reform grounded in Scripture alone, there were other factors which ensured that Scripture was not alone. The conflict in Zürich about baptism illustrates that the availability of scriptural editions, the particular passages chosen for emphasis, the biblical commentary resources used, the timing for implementation of what was understood from Scripture, and the group serving as the magisterium for interpretation and implementa-

---

73. Hubmaier, "Apologia," in *Balthasar Hubmaier: Theologian of Anabaptism*, pp. 303-4.
74. Hodge and Kress, p. 12.

tion were all factors which contributed to the development of the conflict and its outcome.

Clearly, even with their authoritative groups to validate their interpretations, neither Zwingli, Grebel, nor Hubmaier convinced each other that they understood the truth of Scripture. Neither their written texts nor their debates in person changed the perceptions or actions of the others. None of them accomplished what each set out to achieve. Zwingli did not accomplish his vision of an entire society led by its representatives in church and government working together to implement the truth of Scripture in every aspect of life. Grebel did not achieve his goal of a pure church composed of those who joined voluntarily, willing to risk their lives for the truth. Hubmaier's vision of a voluntarily gathered church blessed by the government also did not succeed. The conflict was not resolved. Instead, different paradigms emerged that succeeding generations used for living in this world under the authority of Scripture.

Scripture, Tradition, and the Church: Reformation and Post-Reformation

D. H. WILLIAMS

On 2 November 1750 the Reverend John Gill, a Baptist minister and theologian, preached at a baptismal service during which he said much more about the Bible than he did about baptism. He urged those gathered to be on their guard against "unwritten traditions" that would usurp the authority of the Bible, since "only the word of God is the rule of our faith and practice."[1] In sharp contrast to decrees of popes, councils, and the writing of the Fathers, Scripture is said to be sufficient and the only external guide for Christian teaching such as the doctrine of the Trinity, the deity of Christ, original sin, or the ordinance of baptism. Gill admits that most of the early Fathers of the first three centuries did not advocate infant baptism, but even if they had, "we should not think ourselves bound to receive it [their teaching], any more than the many absurdities, weak reasonings and silly notions these men gave into." Such skepticism about the early and medieval church was historically self-evident in this preacher's mind: after the apostles, the church became so quickly corrupted that nothing was reliable for determining Christian truth except the Bible.

The kind of priority Gill placed on Scripture against ("unwritten")

---

1. The sermon was not published until fifty years later under the title "The Scriptures; The Only Guide in the Matters of Religion" (Wilmington, Del.: Ronsal and Niles, 1803). Gill is better known to students of theology through his *A Body of Doctrinal Divinity and System of Evangelical Truths, Deduced from the Scriptures*, reprinted since it first came out in 1769.

tradition was hardly unique for his time, and would be recognized by most Protestants today. His view represented a particular instance of a broad legacy that allegedly stemmed from the sixteenth-century Reformation, a legacy which numerous Protestant groups shared in their opposition to Roman Catholics and to other Protestants. But exactly how Gill's construal of the Bible's "sufficiency" over against the church's tradition compares with that of the earliest Reformers is worth asking. Like Gill, when today's conservative and evangelical Protestants pit biblical authority in the name of *sola Scriptura* against the authority of church tradition in the basic form of creeds, councils, and liturgical rites (i.e., the presumed institutional marks of Roman Catholicism), they assume they are honoring the foundational principles of the Reformation and sharing in the restoration of true Christianity. A review of the historical evidence from this period, however, reveals that such perspectives are polemical in scope and owe their substance much more to the era of the post-Reformation (latter part of the sixteenth and the seventeenth century) than to the Reformation (fifteenth and early sixteenth century). It is demonstrable that the earliest stages of the Reformation did not emphasize an "either/or" approach to traditional authority as illustrated in Gill, whereas with post-Reformation Protestantism we encounter a more narrowed and contrarian vision of authority pertaining to Scripture in its relation to the church as part of its response to Roman reform and refutation.

Of course, it is inherently problematic to speak of the post-Reformation era as if it were a uniform movement or a homogenous set of ideas. Just as the Reformation was exceedingly diverse from its earliest days — socially, nationally, and theologically (e.g., Hussite, Lutheran, Anabaptist, Anglican, spiritualist, Reformed, antitrinitarian factions), and was inspired by, if not derived from, earlier medieval reforms (e.g., conciliarism, the Waldensians, the Franciscans, etc.) — so were reforming movements after the sixteenth century variegated in their viewpoints. Hence the line of demarcation between the Reformation and the post-Reformation is admittedly a late modern invention, determined more by a transition of theological emphases than by any one writer or event. However the distinction is made, the theological character of what we call "the Reformation" did not remain static after Luther, Zwingli, and Calvin, but continued to evolve in response to new developments. An obvious marker that signals the beginning of the post-reform period is the pronounced reaction among Protestant writers to the Roman Council of

Trent (1545-63).[2] Trent represents a kind of theological watershed in the Protestant mind, as its adversaries further defined and solidified the "Protestant"[3] identity in response. Indeed, it has been suggested that the unity of the Reformation was first created by the "Counter-Reformation."[4] In the aftermath of Trent, Protestant writings become more defensive in tone, focused on combating the theses which came out of this council and which were soon disseminated throughout Europe.[5]

Scholars have long recognized that a climate of extremes was produced on both Roman and Protestant sides as the controversy intensified over reforming the church.[6] Whereas the early sessions of Trent show a diversity of opinion, among which there were strong proponents of Scripture alone and of the church alone, the need to formulate a defensive re-

2. Other ecclesiastical-political "markers" have been identified, such as the Peace of Augsburg in 1555, when Lutherans and Roman Catholics laid down their arms and accepted the fact of religious division. John O'Malley, *Trent and All That: Renaming Catholicism in the Early Modern Era* (Cambridge: Harvard University Press, 2000), p. 19.

3. The term "protestant" was not used for marking religious affiliation in contrast to Roman authority until late in the second half of the sixteenth century. The term originally referred to the "protestation" of the six princes and fourteen south German cities at the second Diet of Speyer (1529) against the rescinding of the religious freedom guaranteed by the first Diet of Speyer three years earlier. See David Lotz, "Protestantism," in *The Oxford Encyclopedia of the Reformation,* ed. H. Hillerbrand vol. 3 (New York/Oxford: Oxford University Press, 1996), pp. 356-57. To avoid unncessary confusion, I will nevertheless use "Protestant" in its anachronistic sense.

4. According to Dorothea Wendebourg, the rejection of Protestants by the Counter-Reformation fashioned the Reformation into a single phenomenon, without which the latter would have remained a series of widely divergent attempts to reform the church. Other historians have argued that there were certain common denominators to anti-Roman faith which gave it coherency apart from its polemical character. See Scott Hendrix, "Rerooting the Faith: The Reformation as Re-Christianization," *Church History* 69 (2000): 558-61.

5. A Roman catechism, proposed at the council, was published in 1566 and translated into all European languages in order to regulate popular instruction, bringing it into harmony with the council's decisions. Other catechisms and polemical treatises will come into use which were designed with the specific refutation of Protestants in mind. Most prominent was Cardinal Robert Bellarmine's *Disputations on the Controversies on the Christian Faith, against the Heretics of this Age,* 3 vols. (Ingolstadt, 1587-90), which numerous post-reform writers targeted in their refutations of Trent.

6. For the extremes of sentiment and doctrine which emerged within Roman Catholicism in response to Lutheran and Calvinist apologetics, see the penetrating study by George Tavard, *Holy Writ or Holy Church: The Crisis of the Protestant Reformation* (London: Burns and Oates, 1959), pp. 131ff.

sponse against the attacks of anti-Romanists inexorably led to a view of the church's authority that overshadowed all else. In opposition to anyone who declares an interpretation of Scripture according to his own under-standing, the Council of Trent insisted on the preeminence of the "holy mother church, whose it is to judge the true sense and interpretation of the holy scriptures."[7] During its fourth session in 1546, the council made what would become its most controverted statement insofar as later Protestants were concerned, namely, that the saving truth of the Christian faith is found "in the written books (i.e., scripture) and the unwritten traditions" *(in libris scriptis et sine scripto traditionibus)*. One can detect in the post-reform period unto the present day how significantly the Protestant idea of tradition has been shaped by this dualism, which has also been the leading cause for its disavowal.

It is still a matter of debate whether Trent was placing Scripture and tradition on equal footing as two separate sources of revelation; neverthe-less, it is clear that both were considered under the interpretive prerogative of the church.[8] Behind it all lies the question of where the primary inspira-tional activity of the Holy Spirit is to be found after the apostles. Is it located in the church's leadership? In Scripture? In the lives of believers? From the Roman perspective the church had received power by the Spirit to discern the tradition of God from traditions of men, which meant that the ultimate task of defining the faith rested upon those who spoke for the church, or the magisterium. Under this interpretation the church is an unerring and anointed mouthpiece, whose proclamations are authorized not simply be-cause of their basis in Scripture or in the catholic tradition, but by virtue of the fact that the church (the pope and his cardinals) is the ongoing locus of the Holy Spirit's ministry in the world. Since the Spirit of God is always free to institute articles of faith, the church's tradition should be seen as nothing less than the Spirit's witness spoken outside of (or beyond) Scripture. To claim (as anti-Roman communions did) that the chief work of the Spirit resides in every believer raised the unacceptable scenario of allowing every believer to be his own final authority, free to use or abuse the historic faith as "God led him" to do. This sort of spiritual anarchy was among the great-

---

7. "Decretum de canonicis scripturis," from the fourth session of the council.

8. The "Profession of Faith of Pius V" (issued 13 November 1564) sums up the essen-tial doctrines promulgated by the Council of Trent. In the second article, only the "holy mother church is the judge of the true meaning and interpretation of the Sacred Scriptures."

est fears of the participants at Trent about the multiplying host of "protestantisms" they were facing.

In reaction to the Roman Church's teaching that saving faith could be planted in the human heart under the aegis of the church with or without Scripture, post-reform thinkers concentrated more intently on Scripture as the sole and only means of knowing God's will. Scripture, not the church, is the unerring and anointed mouthpiece for guidance that leads to salvation. The polemical character of this teaching was apparent. *Sola Scriptura* became less an affirmation of scriptural authority within the church, as it had been for the earlier Reformers, and more a principle of negation: all else was unnecessary or disallowed in the construction of saving faith. Concurrently, the early Protestant valuation of tradition atrophied, especially as it concerned the writings of the early Fathers and councils, the determination of doctrinal truth not found directly in Scripture. For example, although the post-reform theologian William Whitaker makes hundreds of citations in his *Disputation on Holy Scripture* (1588) from the early Fathers in defense of his attacks on Tridentine theology,[9] he is broadly critical of the notion of tradition. The Fathers are said to have used no other authorities than Scripture, and their view of Scripture-alone negates any Roman appeal to the authority of unwritten traditions. That the early Fathers present tradition in a way unlike the medieval papacy, or that the Fathers are the major source of the Christian tradition, is never addressed. Rather, Whitaker closes his massive tome with an ironical conclusion: "Therefore, if we would keep the tradition of the Lord, we must always return to the Scriptures alone" (p. 692).

The developments within post-Reformation Protestantism, in effect, represented a slow hardening or calcifying of the views articulated by Luther and Melanchthon, Zwingli and Bullinger, Calvin and Bucer. Symptomatic of this process of calcification is how the very nature of the sixteenth-century Reformation shifted from the affirmation of a *non–Roman Catholic faith* to an *anti–Roman Catholic faith*, which, among other things, meant in practice a more polemical and rationalist approach to the Bible, thus reducing the concept of tradition to a superfluous by-product of human authority.

I have suggested elsewhere that contemporary Protestants generally

---

9. In *A Disputation on Holy Scripture, against the Papists, especially Bellarmine and Stapleton* (1588).

have understood the Reformation by reading it through the "lenses" of the post-reform era.[10] What this amounts to is a "reading" of the early Reformers and the purposes of the Reformation that fails to see its assertive catholic and traditional character, and that utilizes the Scripture-only principle as a warrant to separate the Bible's authority and its interpretation from the history of the church. In sharp contradistinction to the Roman Church's insistence upon the equal authority of unwritten traditions, the Bible came to be treated in the post-Reformation reaction as an objective and sole standard, possessing its own divinely inspired and infallible value. Therewith the history of the Bible took its own direction on a path apart from that of the church's Tradition; this division has been simplified to a matter of what is inspired versus what is not, and what is needful for informing the Christian faith versus what is superfluous. The unfortunate result is that the use of the Bible became increasingly divorced from its original patristic and canonical "home."

While exploring this process in greater detail, I wish to argue that the initial stages of what would become the Protestant Reformation were not about Scripture versus tradition, but at root a conflict with the Roman Church over the discernment between (human) traditions and the catholic Tradition, or between "false" and "true" tradition(s). The former was associated with canon law, papal pronouncements, and recent conciliar decisions that had no biblical or historical warrant; the latter had to do with ancient ecumenical creeds and writings of the early Fathers (hence the capital T),[11] which were perceived for the most part as faithful interpretive extensions of scriptural teaching. This is not to say that the early Reformers were interested in simply repristinating early Christianity, since there was much about patristic practice and thought that they rejected. But it is equally wrongheaded to think that it was the rejection of tradition that led the Reformers to the doctrine of *sola Scriptura*, a long-standing and erroneous viewpoint that has introduced much confusion into the Protestant identity.

---

10. Chapter 6 in my *Retrieving the Tradition and Renewing Evangelicalism: A Primer for Suspicious Protestants* (Grand Rapids: Eerdmans, 1999).

11. Williams, *Retrieving the Tradition*, pp. 6, 34-37.

Early Church

The ancient church Tradition was certainly catholic, not Roman Catholic, and it formed the platform of religious authority on which the New Testament stood. From the days of the patristic church and for most of the Middle Ages, the Tradition and Scripture formed not two but one mutually inclusive authority. Doctrinal historians have referred to this symbiotic-like relationship between Scripture and the Tradition as "co-inherence" (or "coincidence"),[12] since the content of the church's confessional tradition co-inhered with the content of Scripture. It is according to this understanding that Cyprian adjured fellow clergy to instruct the congregation "according to the authority of Scripture [and] the discipline of the Church" (*Epistle* 5.2). While Scripture had the primacy of place for the Fathers, there was no category in their minds in which Scripture could or should function in the life of the believer apart from the church's teaching and language of worship, i.e., Tradition. In other words, the Tradition was not a novel set of beliefs and practices made as an addition to Scripture, as if it were a separate and second revelatory source.

Tradition was not from outside the faith, but was regarded as the essential teaching or purport of the Bible. So, Tertullian maintained, the Tradition had been kept "as a sacred deposit in the churches of the apostles. . . . Let us see what milk the Corinthians drank from Paul; to what Rule (of faith) the Galatians were brought for correction; what the Philippians, the Thessalonians, the Ephesians read by it; what utterance the Romans give" (*Against Marcion* 4.5). Tertullian, along with other second- and third-century writers, was convinced that the authors of Scripture shared an agreement about the particulars of the church's Tradition or rule of faith for the simple reason that they believed the rule was the *ratio,* or "scope," of scriptural revelation.

By the third and fourth centuries, the Tradition had become embodied in catechetical instruction, baptismal confessions, the language of worship, and later, in the great or ecumenical creeds. These confessions of faith after the time of Constantine were formulated and understood as proper

12. A. N. S. Lane, "Scripture, Tradition and Church: An Historical Survey," *Vox Evangelica* 9 (1975): 37-55; Richard Bauckham, "Tradition in Relation to Scripture and Reason," in *Scripture, Tradition, and Reason: A Study in the Criteria of Christian Doctrine,* ed. R. Bauckham and B. Dewey (Edinburgh: T. & T. Clark, 1988), pp. 117-45.

extensions of biblical teaching. The creed of Nicaea, for example, was propounded as the most suitable and concise statement of biblical revelation pertaining to the relation of the Father and the Son. It was obviously not meant as an exhaustive proclamation of the biblical God, but was supposed to serve as a plumb line of Christian truth; or, as Hilary of Poitiers described it, "the teaching of the gospels and the apostles were unfolded and the perfect light of catholic unity was raised aloft."[13] This notion of the Tradition could not always be sharply distinguished from human traditions that adorned local customs of Christian communities, and some ancient writers will defend a particular point of practice using the same language of "tradition."[14] Most, however, exhibited a sensitivity toward the differences that existed between that Tradition which had been generally received by the church from antiquity and those traditional aspects which were more peripheral to its central teaching.

Tradition and Traditions

The early Reformers were cognizant of the distinction between particular ecclesiastical traditions and the Tradition located in the early Fathers, a distinction they amplified as an indispensable means for discerning true doctrine from false. Given the fact that any reform of the church had to be built upon a solid foundation of church history, it was important to the Reformers that they show themselves in continuity with the historic teaching of the faith. Important precedents for this method of argumentation were already at hand. Wycliffe had argued for a difference between the true church of the early period and the church of simony and ignorance of his own fourteenth century.[15] His insistence that Scripture should act as the authoritative judge in all matters concerning faith and practice was based on the precedent of Augustine, who, according to Wycliffe, had taught the very same thing (*The Eucharist* 13). Contemporary Roman conciliarist theologians such as Marsiglio of Padua, Henry of Langenstein, and Dietrich of Niem also had sought reform by declaring that the pope's authority was

13. Hilary, *Against Valens and Ursacius* 1.8.7.

14. Tertullian, *The Chaplet* 3; Basil of Caesarea, *On the Holy Spirit* 66-67.

15. Wycliffe, *On the Truth of Holy Scripture* 21: "How neglectfully the ordinances of the church, which are so useful, have been thrown aside! Certain it is, the ordinances of Christ and the primitive church are better than those of the modern."

not supreme but subject to that of a general council composed of representatives elected from clergy and laity of the entire church. In accordance with the patristic model and the authority of Scripture, they argued that a general council should be the basis of achieving doctrinal and ecclesiastical orthodoxy in unity.[16]

By the fourteenth century the very concept of tradition was in a state of transition that had been going on for several hundred years. Making fundamental distinctions within it was necessary, partly because of the abuses of the papal office, which seized upon any traditional precedent for legitimizing its decisions, and partly because the scope of the church's tradition had drastically changed (mainly by accretion) in the centuries following the patristic era. Throughout the Middle Ages tradition in the form of church practices, conciliar decisions, papal decrees, theological opinion, etc., had accumulated in various and (sometimes) massive collections with no particular guiding principle in the overall scheme of things.[17] It was therefore exceedingly difficult, except for the most learned, to distinguish between early or the foundational tradition and the layers of subsequent tradition that had been appended by unknown legal and ecclesiastical authorities. Foremost in size and influence was the *Harmony of Discordant Canons,* later known as the *Decree of Gratian,* a diffuse collection of canon law and theological commentary compiled around 1140 in Bologna.[18] Because it was issued as a textbook and teaching guide that encouraged widespread usage, it was reedited in the sixteenth century and was well known to and utilized by the Reformers.

The relativization of *auctoritates* (authorities) in the *Decree* came to mean in practice that papal interpretation of the various texts should have

16. Henry of Langenstein, *A Letter on Behalf of a Council of Peace* (1381), chap. 13; Dietrich of Niem, *Ways of Uniting and Reforming the Church* (1410), asserts that the Roman Church is subsumed under the broader category of the Catholic Church, and that the Roman Church, whose head is the pope, may err and has erred, may suffer schism and heresy. The Catholic Church is defined by the patristic creeds, whereas the latter was qualified by the apostolic see.

17. Lotte Kéry, *Canonical Collections of the Early Middle Ages (ca. 400–1140): A Bibliographical Guide to the Manuscripts and Literature* (Washington, D.C.: Catholic University of America Press, 1999).

18. For an English translation of one part of the work, see *Gratian: The Treatise on Laws (Decretum DD 1-20) with the Ordinary Gloss,* trans. A. Thompson and J. Gordley (Washington, D.C.: Catholic University of America Press, 1993). The editor Gratian compiled material, probably from earlier compilations, ranging from the Old Testament Decalogue to the enactments of recent councils and papal letters.

a place of priority. Whichever writers had been approved or rejected by the decree of Roman pontiffs, a precedent was set by the fifteenth century "so today what the Apostolic See approved is taken as received and what is rejected is now considered of no force."[19] By virtue of the authority attributed to the Roman and apostolic office by "the blessed Apostle Peter," papal decrees were to be obeyed whether or not they were in keeping with the historical consensus of the faith.[20] It was for this reason that Luther, despite his dependence on its ancient historical sources, happily burned the *Decree* in 1520, as he described in a letter to Georg Spalatin.

What one finds then among the earliest Reformers is not a wholesale rejection of the church's tradition(s), but a sense that the body of tradition was in need of paring down. Overall, it had become too unwieldy, and its contents, whether canonical, papal, or select writings of early Fathers, were treated equivocally as "authorities." This made any part of the tradition easily subject to exaggeration by elevating some points over all others with no consideration of Scripture. Some scheme of discernment for interpreting this mass configuration of sources was imperative, necessitated by the crisis of reforming the church.

Early Reformers

The primary issues underlying Jan (John) Hus's reforming efforts and eventual condemnation at Constance on 6 July 1415 can hardly be reduced to a Scripture versus tradition model of conflict. He was himself a catholic, convinced that the catholic church had within itself the "tools" for its restoration. In many ways he shared similar views with contemporary conciliarist (Roman) theologians, namely, that the ecclesiastical power of the pope and his cardinals was limited, that the church did not consist merely of the pope and his cardinals, nor that they were the head of "the whole body of the holy, universal, catholic church."[21] The church could

19. *Decretum,* pars I, dist. XIX. 1.

20. *Decretum,* dist. XIX. 3-4.

21. Hus, *The Church,* chap. 7 (D. Schaff, trans., *The Church by John Huss* [New York: Charles Scribner's Sons, 1915], p. 66). Hus argued on historical precedent of the ancient church that the Roman church consisted of one company of Christ's faithful living under obedience to the Roman bishop, just as the Christians in the Antiochian, Alexandrian, and Constantinopolitan churches lived under their respective bishops.

also fall into heresy, as it had in recent history, which meant that the pope could err.[22] That primacy bestowed by the medieval decretals and canons (such as in Gratian's *Decree*) on the Roman pope, Hus asserted, was misguided since it granted arbitrary authority to the pope to "teach the faithful whatever he wishes," contrary to the teaching of the early church (*The Church*, 13). However, Hus was not advocating a rejection of the Roman episcopal system, and was certainly not articulating a view that placed the authority of Scripture in antithesis to the institutional church.

It is true, of course, that Hus advocates the superiority of Scripture's authority when he explains what is necessary for true belief. In clear opposition to the papal claim that the Holy Spirit has endowed the church (i.e., the pope and his cardinals) for discerning all matters of Christian truth, he argues that the highest form of knowledge for our faith is to be found in Scripture because it is explicitly and implicitly the voice of the Holy Spirit. While he believed completely the patristic dictum that the true faith would always be found in the catholic church, and that the pope is the "true and manifest successor of Peter" to whom one should appeal in cases of doubt or difficulty in ecclesiastical matters, Hus claimed that papal decrees are to be followed only to the degree that "they speak out of Scripture, or in so far what they say is founded in Scripture."[23] The issue is one that will distinguish early "Protestant" reformers from most other "Catholic" reformers of the age: the locus of the Holy Spirit's working is found *always* in Holy Scripture, and *often* in the pope and his cardinals (considered the "church" in Romanist thinking); however, the latter is authenticated by the former and never the other way around.[24] Where there is conflict between the two, Scripture should have the primacy.

At the same time, Hus was careful not to dilute the strength of his position by exalting the privatization of scriptural interpretation, as opponents frequently charged. Certain Bohemian clergy, himself included, were accused of "wishing to have Scripture for the only judge . . . interpreted ac-

---

22. Like the conciliarists, Hus was horrified at the papal schism (1378-1409) which entailed the transfer of the papacy from Rome to Avignon, the simultaneous governance of two and three "popes," the papacy of Agnes, who, under the name of John VIII, occupied the papal office for two years and during which time gave birth to an illegitimate child.

23. Hus, *The Church* 8 (D. Schaff, p. 71).

24. Hus, *The Church* 16. I say "most" other Roman reformers because there were some voices, before and during Trent, that advocated a Scripture-only principle. See Tavard, pp. 172-84.

cording to their own heads, not caring for the interpretation accepted by the community of wise men in the church."[25] But this is not a fair representation of Hus's views. He sternly denounces the assertion that he uses Scripture alone for judgment in faith and practice as a lie. Although he will not accept any canonical statement or decretal unless it is "grounded in Scripture or reason," it is erroneous to think that Scripture can be rightly understood apart from the life of the church. The work of the Spirit is indeed necessary for ascertaining the truth, but this too is a work realized in the activity of the corporate wisdom of the early church, apostolic and patristic. Of importance is Hus's meaning of "church" which has a strong, though not untypical, historical sense. The superintending of the Holy Spirit thus applies not merely to the apostolic period, but to the subsequent and foundational period wherein Scripture was rightly interpreted and employed for the construction of doctrine. "[W]e do not intend to explain Scripture otherwise than the Holy Spirit requires and than it is explained by the holy doctors to whom the Holy Spirit gave understanding."

Hus had already declared that the office of the Roman papacy was not essential to the prosperity of the church, since he thought (erroneously) it was not until Constantine that the papacy was instituted as the head of the church.[26] Prior to that time, "Christ and his law [of redemption] did not fail for governing the church, seeing devoted priests ministered this law unto the people, who followed the judgment of holy doctors, which judgment they issued by the indwelling of the Holy Spirit as is clear from the cases of St. Augustine, St. Jerome, St. Gregory and St. Ambrose, who were given after the apostles' death to the church to teach her."[27] Hus

25. Hus, *The Church* 16 (D. Schaff, p. 161).

26. Like his contemporaries, Hus assumed that the *Donation of Constantine* was historically genuine. In this spurious document dating from the middle of the eighth century, the emperor Constantine, who was miraculously healed from leprosy by the Roman bishop Silvester, is said to have granted to the "Chair of Peter" and its successors the imperial Lateran palace in Rome; sovereignty over the city of Rome; the provinces, cities, and towns of the whole of Italy and the west; and most of all, supreme authority over all churches in the world, including the chairs of Alexandria, Antioch, Jerusalem, and Constantinople. Whereas attributing to the bishop of Rome religious and civic jurisdiction had nothing to do with the historic Constantine or the Roman episcopacy, it had everything to do with reinforcing early medieval Roman papal theory that governing the empire ought ultimately to rest with the head of the church. Hus refers to the *Donation* several times as known to him through the *Decree of Gratian*.

27. Hus, *The Church* 15 (D. Schaff, p. 149).

got his chronology confused — the four "holy doctors" mentioned above all lived after Constantine — yet his point is clear: the early Fathers were guided by the Spirit such that their use of Scripture and definition of the catholic faith is superior to any of the popes or cardinals. While the patristic Tradition of the Fathers has a secondary authority to that of Scripture, as the Fathers themselves showed by their deferential use of Scripture, it is "more profitable to the church than many popes," and the Fathers are more truly the vicars and successors of Peter and Paul. In fact, Hus goes so far as to state that in whatever doctrinal matters the early Fathers agree, the Roman hierarchy may not lawfully declare the opposite.

Scholars disagree on exactly how much Luther was indebted to Hus's ideas, but it is clear that Luther perceived himself walking in Hus's footsteps, averring in 1520 that "we are all Hussites — even Paul and Augustine are literally Hussites." Hus represented for him a genuine image of the early faith that had to be reclaimed. And although Luther did not emphasize the Spirit's working through the Fathers as did his hero, he did make a distinction between the normative Tradition laid down in the early church and the practices espoused by the Roman Church in the name of tradition.

Exemplifying this distinction, Luther writes in a letter to the Christians at Halle, "I shall not cite here the sayings of the other saintly fathers, such as Cyprian . . . or Irenaeus, Tertullian, Chrysostom, etc. Rather I wish to confine myself solely to the canon law of popes and the Roman church, upon whose ordinances, usages, and tradition they so mightily depend and insist. They have to admit that they stand in contradiction to God's word, Christ's ordinances, Paul's teachings, and the usages of earlier popes and the usages of the early Roman church, and all the holy fathers and teachers."[28] It has been rightly proposed that the Reformation was essentially about reclaiming sacred history which had repeatedly fallen away from its original foundations and stood in need of correction.[29] For some reforming movements, such as many "Anabaptist" groups, the utter corruption of the church required a radical revision of history that nullified the reality of most of it. In Luther's mind, however, drawing on the church's past was the

28. *Luther's Works* (= *LW*), gen. ed. H. T. Lehmann (St. Louis: Concordia, 1955-), 43:156.

29. Bruce Gordon, "The Changing Face of Protestant History in the Sixteenth Century," in *Protestant History and Identity in Sixteenth-Century Europe,* ed. B. Gordon, vol. 1 (Aldershot, U.K.: Scolar Press, 1996), pp. 3-4.

vital "stuff" of reformation. To address the corruption of the present church meant that a viable and tangible means of discerning a continuity with the early church was necessary. In fact, the basis of reform in the sixteenth century can be construed largely as a contest over who had the rightful authority to claim early church Tradition as its legitimate heir. Both Roman and non-Roman catholics contested with each other over this prerogative. Given the Roman charge of innovation against the reformers, that is, of inventing a new church (no more defamatory charge could be cast at one's opponents in the medieval ages), the latter could not afford to jettison church history and maintain a credible ecclesiology. So the reform of the church for Luther was a constituent part of establishing the Word of God as authoritative in the world and its history.

Moreover, the Word of God or the message of the gospel could be found in the Bible and was illustrated in the ancient or catholic Tradition, and in this sense the Word was that which revealed the Roman distortions of that Tradition. In effect, the struggle was over identifying the Tradition versus the traditions, for which Scripture, not the church or the episcopacy, acted as the chief arbiter of discerning between the two. As Jaroslav Pelikan has noted, there was an inner ambiguity in Luther's attitude toward the relation between tradition and Scripture. On one hand he claimed to be defending Scripture against the tradition (i.e., the Fathers), and on the other hand he claimed to be defending the Fathers against perverters of the ancient tradition (i.e., Rome). This ambiguity is a general hallmark of the early Reformation: simultaneously defending and criticizing the tradition of the church, sometimes setting the Word of God in opposition to the tradition, sometimes seeming almost to equate the Word of God with the Fathers' teaching.[30]

Until the end of his life Luther maintained that a reform of the church could be accomplished by convening a general council. This is essentially the burden of his best-known treatise, *An Appeal to the Ruling Class of the German Nobility*, in which he repeatedly calls for a genuinely free and ecumenical council, as well as what subjects should be its focus. As the conciliarists had been arguing, he too maintained that the authority of all popes and clergy ought to be subject to the decisions of a council, composed of delegates from all churches. And the proposed council ought to be grounded on the authority of the four great councils: Nicaea (325), Constantinople (381), Ephesus (431), and Chalcedon (451), which had es-

30. J. Pelikan, "Luther the Expositor," in *Luther's Works*, 1:75.

tablished the norm for Christian doctrine.[31] Luther did not dispute the recognition of the church's early creeds and doctors, despite the fact that Rome claimed to represent that tradition. He contended, rather, that Rome had abandoned the ancient faith in its preference for canonical law: "the present position of the church in the papacy is woefully at variance (as is evident) with the ways of the councils and the Fathers."[32]

Luther's rationale for upholding the four councils and their creeds was that they established no new articles of faith but merely defended what had been given by the Holy Spirit to the apostles at Pentecost.[33] Because the message of these creeds was completely commensurate with the message of the gospel as found in Scripture, all subsequent conciliar decisions must be judged according to their doctrinal standards.[34] Luther was pessimistic about the realization of a general council which would act on these principles since, if the papacy were to follow the precepts of the Nicene council, he said, it would have to burn all its bulls and decretals. Yet he was convinced that his reforming efforts mirrored and refined the faith of the ancient church, which would restore true catholicity.

One might expect that because the Reformers dismissed the *traditiones* of "human institutions" which was associated with the Roman Church, they would have discounted the early Fathers and creeds as exemplary of worldly wisdom. This was not the case, however. The Protestant assault on sundry Scholastic theologians of the Middle Ages and "papal books," as Luther called papal decrees and canon law,[35] was not understood as an attack on or break with the catholicity or wholeness of the Christian faith as exhibited in Scripture, epitomized in the ecumenical creeds, and expounded by the early Fathers. The writings and confessions of the Fathers, distinguishable from the teaching of the Roman Church, served as critical links to the Reformers' own theology.

---

31. Henry of Langenstein, *Council of Peace* 13; both Henry and Luther are dependent on the *Decretum*, pars I, dist. XV. 1, which declares that the "four venerable synods, before all others, shelter the whole of the faith, like the four Gospels or the like-numbered rivers of Paradise. . . . These four chief synods proclaim most fully the doctrine of the faith."

32. *LW* 41:14.

33. *LW* 50:551, 607.

34. *LW* 41:121-22. In *The Three Symbols or Creeds of the Christian Faith* (1538), he published his own edited versions of the Apostles' and Athanasian creeds, as well as the *Te Deum* (a hymnic confession), to which the Nicene Creed was appended.

35. *LW* 48:286.

Luther's intellectual disciple, Melanchthon, makes a similar sort of emphasis in the conclusion to part I of the Augsburg Confession (1530): "This is the sum of doctrine . . . nothing which is discrepant with Scripture or with the church catholic or even with the Roman church as far as that church is known from the writings of the Fathers" (article I.22). The point of dissension, says this confession, is "concerning certain traditions and abuses, which without any clear authority have crept into the churches." The consensual Tradition, which had been received by churches as an authority for the last millennium, is not being rejected; rather, being rejected is the arbitrary introduction of doctrines or "observations" that dissent from the Holy Scriptures or the church catholic (II. prol.). Such inventions are called "traditions"[36] which stand in distinction to that faith which had been expressed through the great councils, creeds, and theology of the ancient church.

Heinrich Bullinger, Zwingli's successor in Zürich,[37] was no less cognizant in making a distinction between the Roman Church and the enduring marks of the catholic church. In his sermon "Of the Holy Catholic Church," Bullinger asserts that although the ancient church rejected the heretical churches, it still acknowledged that heretics did use elements of the faith (i.e., baptism) that belong to the true church. In the same way,

> we do not acknowledge the upstart Romish church of the pope (we are not speaking now of the old apostolic church) to be the true church of Christ, but we do not rebaptize those who were baptized by priests imbued with popish corruption, for we know that they are baptized with the baptism of Christ's church, and not of the pope, in the name of the Holy Trinity, [and] in the articles of the catholic faith. . . . Similarly, we do not refuse the Lord's prayer or the Apostles' creed or finally the canonical scriptures themselves simply because the Romish church uses them.[38]

36. Distinction 9: "And it is very apparent, that through this persuasion traditions grew into an infinite number in the Church . . . thereupon were new holidays made, new fasts appointed, new ceremonies, new worships for saints instituted" (P. Schaff, ed., *Creeds of Christendom* [Grand Rapids: Baker Books, 1983], 3:64-65).

37. For Zwingli's approach to the early church, see the previous essay by Phyllis Pleasants.

38. Bullinger, "Of the Holy Catholic Church," in *Zwingli and Bullinger*, trans. G. W. Bromiley (Philadelphia: Westminster, 1953), p. 304.

That God is sovereign insured the fact that the church always retained the marks of catholicity even in times of corruption when certain of these "marks" are used in support of falsity or abusing the faith. Scripture and the articles of the catholic faith are not properly used in isolation from each other, nor are they supposed to be detached from the church.[39]

Like most non-Roman reformers, Bullinger accepts only the first four general or ecumenical councils, whose teaching is said to be "out of the canonical Scriptures, the true and ancient confessions of faith." The creeds from these councils, alongside the Apostles' and "Athanasian" creeds, as well as citations of the rule of faith from Irenaeus and Tertullian, are constitutive of the Christian foundation of faith: "It behooveth us to know those chief principles of that lively tradition, delivered by the holy fathers at the appointment of God."[40]

Enough has been written about Calvin's extensive use of the ancient Fathers and the Tradition to not require much elaboration here. Suffice it to say that Calvin's training as a humanist made him particularly sensitive to the historical connection between the apostolic and patristic roots of the church and its reform. As his "Reply to Cardinal Sadoleto" (1539) shows, Calvin is convinced that the Reformation movement was in line with the doctrines of the early church. "But here you bring a charge against us. For you teach that all which has been approved for fifteen hundred years or more, by the uniform consent of the faithful, is, by our headstrong rashness, torn up and destroyed. . . . You know, Sadoleto . . . that our agreement with antiquity is far closer than yours, but that all we have attempted has been to renew that ancient form of the church." That true church which the apostles instituted is commensurate with the ancient form of the church exhibited by the writings of Chrysostom and Basil, among the Greek writers, and of Cyprian, Ambrose, Augustine, among the Latins, which is in stark contrast to "the ruins of that church, as now surviving among yourselves."

Yet Calvin rarely spoke about tradition in a positive context. For him tradition was de facto equivalent to the custom and practices of the Ro-

39. In the Second Helvetic Confession (1566), which was penned by Bullinger, the method for interpreting Scripture is said to be Scripture, but not without "the rule of faith and love" (chap. 2). This "rule" is undoubtedly an allusion to Augustine's double principle for scriptural interpretation in *On Christian Teaching*.

40. "Of the Holy Catholic Church," in *Zwingli and Bullinger*, trans. G. W. Bromiley (Philadelphia: Westminster Press, 1953), p. 304.

man Church, or "human tradition."[41] This tradition was not to be confused, however, with the ancient credal teaching that could be found in the first five centuries of the church. For Calvin the Nicene Creed and its language of consubstantiality was "simply expounding the real meaning of Scripture," being the work of the Holy Spirit.[42] Of course, the authority attributed to the ancient Tradition did not imply that Scripture was deficient in conveying the Word of God in its entirety. The witness of the Spirit could be found in creation, in providence, and in the Fathers, but was to be found in its most absolute form in the Bible.

Thus early reformers bequeathed to Christianity an intentional mechanism for validating the patristic legacy, or Tradition, and dividing it from the Roman "traditions." The former was an extension of scriptural teaching, the latter of human artifice and worldly power. One could accept the authority of one without the other.

But the maintaining of such a distinction, so precariously balanced, was not to be. A more simplistic version of this distinction became the paradigm upon which subsequent developments of the Reformation erected a notion of Bible authority, gradually shorn of a positive conception of the church's tradition. And the ambiguity of references to the Word of God as both an expression of Tradition and yet also in defiance of tradition, which was present in the earlier phases of the Reformation, will largely disappear.

Post-Reformation

Space will allow only a few examples in order to illustrate the transition from the "early" to "late" Reformation perspectives of Scripture and tradition. Again the reader should be reminded that this transition is uneven in the sense that there were various responses to the Council of Trent and to Roman reform theology that cannot be neatly categorized into a single pattern of doctrinal evolution.

Martin Chemnitz, a student of Melanchthon and a strong defender of the Augsburg Confession, composed a massive refutation in four volumes of Trent's doctrinal theses beginning in 1565. Trent, he says, is not to

41. Calvin, *Institutes of the Christian Religion* 4.10.18, 23.

42. Calvin, *Institutes of the Christian Religion* 4.8.16. The veracity of the creeds from Nicaea, Constantinople, Ephesus, and Chalcedon is thus reckoned because they contain nothing but "the pure and genuine exposition of Scripture."

be acknowledged as a true, legitimate, and free Christian council that Luther and others had once sought. Unlike the ancient Christian councils which based their decisions on Scripture, the Tridentine judges promulgate their decrees solely on their own authority. To make doctrinal judgments not according to the rule and norm of Scripture is "to thrust canonical Scripture from its place." And not untypically for the post-reform period, Chemnitz begins his refutation with a detailed study of Scripture and its supreme authority.

He argues that the sum of the papalist views as evidenced at Trent is that (1) Scripture is insufficient; that is, it does not confer everything needed for faith and godly living; and that (2) Scripture is in many places ambiguous and obscure, in need of an external interpreter. In particular, Chemnitz is responding to the Jesuit, Jacob Payva de Andrada, who claimed that the norm of faith is not Scripture but the judgment of the church (including the "unwritten traditions"), the latter having equal standing to the authority of the gospel. This interpretation of Trent is an obvious distortion of the council's teaching, but it laid heavy upon Chemnitz, and his goal was to prove the absolute sufficiency of Scripture, such that it would rule out the need for any other source in ascertaining religious knowledge.

While Chemnitz shows himself to be well acquainted with patristic writings and with the way in which the term "tradition" can apply to the preaching and confessions of the ancient church,[43] he is committed to showing the inherent weakness of tradition in relation to the written Scripture. He argues that in every case throughout sacred history (i.e., from Genesis onward), whenever each new deposit of God's revelation to humanity is preserved only through traditions, it soon becomes adulterated and its original meaning eventually becomes completely corrupted. For the first time God's Word is written down in the form of the Decalogue, which was "necessary for restoring and retaining the purity of doctrine."[44] It would be a repeatable pattern as oral tradition gave way to the superior written text. The lesson here is that only Scripture, in its permanent written form, can securely transmit the truth of the faith in the

---

43. Chemnitz treats "Concerning Traditions" in the second topic of volume 1, where he distinguishes eight kinds of uses for the term "tradition."

44. Chemnitz, *Examination of the Council of Trent*, trans. F. Kraemer (St. Louis: Concordia, 1971 [orig. 1565]), 1:50ff.

church. With this theory in hand, Chemnitz dismisses the value placed by the papalist on "unwritten traditions." Our search for authority should always take us to the Scriptures, since they reflect Christ's own priority when he said, "it is written." A later Lutheran theologian makes the application of Chemnitz's approach very clear: "laying aside tradition, we are to adhere to Scripture alone. . . . We infer from the perfection of Scripture that it needs in no way the aid of tradition."[45] While there may be a constructive place for tradition by using it to illustrate scriptural principles, the reaction to Roman emphasis on tradition as a necessity placed tradition in a precarious light that was easily transformed into a polarization between Scripture and tradition.

Best known within the Reformed legacy is the work of Francis Turretin, *Institutes of Elenctic Theology* (1679-85), in three volumes, which coined the term "orthodox" with reference to faithful Protestantism.[46] Turretin certainly knows of and sometimes quotes the ancient Fathers, but there is no discussion about their value here. His overwhelming concern with the authority of tradition as promoted by Cardinal Bellarmine and the Tridentine catechism leads him to condemn any ancient or medieval writer he suspects of asserting an opinion without the express sanction of Scripture. The polemical context disallows consideration of tradition's viability independent of Rome.

An earlier contemporary, Johannes Wollebius, provides us with an equally confrontational approach. His *Compendium Theologicae Christianae* (1626) commences with an explanation of the divine origin and authority of Scripture; this pattern will come to typify theological treatises in the post-Reformation era. In general, we can see a formal "doctrine" of Scripture emerging in the post-Reformation as an independent dogmatic locus. As part of the Protestant response to the reassertion of Roman doctrine on the church's authority, Scripture and tradition, well-ordered chapters or whole volumes on scriptural authority began to be produced which had no precedent in the Middle Ages or the Reformation.[47] This is

45. Heinrich Schmid, *The Doctrinal Theology of the Evangelical Lutheran Church*, 3rd ed. (Minneapolis: Augsburg, 1875), p. 64.

46. A highly analytical and rationalist approach to Protestant faith of the post-reform period is commonly known as Protestant orthodox theology.

47. Richard Muller, *Post-Reformation Reformed Dogmatics*, vol. 2 (Grand Rapids: Baker, 1993), p. 87. While Muller acknowledges that a strict dictation theology was promulgated by a large number of Protestant orthodox thinkers, he claims that the post-Reformation doctrine

not to say that the authority of Scripture was of only incidental interest to Protestant and Roman thinkers before the latter sixteenth century.[48] But one can observe the rise of a theology of the Bible that would permanently stamp the doctrinal priorities of subsequent Protestantism (with some exception given to Anglicanism), as witnessed in the Westminster Confession (1647).[49] Henceforth most Protestant statements of faith will commence with a doctrine of Scripture, which displaces the pattern of Christian theologies and creeds for some thirteen hundred years which usually began by articulating a doctrine of the Trinity. To regard Scripture as the infallible rule of faith, the sole norm for Christian doctrine exclusive to any other authority, including the church, will become the prime watershed of distinguishing orthodox Protestantism from "heretical" Protestantism or Romanism.

For Wollebius the primary witness to the truth of Scripture is not the church but the Holy Spirit speaking in the mind and heart of the believer. Calvin's priority of the Spirit's testimony to truth is preserved, but in a much more internalized and rationalized form. While the church can only offer opinion, the divine character of Scripture is revealed by how it opens the believer to God (chap. 9). Methods of biblical interpretation are described according to principles of reason and procedure; nothing is said about the hermeneutical guidance provided by the Fathers, as one finds in Calvin or his successor, Martin Bucer. In fact, Wollebius makes no citations whatsoever in this work from the early Fathers or ancient creeds. This absence does not mean he is unaware of such sources; rather, it speaks to the lack of importance they hold in the construction of sound Christian doctrine.

In a commentary on the Apostles' Creed (1681), Herman Witsius intentionally writes to refute Trent and "the Doctors of the church of Rome"

---

of Scripture stood in substantial continuity with the views of medieval and Reformation thought (p. 540). In a limited sense this is true. Numerous thinkers, Roman and otherwise, were committed to a view of Scripture as the highest and final authority in the church. But the basis for this "substantial continuity" is what Muller unconvincingly calls "a fundamental doctrinal intentionality." Virtually all intellectual Christians whose writings survive, Catholic and Protestant, were vitally interested in matters related to doctrine and history.

48. For example, anti-Lutheran polemicist Johann Cochlaeus wrote *On the Authority of the Church and Scripture Against Luther* (1524), and Johannes Dreido, *On the Church's Scripture and Doctrines* (1533).

49. Chapter 1 of the document begins by asserting a doctrine of Holy Scripture, which is called the "Word of God" and is in reference to the canonical writings (excluding the Apocrypha), because only they are infallible.

(or "papists"), who allegedly declare the creed to be as authoritative for the Christian faith as Scripture. The distinction of the early Reformation is not wholly absent, since Witsius does make various quotations from the Fathers in support of various articles of the faith. He is not so much anti-patristic as he is against Rome and its use of the Fathers' testimonies. But it is the latter which reveals the polemical nature of the work, as Witsius subjects the ancient Tradition to much negative criticism. First, he points out the existence of conflicting opinions among the Fathers, asserting that "In some instances even the most ancient Fathers were wretchedly deceived by pretended tradition." Witsius is, secondly, concerned with the lack of distinctions within the massive body known as tradition. Unlike the position taken by the earlier reformers, he is prepared to eject virtually all of the early tradition because it is too difficult to tell genuine tradition from the spurious: "the whole subject of traditions is so involved in the thickest shades of darkness that they are incapable of proving anything."[50] A third argument has to do with the limitation of the early Fathers. While the Apostles' Creed is useful for instruction in the Christian faith, it is reliable only because it agrees with Scripture. Any ancient confession or writing "is merely a human writing" and not to be accounted the authority given to Scripture. Of importance here is the characterization of the early church tradition as that which is human and subject to error — a familiar theme of the Reformation — but also of its minimalized significance for Christian doctrine versus Scripture, which is alone divine revelation and infallible, mostly stripped of its patristic history and canonization within the life of the church.

The above writers are only a few of a multitude of witnesses to the attitudes of this post-reform period, but it is clear enough that a common theme of seventeenth-century anti-Romanist or anti-Tridentine arguments is an identification of the Word of God *solely* with the written words of Scripture. In effect, the theological argument of Scripture's divine inspiration and the historical issues of canonicity have been merged into a single platform, making it much easier to place the unwritten word of the Roman Church in opposition and subservient to the written Word of God.

In the polemical atmosphere of the post-Reformation, particularly of the seventeenth century, the focus on Scripture became a matter of de-

---

50. *Sacred Dissertations on What Is Commonly Called the Apostles' Creed,* trans. D. Fraser (Edinburgh: A. Fullerton & Co., 1823 [orig. 1681]), pp. 8-9.

fending the very text itself as the locus of divine revelation and inspiration.[51] There is a gradual departure from emphasizing the Word of God as
a hermeneutical principle or as the essential teaching of the gospel such as
Luther or Calvin had taught. The dynamic of the Word shifts from the
Holy Spirit–inspired activity of the gospel in history, supremely manifested in Scripture, to the Word now equated with the texts of Scripture.
Against the Roman contention for an unwritten and inspired Word, Scripture becomes the one and only vehicle of God's revelation, the very words
themselves being superintended by the Holy Spirit, without error of any
kind. It seemed the more Rome asserted the church's traditional authority,
the more calcified the Protestant view of Scripture became.

Another implication is that post-reform writers will speak of the
perfection or sufficiency of Scripture in a qualitative sense; that is, Scripture teaches all we need for salvation and theological understanding. In
this sense did Turretin call Scripture the total and adequate rule of faith
and practice. But it was then a small step for the qualitative sense of the Bible's sufficiency to be applied in a quantitative sense. This absolutist version of sufficiency ruled out all other sources of religious knowledge except the Bible. Scripture is completely sufficient in that no additional rule
of faith or precepts of tradition are necessary. It was automatic, therefore,
to claim that no tradition could be equal or superior to the Bible, which
meant, in effect, that the church's tradition is a human enterprise. As Samuel Des Marets (spelled also Maresius) maintained in his *Collegium
theologicum, sive Systema Breve Universae Theologicae* (1649), only the perfection of the Word of God could be admitted as the norm of faith,
whereas the normative nature of all church traditions should be rejected.[52]
While the early Fathers would continue to be regarded as useful witnesses
to scriptural truth in the age of the post-Reformation, the category of the
church's tradition, which also contained the writings of the Fathers, was
perceived as antithetical to the authority of Scripture. The once fruitful relationship of co-inherence between Scripture and tradition, integral to the
reading of the Fathers, had a much smaller place in this new Protestant
world. Most often the term "tradition" will be used synonymously with

---

51. For an instructive survey of writers during this critical period, see John F. Robinson, "The Doctrine of Holy Scripture in Seventeenth Century Reformed Theology" (Thèse
de Doctorat, Faculté de Théologie Protestante Université de Strasbourg, 1971).

52. Robinson, p. 128.

Trent's "unwritten traditions," that is, identified with teaching that was not in the Bible. "Tradition" would ever after have a negative connotation.

One further implication deserving brief mention is how the sufficiency of Scripture led to a diminishing sense that the canonical development of Scripture stemmed directly from the patristic church's worship and intellectual life. So urgent was the need to absolutize Scripture over the authority of the church, that the church's role becomes that of a corollary witness to Scripture. Ultimately the concept of the Spirit's inspiration, which had once been a fundamental part of ecclesiology, becomes subordinate to the subject of scriptural infallibility. The Bible is not in any sense a human book; it is the literal word of God in all parts, having been dictated by the Holy Spirit. Biblical authority, therefore, while always in a complementary relationship with the witness of the church, exists in its own and separate sphere, capable of functioning independent of the history of the church.

To Conclude

Nearly fifty years ago the French ecumenist George Tavard called for a reappraisal of the concept of *sola Scriptura,* by Scripture alone, which has been construed by many Protestants as if finding the truth of Scripture is an enterprise best done without the church, or even in spite of the church. Much has been said and written over the years that has brought greater clarity to the integrative role that Scripture has always played with the Tradition and the church; nonetheless, the need for a reappraisal that effectively impacts the faith of Protestant Christians, especially free church Protestants, still persists.

I submit that a more balanced perspective, and one that is amenable to Protestant ears, can be found in the attitude of John Wesley. There was no question in his mind that the only responsible way of interpreting Scripture was through the faith of the early Fathers and the historic expressions of the church. To use Scripture without this Tradition was to make biblical understanding captive to every whim of personal interests and experience. He had learned from reading the Fathers how often the concept of Scripture alone had been used as a platform for supporting heresy.[53] That is no less

53. For the "Arian" use of Scripture in just this way, see D. H. Williams, "The Search

true today. The Scripture-only principle is no guarantee for establishing Christian truth, nor is it immune from pious and well-intentioned believers whose use and presentation of the Bible holds little connection to historic Christianity.[54]

As a true descendant of the Reformation, Wesley argued for the importance of asserting the *sola* in *sola fide* and *sola Scriptura*. He noted, however, that *solus* should be interpreted as "primarily," rather than "solely" or "exclusively." The guiding principles of Scripture and faith were never meant to be taken in isolation from the consensual and foundational Tradition of the church.[55] While there were surely mistakes and some ill-conceived conclusions in the writings of the early Fathers, especially after the time of Constantine, nevertheless Wesley declared that he greatly reverenced and esteemed them in love "because they describe true, genuine Christianity, and direct us to the strongest evidence of the Christian doctrine."[56]

Reforming initiatives within the church have never stood still, which

---

for *Sola Scriptura* in the Early Church," *Interpretation* 52 (1998): 338-50. Against the Moravians, Wesley adamantly rejected the idea that personal union with God is a reliable guide to interpreting the Bible.

54. Of course, the Scripture-only principle could and did backfire on its adherents. Using virtually the same kinds of arguments, Thomas Worcester in 1813 rejected all the major creeds of the early church, declaring the Bible the sole and supreme authority, in order to defend the doctrinal legitimacy of Unitarianism (*Divine Testimony received without any Addition or Diminution* [Hanover, N.H.: Charles Spear, 1813]). Worcester is emphatic that the church had abandoned the simplicity of the gospel since the apostles and had lain in darkness, error, and degeneracy. Even Luther and Calvin, who were instruments of a "great reformation," retained too many of the formulas and words of the church's fourteen-hundred-year corruption. These were illicit additions to divine testimony that needed to be purged from the church's faith, relying on scriptural words alone. Antitrinitarian theology of this time was largely built on the platform of a "return" to the primitive or apostolic church, as the writings of John Locke, Isaac Newton, and Joseph Priestly bear witness. The famous philosopher John Locke had made a similar case for the same reasons. In accordance with the views of Isaac Newton and William Whiston, both of whom had been accused of "Arianism," Locke was committed to the plain text of Scripture, referring to the Council of Nicaea as the representative episode of the church's "fall" into doctrinal corruption and loss of the gospel's simplicity.

55. Wesley writes of his own early spiritual pilgrimage: "But it was not long before Providence brought me to those who showed me a sure rule of interpreting Scripture, viz., 'Consensus veterum: quod ab omnibus, quod ubique, quod semper creditum'" ("An Early Self-Analysis," in *John Wesley*, ed. A. Outler [New York: Oxford University Press, 1964], p. 5).

56. "A Plain Account of Genuine Christianity," 3.12, in Outler, ed., *John Wesley*, p. 195.

is a wonderful mechanism of the Spirit's activity in his people. And the Christian faith is rightly subject to a periodic course correction or revision, as Protestants have vigorously defended. Thus a "reading" of the Reformation through the "lenses" of the post-reform period is not necessarily negative, and in many ways it cannot be helped. But we need to be aware that we are doing so, and acknowledge that subtle but definite shifts took place that impact the present-day understanding of the Reformation, and which may require some readjustment and redirection on our part. When it comes to the notion of tradition, we need to reconsider how much of the catholic "baby" has been thrown out with the Roman Catholic "bathwater" in the post-Reformation. To look into the heart of Protestant faith is to find not simply a reactionary faith — whether it be to Trent or any later developments of the Roman Church — but a clear and positive affirmation of the Christian faith that bears witness to the apostolic message.[57]

As we have seen, many of the earliest impulses behind the Protestant Reformation were linked to the patristic heritage of the Christian faith as an indispensable part of that faith's future direction. If Protestants of all kinds are going to understand better the Reformation's idea of authority as it relates to Scripture, the Tradition, and traditions, they will have to come to terms with its catholic character and its affirmation of the historical worshiping and confessing church. In effect, the path of renewal is found through mimicking our earliest Protestant ancestors, namely, by rediscovering the roots in the church's early spirituality and theology. Herein we will find an avenue that leads not to the loss of our distinctiveness as Protestants, but, as the sixteenth-century Reformers found, to the resources necessary to preserve a Christian vision of the world and its message of redemption.

---

57. As the primary meaning of the Latin verb *protestare* indicates: one who seeks "to bear witness," or "to declare openly."

TRADITION AND THE CHURCH

The "Congregationalism" of the Early Church

EVERETT FERGUSON

"All politics is local." So said "Tip" O'Neill, at the time representing Massachusetts in the U.S. Congress and serving as Speaker of the House of Representatives. All church life too is local. This paper addresses some aspects of the early church's emphasis on the local congregation of believers. Professor George Williams of Harvard, while lecturing on ancient church history, made one of the casual asides that university teachers sometimes make. He referred to the "congregationalism" of the early church.[1] Since he came from a Congregationalist/Unitarian background, the remark may have reflected that perspective. However, the comment stuck in my mind, and now, over forty-five years later, I have occasion to explore it. I do not present my development of the theme as reflecting Professor Williams's viewpoint; in fact, all I remember is the impression his remark made on me, so I cannot claim to represent what he had in mind.

A feature of free church polity has been a basically congregational church organization. This is often modified in practice by synods or conventions, but even these extracongregational bodies are typically not structured in layers as they are in more hierarchically organized churches. With this emphasis on the local congregation, free churches have been sus-

1. George Williams's detailed account of the organizational development of the early church (and much more) is found in his two articles, "The Ministry of the Ante-Nicene Church (c. 125–325)" and "The Ministry in the Later Patristic Period (314-451)," in *The Ministry in Historical Perspectives*, ed. H. Richard Niebuhr and Daniel D. Williams (New York: Harper and Brothers, 1956), pp. 27-81, 290-301.

picious of the church that emerged in the early centuries. They have viewed it as dominated by a clergy understood in priestly terms, as ruled by bishops, and as developing according to a strictly hierarchical model. This, however, is not a wholly accurate picture. There are several elements worth noting of "congregationalism" in the early church, that is, viewing the church essentially in terms of the local congregation of believers.

Professor Williams's comment was to the effect that the congregationalism of the early church had no structure for solving interchurch conflicts. When a conflict was larger than the local congregation, representatives of one congregation went to another congregation to discuss the problem. This was what occurred in Acts 15, when the church at Antioch was troubled by representatives from Jerusalem insisting on the circumcision of Gentile converts to Christ. This meeting became the scriptural basis appealed to as a precedent for church councils, but what took place was essentially a meeting of representatives of one church with another church. Such consultations continued to occur. When there was dispute between the churches of Asia and the church of Rome over the date for observing the Pasch, Bishop Polycarp of Smyrna went to Rome about the year 155 to consult with Bishop Anicetus in an effort to resolve the conflict.[2]

The failure of this meeting to reach agreement on a common observance of the Pasch resulted in the parties agreeing to disagree, both maintaining their own practice but preserving fellowship. In the words of Irenaeus later, "The disagreement on the day of fasting confirmed the agreement in the faith."[3] This disagreement in practice was a factor in the development of regional councils of bishops. When Bishop Victor of Rome (ca. 189–ca. 198) no longer followed the peaceful policies of his predecessors but pushed for a common paschal observance in the churches, "Synods and assemblies of bishops were held on this point."[4] There survived to Eusebius's day (ca. 260–ca. 339) letters reporting practices on this question sent by bishops who assembled in various provinces — Palestine, Rome, Pontus, Gaul, Osrhoene, and Corinth.[5]

Regional meetings to deal with a common problem had begun a few years earlier. The first notice of such gatherings relates to the outbreak of

2. Eusebius, *Ecclesiastical History* (= *HE*) 4.14.1.
3. Quoted by Eusebius, *HE* 5.24.13 and 16.
4. Eusebius, *HE* 5.23.2.
5. Eusebius, *HE* 5.23.3-4. Eusebius had his faults as an historian, but where he collects and preserves earlier sources he is extremely valuable.

the New Prophecy, called by its opponents the "Phrygian Heresy" and better known today as Montanism. One of its early literary opponents, Apollinaris of Hierapolis, writing about 180, says, "The believers in Asia coming together many times and at many places" rejected the Montanist heresy "so that they were driven out of the church and excluded from fellowship."[6] Tertullian a few years later mentions mandates by bishops in regard to fasting and councils of the churches in Greece that "handled deeper questions for the common benefit."[7]

From such ad hoc meetings developed the practice of regular, usually annual, synods of bishops in a province or region. The correspondence of Bishop Cyprian of Carthage indicates that by the mid–third century synods of bishops in North Africa were highly developed institutions. Some of the letters in his correspondence were written on behalf of councils of North African bishops.[8] Provincial synods provided a precedent for Constantine to call together bishops from the territory under his control to consider problems threatening the peace of the churches — at Arles in 314 to deal with Donatism and at Nicaea in 325 (the first "ecumenical" council) to deal with the teachings of Arius.

Even ecumenical councils did not have inherent authority. The frequent councils of the fourth century that drew up competing creeds show that Nicaea did not receive general acceptance for some time. The authority of the councils depended on their reception by the churches, and conciliar decisions had to be accepted and implemented by Christians. One of the principal sources of information about the Council of Nicaea in 325 is the letter of Bishop Eusebius of Caesarea, the church historian, to his home church. The letter is a justification of Eusebius's part in the proceedings at the council. In an effort to win support from his home church, he offered an extended explanation of key terms in the creed that was adopted.[9] Eusebius needed to make this explanation because the terminology of the creed and the conceptual basis for it did not correspond to the teaching he and presumably his congregation had previously supported. His orthodoxy was already under suspicion in several circles, and his

---

6. Quoted by Eusebius, *HE* 5.16.10.

7. Tertullian, *On Fasting* 13.

8. Cyprian, *Letters* 57[53], 64[58], 67, 71[69], 72[71]; cf. *Judgment of Eighty-seven Bishops*.

9. The letter is quoted by Socrates, *Ecclesiastical History* (= *HE*) 1.8, and Theodoret, *Ecclesiastical History* (= *HE*) 1.11-12.

agreeing to accept the creed of his opponents would now jeopardize his position with his previous allies. The emperor and over 200 bishops[10] carried a lot of weight (and Eusebius makes the most of the emperor's endorsement of the creed and of explanations that would put the most favorable light on it in the eyes of potential critics). However, even such an assembly did not automatically have the authority that would be accepted without examination.

Reception by the church at large has remained an important part of the Eastern Church's theory of conciliar authority.[11] The councils of the early church were not canonical institutions but rather "*charismatic events*," and "no council was accepted as valid in advance."[12] The so-called Robber Council of 449 was an impressive gathering summoned by the emperor, but it was rejected by a majority of the churches. The ancient church developed no theory of reception in regard to conciliar authority; the consensus of the faithful in fact determined the acceptance of doctrines. Reception of conciliar decisions may justly be regarded as an expression of congregationalism that lingered in churches not usually thought of as "congregationalist."

Another indication of the congregationalism of the early church is found in its correspondence. The earliest noncanonical Christian letter is from "the church of God that sojourns in Rome to the church of God that sojourns in Corinth" (1 *Clem.* 1.1). The document is accurately named 1 *Clement,* but we know the name of the actual writer not from the document itself but from the manuscript tradition and the testimony of Dionysius of Corinth less than a century later.[13] The letter presents itself as the writing of one church to another. If Clement was something like what

10. There were about 220 signatories to the creed, but the orthodox convinced themselves that there were 318 bishops present, based on number symbolism derived from Gen. 14:14.

11. Georges Florovsky, "The Authority of the Ancient Councils and the Tradition of the Fathers: An Introduction," in *Glaube, Geist, Geschichte: Festschrift für Ernst Benz,* ed. G. Müller and W. Zeller (Leiden: E. J. Brill, 1967), pp. 177-88, reprinted in E. Ferguson, ed., *Church, Ministry, and Organization in the Early Church Era,* Studies in Early Christianity, vol. 13 (New York: Garland, 1993), pp. 211-22, makes the case that councils did not have authority over the church but were representations of the church. Hermann Josef Sieben, *Die Konzilsidee der Alten Kirche* (Paderborn: Schönigh, 1979), pp. 306-43, discusses the difference of Western and Eastern views on councils and their reception.

12. Florovsky, p. 179.

13. Quoted by Eusebius, *HE* 4.23.11.

would later be called a bishop, he does not present himself as such and speaks with the collective authority of the church, not personal authority. Clement's role was that of secretary for the church, and he writes in the name of the church, not his own name.[14] The letter was written with authority and expects to be heeded, but no hierarchy of individuals or churches is appealed to, only that the message is what the Holy Spirit would have said in the situation (1 *Clem.* 63.2). A few years later Ignatius wrote six letters to churches and one letter to a fellow bishop, Polycarp. The latter is a personal letter to Polycarp, although the contents were intended for the church as well.[15] Ignatius sent a separate letter to the church at Smyrna, where Polycarp served. The significant fact is that churches were communicating with churches, or an individual was communicating with churches; bishops were not communicating with churches primarily through their bishops.

The two most important early accounts of martyrdom were letters from churches. The *Martyrdom of Polycarp* (probably about 156) is actually a letter, employing the same phraseology as 1 *Clement,* from "The church of God that sojourns in Smyrna to the church of God that sojourns in Philomelium and to all the communities of the holy and catholic church in every place" (pref.). The account of *The Martyrs of Gaul* (177) comes from two churches and is more broadly worded in its address. It is a letter from "The servants of Christ who sojourn in Vienne and Lyons in Gaul to the brothers and sisters in Asia and Phrygia who share with us the same faith and hope of redemption."[16] Again, churches are writing to churches. In both of these cases the bishops had died in the persecution and so could not write; nevertheless, the point is that the churches did not write to bishops but to other churches or Christians in order to inform them about events.

The collection of letters of Dionysius of Corinth available to Eusebius included letters to churches and letters to bishops intended for the churches.[17] These letters may represent a transitional stage. By the mid–third century, Cyprian's correspondence to people outside of Carthage was with bishops, if there was an occupant of the episcopal chair of the church

14. Cf. Hermas, *Vision* 2.4.3 (= 8.3), for a Clement whose task was to correspond with other cities.

15. Note the address to the church in Ignatius, *Letter to Polycarp* 6.

16. Eusebius, *HE* 5.1.3.

17. Eusebius, *HE* 4.23.1-13.

at the moment.[18] When there was no bishop or if the bishop was guilty of misdeeds, he wrote to the other clergy. Even letters to his own church in Carthage, apart from the letters to martyrs, are for the most part addressed to the clergy. Bishops were now writing to bishops and other clergy instead of directly to churches. Cyprian, furthermore, pioneered the idea of bishops being bishops of the church at large and not simply in a church (on his view of bishops, more below). This is carried further in the large collections of letters of Basil of Caesarea and Gregory of Nazianzus in the fourth century, where the bishop addresses individuals in many churches.

In regard to organizational matters, we should note that in the early history of Christianity there was congregational selection and commissioning of ministers. Our earliest notices refer to election by local congregations. There was precedent for this in the New Testament, as in the choice by the community of believers of the seven servants of the church at Jerusalem in Acts 6:1-6 and the commissioning by the church in Antioch even of those chosen by the Holy Spirit in Acts 13:1-3. Our earliest post-canonical documents reflect local choice. 1 Clement 44 referred to bishops appointed "by eminent men with the consent of the whole church." And Didache 15 instructed Christians "to elect for yourselves bishops and deacons." The church orders continued to describe procedures involving election by the local congregation. "Let the bishop be ordained being in all things without fault chosen by all the people. And when he has been proposed and found acceptable to all, the people shall assemble on the Lord's day together with the presbytery and such bishops as may attend" (Hippolytus, Apostolic Tradition 2.1-2). This statement is typical of instructions in the church-order literature, both in the expectation of popular election and in the description of the public nature of the ordination. Not only the selection but also the appointment occurred in the gathering of the church in which one was called to serve.

Election of their bishops by the local churches continued to be the norm in the third century and at many places for some time later.[19]

18. Persecution often left churches without a bishop for a period of time, for example, in Rome for over a year in 250 to early 251.

19. E.g., Cyprian, Letters 59[54].5-6; 67.3-5; Gregory of Nyssa, Life of Gregory Thaumaturgus 62-72 (Patrologia Graeca 46:933B-940B = Gregorii Nysseni Opera X.1.36,3–41,15). Origen knew other methods of selection in addition to election in the third century (Hom. 13 in Num. 4) — see Everett Ferguson, "Origen and the Election of Bishops," Church History 43 (1974): 26-33.

Bishops in turn selected the lesser clergy, as the *Apostolic Tradition* indicates, sometimes even the presbyters,[20] but in this case with the approval of the congregation.[21] A congregation's selection of its own ministers was a firmly established principle of the early church, and that is a distinctly congregationalist principle.

The *Apostolic Tradition* from the beginning of the third century assumes the presence of bishops from other churches at the ordination. Canon law later required the presence of three bishops at the ordination of a bishop.[22] This requirement related the appointment of a bishop to the universal church through the presence of representatives of other congregations. The involvement of other bishops in ordination led to the initiative in the selection of the bishop moving outside the congregation, either to the other bishops of the area or to the metropolitan bishop, who at least had to give his approval, but local consent to the choice remained crucial.[23]

During the fourth century imperial involvement in the selection of bishops, especially at important churches, became an increasing problem. Nevertheless, the older sentiment remained strong. Western bishops at Sardica in 343 wrote to Emperor Constantius II that each community should be allowed to choose its own bishop.[24] A vivid account of popular election in a situation complicated by competing ecclesiastical parties concerns Ambrose of Milan.[25] There was disturbance in Milan after the death of the Arian bishop Auxentius, and Ambrose as governor of the province went to the church to restore order between the Arian and Nicene factions. When he was addressing the people, the voice of a child called out, "Ambrose bishop." The people took this as a divine sign and, although Ambrose was not even baptized yet, both catholics and Arians agreed on his election. Ambrose was reluctant to accept the call but, finally persuaded, was baptized and ordained.

A corollary of congregational election was that a person was a minis-

---

20. *Didascalia* 9.

21. Cyprian, *Letter* 38[33].1f.

22. Arles, can. 20; Nicaea, can. 4; *Apostolic Constitutions* 3.20.

23. For some instances in the fourth century of selection of a bishop by other bishops, see Theodoret, *HE* 2.28 at Antioch; 5.19.14 at Constantinople.

24. *Liber I ad Constantium* 1.1-4 (Hilary of Poitiers, in Corpus Scriptorum Ecclesiasticorum Latinorum 65:181-187); see R. P. C. Hanson, *The Search for the Christian Doctrine of God: The Arian Controversy, 318-381* (Edinburgh: T. & T. Clark, 1988), p. 853.

25. Paulinus, *Life of Ambrose* 3.6.

ter in the church where chosen to serve and only in a limited sense a minister in the universal church. The implications of decisions made at Nicaea concerning the status of clergy from schismatic groups reconciled to the catholic church have not attracted sufficient attention.[26] When followers of Melitius, Novatian, and Paul of Samosata who held clerical office came into the catholic church, they were entitled to the same position in the catholic church that they had formerly held in the schismatic or heretical community, but they first had to receive a new ordination.[27] Their previous ordinations were not recognized, although the baptisms of the Melitians and Novatianists (but not those of the Paulianists) were recognized. This practice suggests the possibility of a new ordination when a clergyman moved from one catholic church to another. Such might be the implication of a canon adopted at Nicaea: "If anyone shall dare surreptitiously to carry off and ordain in his own church a man who belongs to another church without the consent of that person's bishop from whose clergy list he was separated, the ordination will be void" (Nicaea, can. 16). Since in most cases this involved a promotion, a new ordination would have been to the new rank in the ministry, and so this canon may not be indicative of a repeated ordination. We lack details about what was done when the same function was accepted at another congregation. However, since normally what is forbidden somebody is doing, some significance attaches to the following decree from the late fourth century: "If any bishop, presbyter, or deacon receives a second ordination from anyone, let him be deprived, and the person who ordained him, unless he can show that his former ordination was from the heretics; for those that are either baptized or ordained by such as these, can be neither Christians nor clergymen" (*Apostolic Canons* 68). This prohibition of a second ordination (to the same rank in the clergy) was an important step toward viewing ordination as a permanent endowment, a result achieved in Augustine's doctrine of the indelibility of orders.

When Polycarp, bishop of Smyrna, visited Bishop Anicetus of Rome

26. See my paper, which was disturbing to champions of a conventional episcopal understanding of the organization of the early church, "Attitudes to Schism at the Council of Nicaea," in *Schism, Heresy, and Religious Protest,* ed. Derek Baker, Studies in Church History, vol. 9 (Cambridge: Cambridge University Press, 1972), pp. 57-63.

27. On the Melitians, the letter of the Council of Nicaea to the Egyptian churches preserved in Socrates, *HE* 1.9, and Theodoret, *HE* 1.9.7ff.; on the Novatians and Paulianists, canons 8 and 19 of Nicaea.

(discussed above), "Anicetus, showing his respect for Polycarp, allowed him to celebrate the eucharist in the church."[28] This was a particular favor and sign of fellowship, and it was referred to by Irenaeus of Lyons later as a demonstration of peace and intercommunion. Polycarp had no inherent right to preside at the Lord's Table in another church. One was originally viewed as a bishop in a particular church, not a bishop "at large" or a bishop in the universal church, although one church honored the leader of a sister church. It was only in the mid–third century with Cyprian that another theory of church office was promoted. In his view the bishops were not simply bishops of individual churches but jointly shared an episcopate over the whole church.[29] Such a view gave a theoretical basis for what was already taking place, that is, bishops in council speaking for the churches they represented.

The expectation of the early church was that a person would remain in the church for which he was ordained. One was not ordained to be a clergyman at large, but for ministry in a particular church.[30] The attitude is summed up in the canons of the Council of Chalcedon in 451: "Neither presbyter, deacon, nor any of the ecclesiastical order shall be ordained at large, nor unless the person ordained is particularly appointed to a church in a city or village, or to a martyrion, or to a monastery. And if any have been ordained without a charge, the holy Synod decrees, to the reproach of the ordainer, that such an ordination shall be inoperative, and that such a person shall nowhere be allowed to officiate" (Chalcedon, can. 6). The principle was much older than Chalcedon. An important reflection of the view that the clergy were identified with a particular congregation was the position that there was to be no translation of bishops from one church to another. "On account of the great disturbance and discords that occur, it is decreed that the custom prevailing in certain places contrary to the canon, must wholly be done away, so that neither bishop, presbyter, nor deacon shall pass from city to city. And if any one, after this decree of the holy and great synod, shall attempt any such thing, or continue in any such course, his proceedings shall be utterly void, and he shall be restored to the church

28. Letter of Irenaeus of Lyons to Victor of Rome, quoted in Eusebius, *HE* 5.24.17.

29. "The episcopate is one, each part of which is held by each one for the whole" (Cyprian, *On the Unity of the Church* 5).

30. Developments affecting this principle are surveyed in Bernard Callebat, "Origines et fondements du droit de la stabilité des ministres ordonnés dans l'Église d'Orient (Ier-Ve siècles)," *Bulletin de Littérature Ecclésiastique* 98 (1997): 211-33.

for which he was ordained bishop or presbyter" (Nicaea, can. 15). The practice of transferring from one church to another was thus applied to presbyters and deacons as well as bishops, but it was the translation of bishops that drew frequent prohibition in the canons of various councils. "A bishop may not be translated from one parish to another, either intruding himself of his own suggestion, or under compulsion by the people, or by constraint of the bishops; but he shall remain in the church to which he was allotted by God from the beginning, and shall not be translated from it, according to the decree formerly passed on the subject" (Antioch [341?], can. 21).[31] The feeling was strong that a minister must remain in the place where he was ordained. At a time when the hierarchy of bishops and synodal procedures were being institutionalized, the church preserved a basically congregational consciousness of its organization and ministry.

Whether the initiative was with a person who tried to transfer to another church (Nicaea, can. 15 above), with a church that tried to carry off someone from another church to serve them (Nicaea, can. 16), or with bishops trying to strengthen their party by placing someone of their persuasion in a given church, the canonical legislation opposed the moving of ministry from one place to another. A person certainly had the rank of his office wherever he went, and he did not lose the right to exercise his ministry with the permission of the bishop of the church where he was visiting, but canon law sought even the limitation of the period of time a clergyman could visit another church.[32] The primary conviction was that the minister was considered wedded to the church where he was ordained.[33] His ministry was to be for a particular people at a particular place.

The frequently repeated prohibition of translation from one church to another shows, however, that the practice was common and was not eliminated by conciliar canons. Churches wanted proven men from other churches, and ambitious men (and probably others who sincerely felt called) wanted advancement to larger or more prestigious churches. The

31. Not everyone, of course, agreed with the prohibition. The historian Socrates Scholasticus cited many instances when "bishops have been transferred from one city to another to meet the exigences of peculiar cases" (*HE* 7.35-36, 40).

32. Sardica, can. 11 and 16, placed a limit of three weeks for a bishop, presbyter, or deacon to be away from his home church.

33. A singular extension of this idea comes in the charge that someone translated from one church to another was guilty of spiritual bigamy or adultery (Athanasius, *Apology against the Arians* 6; cf. Jerome, *Letter* 69.5).

troubled ecclesiastical conditions caused by the doctrinal conflicts of the fourth century created situations that encouraged "clergy at large" without assignment to a particular church. One of the canons adopted at Antioch (usually assigned to the council of 341 but probably from another council) pointed to the kind of situation that could (and did) arise: "If any bishop ordained to a parish shall not proceed to the parish to which he has been ordained, not through any fault of his own, but either because of the rejection of the people, or for any other reason not arising from himself, let him enjoy his rank and ministry; only he shall not disturb the affairs of the church which he joins; and he shall abide by whatever the full synod of the province shall determine, after judging the case" (can. 18).[34]

The fourth century saw increasing occasions when one party in the trinitarian disputes of the age covertly ordained someone of their persuasion and tried to force that person on a given church. Such a divorce of ordination from the local church is illustrated by a comment by Jerome, defining the Greek word for ordination, *cheirotonia*: "That is, the ordination [*ordinatio*] of the clergy which is accomplished not only at the verbal prayer but at the imposition of the hand (lest indeed in mockery someone be ordained ignorantly to the clergy by a secret prayer)."[35] Jerome refers to the two principal actions in ordination — prayer and the laying on of hands. His comment shows that prayer was the central element of the ordination and the laying on of hands an accompanying circumstance.[36] He offers a practical reason why the laying on of hands was also necessary. His explanation in regard to the possibility of secret ordination may be hypothetical, but his very entertaining of the thought shows that what would have been inconceivable in an earlier period, when ordination was done in the context of the assembly of the church for whose service one was being ordained, was now conceivable.

The attitude that would forbid the transfer of bishops (and other clergy) from one church to another was more strongly affirmed in the East,

---

34. Canon 17 had called for the excommunication of someone ordained as a bishop for a given church who would not accept the ministry. The Council of Ancyra (314), can. 18, had already had to deal with the problem of bishops "not received by the parish to which they were designated."

35. Jerome, *On Isaiah* 16.58.

36. Everett Ferguson, "The Laying on of Hands: Its Significance in Ordination," *Journal of Theological Studies*, n.s., 26 (1975): 1-12; reprinted in Ferguson, *Church, Ministry, and Organization in the Early Church Era*, pp. 147-58.

where it still obtains, than in the West. For instance, Gregory of Nazianzus had to resign as bishop of Constantinople on the charge that his appointment was illegal since he had been ordained as bishop of Sasima (although in fact he never served there). A basis for modification of the legislation against transfer of bishops was already present in Cyprian's theory of the episcopate belonging to the whole church, and the premise of the old view was changed by Augustine's view of ordination as a permanent possession not tied to the action of a local congregation.[37]

A modern Benedictine, in introducing his translation of a work by a Father of the Greek Church, Maximus the Confessor (580-662), expressed the viewpoint of the Greek Church in a statement that those of a congregational polity would also endorse: "The Church is not made up of the sum of its parts, but all of it is present in each of its parts."[38] A modern Greek Orthodox theologian defines the church in terms of the local eucharistic community, each in full unity with other communities by virtue of the whole Christ represented in each.[39] Congregational church polity has attempted to carry out consistently the implications of this insight.

Free churches have things to learn from the ancient church, as other essays in this collection will argue. From the perspective of this essay, it is also true that much in the ancient church is congenial with or even supportive of emphases found in free churches. These include the local congregation as the basic organizational unit of the church, the local congregation as the essential decision-making body, congregations related directly with one another and not through their leaders, and the right of the local congregation to choose its own ministers. The convictions and practices of the early church remind all church communions to focus on the church, not only as an institution, but as the gathered community of believers.

37. Augustine, *On Baptism against the Donatists* 1.1.2.
38. Dom Julian Stead, *The Church, the Liturgy, and the Soul of Man: The Mystagogia of St. Maximus the Confessor* (Still River, Mass.: St. Bede's Publications, 1982), p. 16.
39. John D. Zizioulas, *Being as Communion: Studies in Personhood and the Church* (London: Darton, Longman and Todd, 1985), p. 157.

The Authority of Tradition: A Baptist View

E. GLENN HINSON

Few Baptists would claim to represent *the* Baptist view on any subject, much less *the* Baptist view on an issue as debatable as the authority of tradition. Indeed, within Christian tradition as a whole one may find a variety of attitudes and within Baptist tradition representatives who will agree with each: (1) Scripture alone (the view of the magisterial Reformers); (2) tradition as authoritative as Scripture (the pre–Vatican II Roman Catholic view); (3) selected earlier tradition as authoritative as Scripture (the Greek Orthodox view); (4) the living contemporary tradition as superior to Scripture (the early Gnostic view); and (5) Scripture and tradition as a single source of authority (the view adopted at Vatican II).

In the main, Baptists have inclined more toward the "Scripture alone" end of the spectrum and have disclaimed the authority of tradition. However, there has not been thorough consistency on this view. The same group of Baptists can sing "Faith of Our Fathers" and "Holy Bible, Book Divine" with equal élan. Or they can publish a confession of faith which asserts that "The Holy Scripture is the only sufficient, certain, and infallible rule of all saving Knowledge, Faith, and Obedience" and yet frames its statement about God in terms of the Nicene-Chalcedonian formula.[1] Or they can assert that "no decrees of popes, or councils, or writings of any person whatsoever, are of equal authority with the sacred scriptures" while insisting that the Nicene, "Athanasian," and Apostles' creeds "ought thoroughly to be re-

---

1. Second London Confession I.1; II.3.

ceived, and believed."[2] The fact is, Baptists have not really given serious overt attention to the authority of tradition, even their own tradition. Tradition, therefore, exerts usually an undefined and possibly even unadmitted influence in the interpretation of Scripture, in shaping theological views, or in forming or conserving ecclesiastical observances. It is tradition, for example, which convinces many Baptists that their congregational polity is the only true New Testament polity and that episcopal or presbyterian polities have no grounds in the earliest period of church history.

Recognizing the diversity of Baptist views and the lack of sophisticated attention to the question of tradition hitherto, I doubt whether it will be profitable to review Baptist views of tradition at any length. Rather, I think we may produce more fruit by asking to what extent a Baptist might accept the view of the authority of tradition put forth in the *Dogmatic Constitution on Divine Revelation* at the Second Vatican Council, namely, as related to the "one source" concept of revelation. Methodologically this will mean a critique of this concept from the perspective of the nature of God's self-disclosure. The chief issue is: can God disclose God's Word, God's person, and God's purpose, through tradition which is found elsewhere than in the canonical Scriptures? Many Baptists would answer no unequivocally. However, I am going to argue that, with some qualifications, Baptists can accept the "one source" concept without doing violence to their fundamental conviction that the Scriptures contain (I hesitate to assert without qualification that they are) the Word of God.

The Definitive Authority: Revelation Itself

From a Protestant perspective the *Dogmatic Constitution on Divine Revelation* starts in the right place, viz., with revelation itself. Most Protestants will acquiesce with the significance attached to special as opposed to general revelation, with the finality ascribed to the revelation which has occurred, and with the description of the way in which revelation has occurred. Disagreements will arise chiefly with respect to those particulars on which Protestants disagree with other Protestants.

To look at points of agreement more closely, first of all, Protestants

2. "The Orthodox Creed," 1678, art. 37, 38, in *Baptist Confessions of Faith*, ed. William L. Lumpkin (Valley Forge, Pa.: Judson, 1959), p. 326.

will concur with this document in emphasizing the reliability of *special* as opposed to *general* revelation. While Protestants have typically denied the assertion that "God, the beginning and end of all things, can be known with certainty from created reality by the light of human reason," few would dispute the general tenor of the assertion that "it is *through His revelation* that those religious truths which are by their nature accessible to human reason can be known with ease, with solid certitude, and with no trace of error, even in the present state of the human race" (I.6).[3] Later on we will query whether suggestions of inerrancy and infallibility do not go too far. At this point, however, it suffices to affirm the intent of the document to give a normative significance to special revelation.

In addition to approving this intent, secondly, most Protestants will also subscribe to the *finality* which the constitution attaches to the revelation already given. "The Christian dispensation, therefore, as the new and definitive covenant," the constitution states, "will never pass away, and we now await no further new public revelation before the glorious manifestation of our Lord Jesus Christ" (I.4). The use of the word "public" would not, I assume, exclude *private* experiences which would be authoritative to the persons who experienced them. Through the centuries, as a matter of fact, the church has acknowledged and affirmed mystical experiences recorded by martyrs such as Perpetua or saints such as Augustine or Francis of Assisi or Catherine of Siena. It has even approved the significance which many faithful attach to such persons and their experiences. However, this statement seems to say that the church would not see them as normative for the church corporate. That revelation which is fundamental for Christians has already occurred.

Protestants, too, I should think, thirdly, would agree generally with the constitution's understanding of the *nature* of divine revelation — through nature *but* especially through historical events, and through prophetic insight into the revelatory significance of the events. It is said that "the deeds wrought by God in the history of salvation manifest and confirm the teaching and realities signified by the words, while the words proclaim the deeds and clarify the mystery contained in them" (I.2). Even more significantly, the finality of the divine revelation in *Christ* is made clear in a manner that would please Karl Barth himself. "By this revelation,

---

3. All citations of *The Dogmatic Constitution on Divine Revelation* will be from *The Documents of Vatican II*, ed. Walter M. Abbott (New York: Guild Press, 1966).

then," it is said, "the deepest truth about God and the salvation of man is made clear to us in Christ, who is the Mediator and at the same time the fullness of all revelation" (I.2).

Points of debate seem to me to have nothing to do with Catholic-Protestant or Catholic-Baptist perceptions but with Christian-Christian perceptions. The emphasis on natural or general revelation is, to my mind, a wholesome one, though many astute Protestant theologians, from Calvin and Luther to Barth, have denigrated it on the ground that humankind's "fall" so marred human reason as to render it virtually useless in knowing God's will. Where I find myself quibbling with the views of this document is the same place I quibble with conservative Protestants about the Bible. Can we be so confident "that those religious truths which are by their nature accessible to human reason can be known by all men *with ease, with solid certitude, and with no trace of error,* even in the present state of the human race" (I.6)? Any objective look at human experience should incite caution. The same caution is needed when we look at the use of the term "infallibility" in the *Dogmatic Constitution on the Church.* "This infallibility with which the divine Redeemer willed His Church to be endowed in defining a doctrine of faith and morals extends as far as the deposit of divine revelation, which must be religiously guarded and faithfully expounded" (III.25).[4] This assertion, like that concerning an infallible Bible, seems not to take adequately into account the *human* side of receiving and handing on the revelation. On this matter I would side with Hans Küng in his argument for "indefectibility" as opposed to "infallibility" in describing any receiving and handling of God's self-disclosure.[5] After all, modern theology is teaching us to apply the word "infallible" to God with some caution. Can we apply it at all, then, to *our* knowledge of God and God's purpose for humankind?

The Transmission of Divine Revelation

In the final analysis, the Vatican II statement about revelation probably contains more elements with which Baptists can agree than with which

---

4. All citations of *The Dogmatic Constitution on the Church* will also be from *The Documents of Vatican II.*

5. Hans Küng, *Infallible? An Inquiry,* trans. Edward Quinn (Garden City, N.Y.: Doubleday, 1971).

they have to disagree. The same may be said of the statement concerning the transmission of divine revelation. The one-source theory and the tripolar conception of authority (of Scriptures, tradition, and the church's magisterium), properly understood, are amenable with a Protestant perspective of authority based on the Word of God. The chief points of dispute are related to that mentioned above regarding revelation, viz., how final and absolute the church's own claims may be. On some points the constitution appears to contradict itself.[6]

To look first at the positive side, the document falls into line with modern biblical studies in asserting the "close connection and communication between sacred tradition and sacred Scripture" (II.9). The fact is, the reason the scriptures of the New Testament were assembled into an authoritative collection by the early churches is because they contain *the apostolic tradition,* the original deposit of or about Jesus which was preserved by the first witnesses. This, rather than apostolic authorship, was almost certainly the chief criterion of "canonicity." Early missionaries committed to memory some fundamental elements of tradition which they could instill in their converts. How uniform this original fund was cannot be determined exactly. Fragments of it, however, stick out in the New Testament. In 1 Corinthians 15:3ff., for example, Paul reminded the Corinthians that he had handed on *(paredoka)* to them the tradition he had received concerning Christ's death, resurrection, and appearances. The material itself bears the stamp of formal, catechetical usage. In speaking of "tradition" in this sense, of course, we are talking about the fundamental, essential, *sine qua non* message of God's self-disclosure in the Christ event. It may be distinguished, albeit with great difficulty, from the forms in which it has been enclosed in various cultures as the church has carried out its mission. As the essential message, *tradition* must always exist. To depart from it is to depart from the source of the church's very existence.

The *Dogmatic Constitution on Divine Revelation* is also right in saying that this single source has existed all through the centuries. Overlooking for the moment the historical problems, we can agree with the general schema set forth in chapter II regarding "the Transmission of Divine Revelation." Christ, "in whom the full revelation of the supreme God is brought to completion," commissioned the apostles "to preach the gospel and to impart gifts to men" (II.7). The apostles, discharging their com-

---

6. Some of the contradictions will be noted later.

mission by oral preaching, by example, and by ordinances, "handed on what they received from the lips of Christ, from living with Him, and from what He did, or what they had learned through the prompting of the Holy Spirit" (II.7). Other "apostolic men" and then "bishops" succeeded them. "And so the apostolic preaching, which is expressed in a special way in the inspired books, was to be preserved by a continuous succession of preachers until the end of time" (II.8). Agreement with this sketch of the process of transmission should not of course be interpreted as an affirmative judgment about episcopal or apostolic succession.

Any of us who study objectively the actual transmission process within the life of the church will recognize the operation of a magisterium, a teaching office. For Baptists, with their congregational polity, this office is difficult to define. It probably exists in individual interpretation; in congregational worship and Sunday school instruction; in denominational agencies, especially the seminaries; and in various "leaders" within a democratic political body. It is this indefiniteness which in part causes many Protestants to deny that they have a magisterium. More than that, however, many shudder at the ominous sound of the word, which provokes images of papal pronouncements and inquisitors. Nevertheless, it is time for us to admit that a teaching office has to exist somewhere, as the constitution says, in order to preserve the Word of God faithfully, to explain it, and to make it widely known.

With the basic tenor of the one-source concept and the tripolar view of authority Protestants may agree. Questions arise not in regard to these, but in regard to the location of the magisterium, the equality or superiority of one or another of the three poles of authority, and the manner and extent of development of revelation.

First, I doubt whether Baptists, with a long heritage of suspicion of authority, will concede that "The task of authentically interpreting the word of God, whether written or handed on, has been entrusted exclusively to the living teaching office of the Church, whose authority is exercised in the name of Jesus Christ" (II.10), unless the magisterium is seen as located in the whole body of Christ, including the laity. The ultimate court of interpretation among Baptists has been the individual conscience. This was also Luther's judgment when he declared at Worms in 1521: "Unless I am convinced by the testimony of the Scriptures or by clear reason (for I do not trust either in the pope or in councils alone, since it is well known that they have often erred and contradicted themselves) — I am bound by the Scriptures I have quoted and my conscience is captive to the Word of God. I cannot and I will not recant anything, since it is neither safe nor right to go against conscience."[7] We would have to stretch our imaginations to believe that this constitution implies anything so broad as this. As Walter M. Abbott has noted, magisterium means "In its broadest sense all who proclaim the word with authority in the Church," and more narrowly "the Pope and the bishops collectively."[8] The *Dogmatic Constitution on the Church* indeed makes it unmistakably clear that the faithful are to accept and adhere to the teachings of the bishops individually "with a religious assent of soul" and to submit will and mind "in a special way to the authentic teaching of the Roman Pontiff, even when he is not speaking *ex cathedra*" (II.25). Further, when the bishops, though not possessing infallibility individually, speak together with the pope, "they can nevertheless proclaim Christ's doctrine infallibly," especially in synods. Finally, the pope's definitions of some doctrines of faith or morals "of themselves, and not from the consent of the Church, are justly styled irreformable, . . . need no approval of others, nor . . . allow an appeal to any other judgment." When either the pope or the bishops together define doctrine, it becomes "revelation,"[9] and therefore "All are obliged to maintain and be ruled by this revelation, which, as written or preserved by tradition, is transmitted in its entirety through the legitimate succession of bishops and especially through the care of the Roman Pontiff himself" (*Church*, II.25).

This brings us to a second question, one which may be the real crux: *the equality or superiority of one or another of the poles.* What the passages just cited evince is that, in the end, the magisterium, meaning the bishops and the pope, stands above the other two. It hands on to the faithful the infallible and irreformable revelation. To make matters more complicated, this conception of the magisterium in the document on the church emits a strange sound alongside the assurance of that on revelation that "This teaching office is not above the word of God, but serves it, teaching only what has been handed on, listening to it devoutly, guarding it scrupulously,

---

7. "The Speech of Dr. Martin Luther before the Emperor Charles and Princes at Worms on the Fifth Day after Misericordias Domini [18 April] in the Name of Jesus," trans. Roger A. Hornsby, in *Luther's Works*, ed. George W. Forell (Philadelphia: Muhlenberg, 1958), 32:112.

8. In *Documents of Vatican II*, p. 118 n. 26.

9. "Revelation" is evidently used as an equivalent of "authoritative teaching" rather than the more usual understanding of divine self-disclosure.

and explaining it faithfully by divine commission and the help of the Holy Spirit; it draws from this one deposit of faith everything which it presents for belief as divinely revealed" (*Revelation*, II.12). Admittedly, these two positions may be reconciled by saying that all three poles — Scriptures, tradition, magisterium — fall under the Word of God. But the document on the church, and even more, a dogma such as that of the assumption of Mary, seems to imply that for the church, the pope and the bishops can actually produce revelation, viz., the Word of God, without reference to the other two poles.

The accuracy of this judgment is confirmed, I think, in the prospect of a new revelation. To be sure, this is denied explicitly in both the *Dogmatic Constitution on the Church* and the *Dogmatic Constitution on Divine Revelation*. Both disallow "that there could be any new public revelation pertaining to the divine deposit of faith."[10] These statements notwithstanding, the possibility of hitherto undisclosed public revelations being discovered seems to be implied in article 8 of the *Dogmatic Constitution on Divine Revelation*, for it is said that "This tradition which comes from the apostles develops in the Church with the help of the Holy Spirit. For there is a growth in the understanding of the realities and the words which have been handed down. . . . For, as the centuries succeed one another, the Church constantly moves forward toward the fullness of divine truth until the words of God reach their complete fulfillment in her." The crucial question here is whether we can say "This tradition . . . develops . . . ," even granting that the church may grow in its grasp of the divine revelation which has reached its complete expression in Christ. Our answer will depend heavily upon what we mean by "this tradition." If we define it broadly enough, the answer may be yes. If, however, we define tradition as the essential deposit related to the Christ event, then the answer will have to be no. The definition of this word thus becomes our most critical task and merits special consideration.

What Is Tradition?

On this point the *Dogmatic Constitution on Divine Revelation* seems to want it both ways. For the purpose of establishing the authority of tradi-

10. *Church*, II.25, in *Documents of Vatican II*, p. 50; cf. *Revelation*, I.4, in *Documents of Vatican II*, p. 113.

tion it uses the narrow definition, but for the purpose of establishing the authority of the magisterium it uses the broad definition. Is tradition to be understood as the essential deposit of faith (the narrow sense) or as the whole corpus of Christian heritage (the broad sense)?

One has to admit the difficulty of defining tradition in the narrow sense. Can it ever be expressed in an *essential* form, as the "essence" of Christianity? The truth of the matter is that the tradition, as an essential deposit, appears, even in the earliest period, in numerous traditions. We cannot be as confident as C. H. Dodd was, for example, that we can establish the apostolic preaching. You have, as it were, a gospel according to Paul, according to Matthew, according to Mark, according to Luke, according to John, etc. In the early centuries, moreover, the Church Fathers articulated the "rule of faith" in several ways.

This difficulty would seem to argue for adoption of a comprehensive definition of tradition. However, the problem of finding *the* apostolic tradition is small by comparison with that of ascribing definitive authority to the amorphous mass of the Christian heritage. Are we to say that tradition is authoritative if the magisterium declares it to be so? If we say that, can we ever be sure we are not acting on purely subjective whim? Whether it can do so with complete success or not, the church would always seem to need to search relentlessly for an essential deposit of revelation. It is precisely this need which has caused Protestants to place the Scriptures in the preeminent position of authority. Indeed, the Protestant principle, that is, that no human institution can claim finality in the way Scripture can, lies near the surface here. The final thing is not the church, but the Word of God itself. The church lives always on what it has received.

A way around this difficulty has been to distinguish between tradition as the essential deposit and traditions which incorporate it.[11] Such a distinction has the advantage of representing the problem accurately enough; certainly the essential deposit never exists apart from forms which encase it. As in an electric cable, the vital element of each of the traditions is the central tradition. Each of them has authority, therefore, insofar as it contains this tradition.

Still, does this hypothesis eliminate the need to test traditions to see whether they contain *the* tradition? Can we ever assume that all traditions

---

11. So Yves Congar, *Tradition and Traditions* (New York: Scribners, 1966) and *The Meaning of Tradition*, trans. A. N. Woodrow (New York: Hawthorn Books, 1964).

are equally reliable or, indeed, reliable at all? Obviously the answer to both questions is no. At a given time the central tradition may become so vitiated by the form which encases it that it may be wholly ineffective and even counterproductive. Is this not, after all, what the Reformation of the sixteenth century was about? To be sure, we cannot say that the whole church was totally impaired and thus unfaithful. It was impaired, however, to the extent that some of its traditions needed reforming in light of *the* tradition. But where could one discern *the* tradition in a reliable or in its most reliable form? The answer of the Protestant Reformers was, "in the Scriptures."

Tradition and Scripture

This statement offers a suitable juncture for introducing a crucial consideration regarding the authority of tradition as posed by the *Dogmatic Constitution on Divine Revelation;* that is, the relationship between tradition and Scriptures. In general I believe that Protestants would appreciate the attempt of this constitution to maintain a reciprocal relationship in which now Scriptures and now tradition stand guard over one another and help to interpret one another. Nevertheless, there is still reason to question whether we do not need to ascribe a superior place to that tradition found within the New Testament scriptures by virtue of their proximity to the Christ event. In short, is all tradition the same no matter where it comes in the stream, or do we need to test later tradition by the earlier? On this point modern historical criticism forces some qualifications of the uncritical views of transmission of tradition reflected in this document.

To look first at the positive side, we can assume properly that if tradition, defined as the essential deposit of revelation, contains divine revelation, the Word of God, then the church will have held on to the Word of God from the beginning. Wherever we find this essential deposit, therefore, we will find the Word of God and respond to it as our authority as it is contained in the Scriptures, in the Fathers of the church, in medieval writings, in any post-Reformation denomination — whether Roman Catholic, Orthodox, Anglican, or Protestant. In this sense there is a single source of authority, the Word of God, which is found in Scriptures and in the whole Christian heritage. (This is not to say, however, that everything in Scripture or the whole heritage is the Word of God.)

Further, we must assume that the Holy Spirit has aided the church in remaining *faithful* to this tradition during all of these centuries, sometimes despite itself. The Spirit surely guided the church in the writing and collection of the Scriptures. The Spirit guided the church in its proclamation of the Word and in its incorporation and instruction of converts. The Spirit guided the church in its continuous task of interpreting and applying the Word of God to human life during many centuries of shifting cultures and customs. I am inclined to agree with Petrarch's "Jew" who was converted to Christianity after he saw Rome in its most sordid state: if Christianity has survived all of its corruptions and deficiencies, he concluded, then surely it must be of God.

The chief question which has to be raised here is whether later tradition does not have to be checked against earlier tradition, the church's teachers of the postbiblical era against its teachers of the New Testament era. The *Dogmatic Constitution on Divine Revelation* seems to give a negative answer to the question. It does so by an explicit statement which pulls the one-source theory backward in the direction of the two-source theory of Trent.[12]

> To the successors of the apostles, sacred tradition hands on in its full purity God's word, which was entrusted to the apostles by Christ the Lord and the Holy Spirit. Thus, led by the light of the Spirit of truth, these successors can in their preaching preserve this word of God faithfully, explain it, and make it more widely known. Consequently, it is not from sacred Scriptures alone that the Church draws her certainty about everything which has been revealed. *Therefore both sacred tradition and sacred scripture are to be accepted and venerated with the same sense of devotion and reverence.* (II.9; emphasis added)

With one aspect of this statement I am in hearty agreement; that is, in its supposition that the Spirit has continued to guide the church in its handling of tradition. The Protestant emphasis upon Scripture alone is based upon a subtle but erroneous underlying assumption that the Spirit died about A.D. 100 or with the closing of the canon. This position, most forcefully stated in Protestant dispensationalism,[13] sets the apostolic age

---

12. Karl Barth called attention to the same problem in his *Ad Limina Apostolorum: An Appraisal of Vatican II*, trans. K. R. Crim (Richmond: John Knox, 1968), pp. 43-55.

13. Dispensationalism has a long heritage in Christianity. On the basis of an expectation of an era of a thousand years during which Christ would reign over an ideal kingdom, Papias, bishop of Hierapolis during the second century, set forth an outline of history in

apart from the rest of history in respect to miracles and other direct "evidences" of the Spirit. It hardly allows room for a consistent view of God or God's self-disclosure in history.

While assenting fully to this emphasis, however, I would ask once more: does the tradition found in the Scriptures hold a unique place, so to speak, *above* other tradition and even above the church's magisterium? My own answer has to be yes. I trust that it is yes not merely because of our long Protestant tradition of *sola Scriptura* but because this answer agrees with our understanding of divine revelation.

As I noted earlier, it is God's self-disclosure, God's Word, which is authoritative, that is, determinative for faith and practice. Although this self-disclosure occurs in nature, in general history, and in other aspects of human experience, it has been concretized and particularized in the history of Israel, in the life of Jesus of Nazareth, and in the history of the church. It reached its definitive expression in Jesus of Nazareth.

For our contact with this last event we are dependent upon *the testimony or tradition handed down by those who participated in and experienced God's self-disclosure through the eyes of faith.* Not even in this tradition, to be sure, do we have the "bare facts." Rather, we have faith history, the "facts" of the life, death, and resurrection of Jesus in a confessional package. Nevertheless, we are dependent upon this tradition for whatever we know of this event which is the basis of our salvation. Later generations may reproduce the testimony and apply it to their era, but they cannot experience it and give their testimony to it as did the first believers.

There is, therefore, a *chronological* factor in the question of the authority of tradition. The earliest tradition, based as it is upon eyewitness participation, holds a unique place vis-à-vis God's self-disclosure in Christ. As Hans von Campenhausen has argued, the first witnesses' *experience* of the resurrection of Jesus differed in kind from *our belief in* God's raising him from the dead.[14] Consider in support of this observation Paul's recitation of the kerygma in 1 Corinthians 15:3ff. with the appended note that "Last of all, as to one untimely born, he appeared also to me." Paul saw his own experience as unusual, beyond the time for the risen Lord's other

---

seven "dispensations." Protestant dispensationalism began with J. N. Darby, founder of the Plymouth Brethren Church in England. The theory was popularized through the Scofield Bible, first published in 1906.

14. Hans von Campenhausen, "The Events of Easter and the Empty Tomb," in *Tradition and Life in the Church*, trans. A. V. Littledale (Philadelphia: Fortress, 1968), pp. 53f.

disclosures. He seems to have expected no recurrences of this type. "To all appearances," von Campenhausen judged, "he holds the series to be closed — ecstatic experience and whatever 'visions' may have occurred are on quite a different plane."

The distinctive nature of this apostolic tradition, therefore, establishes for it a uniquely normative position for Christian faith and practice. Since the New Testament scriptures, as collected by a process of elimination over several centuries, contain this never-to-be-repeated deposit, the church must continually bring its traditions there for testing. It is a question of returning again and again to the source, *ressourcement*. In formulating its faith subsequent to the apostolic age, the church should never be presumptuous enough to deviate from the *sine qua non* tradition found in Scriptures. It may interpret and expound upon and draw out the implications of what it finds in that tradition, but it cannot create new dogmas which have no basis in it.

The modern historical model suggests a useful paradigm for the issue of authority. An historian distinguishes between primary and secondary sources. *Primary* sources are those which give direct, firsthand testimony about an event. *Secondary* sources are those which give indirect, secondhand testimony. The historian's rule of thumb is to rely insofar as possible on primary sources and "be suspicious of secondary works in history, even the best ones."[15]

Using this historical model, we are obligated to ask whether we are to see all of the Scriptures as *primary* sources? The answer is, of course, negative. Scripture, too, contains both *primary* and *secondary* tradition. What this means is that scripture differs from scripture as regards the value of each in bringing us God's self-disclosure. Some are to be treated as *primary*, others as *secondary*, even if early secondary, witnesses. Indeed, portions of the same writing are to be distinguished in this way.

---

15. Louis Gottschalk, *Understanding History* (New York: Knopf, 1958), p. 116. We should recognize, of course, that even primary witnesses require critical evaluation. However, we are dependent upon the data they contain, however inadequate, for all later reconstructions.

The Use of Tradition

By the above model differing degrees of authority will be accorded to primary and secondary tradition. *Primary* tradition, by virtue of its proximity to the Christ event, will hold a uniquely normative character. The church must continually test its faith and practice by this tradition. Indeed, it will test all traditions by this tradition.[16]

How to apply the authority of *secondary* tradition is a more difficult question. The truth of the matter is that it is extremely hard to decide which portions of the Christian tradition, in the broad sense, one will use in formulating Christian doctrine or practice. In Christian history several answers, both theoretically and practically, have been given:

1. That Which Confirms What We Already Believe

The Protestant Reformers used Scripture and the early Fathers in this way to support Protestant doctrine and to attack the Roman Catholic Church. By the same token they rejected and/or polemicized the medieval Schoolmen, pointing especially to the deterioration of doctrine in their writings.

2. That Which Is Orthodox

Protestants, Roman Catholics, and Orthodox have all employed this approach with somewhat different results. Protestant theologians have used creeds, usually of the first four centuries; the early Fathers; and the Reformers. Anglican theologians, who in some respects bridge Catholic and

16. A question may be raised here about the Hebrew Bible in relationship to the primary tradition. By virtue of chronology, would 1 *Clement* (A.D. 96) or the *Epistle of Barnabas* (ca. 100-120) have greater authority than Genesis or Isaiah? My answer would be no. The Hebrew scriptures were the authoritative writings of the first Christians. They searched them to understand what they had experienced in connection with Jesus. Christians will of necessity view the Old Testament through the lenses of the revelation of God in and through Jesus of Nazareth, but the Christ event can have no meaning apart from the whole story of God's dealings with the Jewish people. God was disclosing Godself long before Jesus entered the picture, and we are the beneficiaries of a tradition which began with Abraham. So those writings, too, are in some sense part of the primary source.

Protestant traditions, have relied especially on writings of the period up to 451, terminated by the Council of Chalcedon, and certain Anglican reformers. Roman Catholics have used the whole western Catholic tradition, but, by way of reaction to Protestantism, have elevated the Scholastic synthesis of Thomas Aquinas, along with about twenty-one ecumenical councils, to the most eminent place. The Eastern Orthodox have employed the first seven ecumenical councils and especially the synthesis of John of Damascus as normative.

3. Christian Thought

It became fashionable in the late nineteenth and early twentieth centuries for more liberal Protestant theologians such as A. C. McGiffert to write histories of Christian thought. Thence, either by critique or by praise, even the "heretics" had a hearing. Many whom earlier generations had condemned, e.g., Origen and Nestorius, were reappraised and restored to places of significance in the formulation of doctrine.

4. That on Which We Agree on the Basis of the Word of God

In the fifth century Vincent, abbot of the monastery at Lérins in the south of France, tried to define catholic doctrine in terms of consensus, "That which has been believed always, everywhere, and by all." On the face of it, such consensus appears unattainable. In the last three decades, however, Jaroslav Pelikan has published a five-volume work on the history of Christian *tradition* in which the matter of consensus has again come to the fore. He defines "the Christian tradition" as "What the church of Jesus Christ believes, teaches, and confesses on the basis of the word of God."[17]

Pelikan's formula may be useful in our discussion here. Notice how his statement both (1) projects the inseparable interrelation of God's self-disclosure and the whole heritage of Christian interaction with it, and (2) assures always the preeminence of the former. In practice this would

17. Jaroslav Pelikan, *The Christian Tradition: A History of the Development of Doctrine,* vol. 1, *The Emergence of the Catholic Tradition (100-600)* (Chicago and London: University of Chicago Press, 1971), p. 1.

mean that we would scrutinize the whole Christian heritage with a view to what it had to teach us concerning the interpretation and application of God's Word throughout the ages, but that we would never become enslaved to any segment of it, for we would at the same time judge it by the self-authenticating Word of God. This approach appears to me to meet the principal objection which Baptists have voiced regarding tradition; that is, that the authority of tradition tends so often to supplant the authority of God's self-disclosure and to lock us into a prison built of credal orthodoxy. Baptists have not opposed the use of tradition, but they have opposed assigning it any normative place alongside Scripture. Thence they have preferred to use the designation "confession of faith" rather than "creed" because it emits a less dogmatic ring.

The preface to the 1925 Baptist Faith and Message, a revision of the 1833 New Hampshire Confession of Faith prepared in the midst of the evolution controversy for use in the Southern Baptist Convention, explains in some detail the reservations Baptists hold with reference to formal statements of faith.[18] According to this preface, confessions are framed and circulated by Baptists with the following understandings: (1) "That they constitute a consensus of opinion of some Baptist body, larger or small, for the general instruction and guidance of our own people and others concerning those articles of the Christian faith which are most surely held among us," without intending to "add anything to the simple conditions of salvation revealed in the New Testament"; (2) that they not be considered "complete statements of our faith, having any quality of finality or infallibility," and be subject always to revision; (3) that any group of Baptists may draw up their own confessions and publish them as they think advisable; (4) that the scriptures of the Old and New Testaments constitute "the sole authority of faith and practice among Baptists," while confessions are "only guides in interpretations"; (5) that confessions "are statements of religious convictions, drawn from the scriptures," which should not be used to hinder "freedom of thought or investigation in other realms of life."[19]

In actual practice, the proposed approach will have an effect upon both our selectivity in the use of our heritage and upon the manner in

18. Both confessions can be found in *Baptist Confessions of Faith*.

19. I should note here that the Southern Baptist Convention (SBC) revised the Baptist Faith and Message in 1963 and again in 2000. The 1963 version stated that Jesus Christ would be the standard for interpreting Scripture. The 2000 version, however, deleted that statement, thus placing interpretation in the hands of a more definite magisterium of SBC leaders.

which we use it. *As regards selectivity,* although the whole Christian heritage will be open for our examination, we will take a particular interest in that which bears upon the interpretation and application of the divine self-disclosure attested in the Scriptures. This principle tends, therefore, to validate the special attention given in the Baptist tradition to the early Fathers and the Protestant Reformers, in that both of these, however successfully, sought to place Scriptures at the center in formulating both faith and practice.[20] Other writers and epochs where the study of the Scriptures has broken through with fresh insight likewise merit special attention. Need one mention monastic piety which has nourished itself on the Psalms, German Pietism, the Wesleyan revival, the Great Awakening, the Barthian epoch, the epoch of John XXIII? Yet a study of these will, of necessity, carry us into the whole stream of the Christian heritage. The whole stream has some fresh water to pour on the church's application of its understanding of God's self-disclosure in Jesus Christ. It would be erroneous to narrow the range too much in view of the fact that we recognize that our fathers, too, have erred in judging their contemporaries.

As regards the manner of use, the larger Christian heritage would seem in the main to offer hermeneutical help. To be sure, Baptists have utilized their own traditional formulae for many reasons. They have formulated confessions of faith, for instance, to defend themselves against false interpretations or slanders, to provide the basis for uniting in associations and conventions, to distinguish and identify themselves in relation to other Protestant or even Baptist groups, to instruct their constituency in Baptist principles, to affirm ecumenical ties with other Christians, and to maintain some standard for determining orthodoxy. In a very real way, however, all of these should have been subsidiary to faithful interpretation and application of the divine self-disclosure recorded in the Scriptures, as virtually every confession has explicitly claimed. Beyond that, everything is annotation. The authority of the Christian heritage is a derivative authority, one that originates in the faithfulness of Christians in various eras under their particular circumstances to God's self-disclosure. None of it is

---

20. I wonder if this was not also the method Roman Catholics applied in the renewal of the church which came to a focus in Vatican II. *The Dogmatic Constitution on the Church (Lumen Gentium),* for instance, has a fully scriptural text footnoted by tradition. This appears to me to be the correct approach.

authoritative in and of itself; it is authenticated by whether it has shown accurate interpretation and application of the Word of God.

This position, I believe, would win an essential consensus both in theory and practice in the history of the church, although there would be periods of deviation. It is not possible to run through the entire history of the church without presenting evidence on both sides, but it may be profitable to offer a brief statement from the patristic era. In this period, as R. P. C. Hanson has shown, the early Fathers normally spoke of confessions and "the rule of faith" or "summaries of faith."[21] In the pre-Nicene period the consistency of confessional statements on major items evidently arose from their dependence upon the apostolic tradition preserved either orally or in the Scriptures, but the Fathers saw an essential link between the two. Thence Irenaeus could say, "If the Apostles had not left to us the Scriptures, would it not be necessary to follow the order of tradition, which those to whom they committed the churches handed down?"[22] It is even clearer that Origen used a summary of what he thought to be essentials of the biblical revelation as "the form of those things which are manifestly delivered by the apostolic preaching."[23]

In the post-Nicene period, as the great theological controversies heightened the concern for doctrinal norms, insistence upon faithfulness to Scriptures increased. Nothing reveals this more clearly than the heated debate over the use of the term *homoousios* in the Nicene Creed. Pro-Arius supporters argued vehemently against its inclusion in the creed on the grounds that it has no scriptural precedent. In response to their contention, Athanasius was careful not to question the centrality of the Scriptures. Instead, he argued that *homoousios* was true, if not to the letter, then to the *sense* of Scripture. The bishops of Nicaea were "compelled on their part to collect the sense of the Scriptures, and to re-say and re-write what they had said before, more distinctly still," in order to cut off Arian subterfuges.[24] If anyone has a complaint about the expression, "let him know that, even if the expressions are not in so many words in the Scriptures, . . .

21. R. P. C. Hanson, *Tradition in the Early Church* (Philadelphia: Westminster, 1962), p. 10 and passim.

22. Irenaeus, *Against Heresies* 3.4.1.

23. Origen, *On First Principles* 1, pref. 4-6.

24. Athanasius, *Defence of the Nicene Definition* 20, in Nicene and Post-Nicene Fathers, 2nd ser., 4:163.

they contain the sense of the Scriptures, and expressing it, they convey it to those who have their hearing unimpaired for religious doctrine."[25]

In the patristic era the creeds functioned in the main, once a collection of the Scriptures existed, as guides to their interpretation and application. There were, of course, varied special usages: catechizing and baptism, worship, exorcism, guidance in persecution, and refutation of heresy.[26] The most salient usage, however, was in catechizing and baptism, and this accounts for most of the credal development of the first centuries.[27] By the fourth century the exposition of the creed involved a phrase-by-phrase scriptural commentary. In his famous *Catechetical Lectures,* delivered in 348, Cyril of Jerusalem lets us know that he considered the creed to be derived from Scriptures and to point to them. Having commented from Scriptures in a summary way on each article of the creed, he noted that "the remaining subjects of our introductory teaching" are taught by "the divinely-inspired Scriptures of both the Old and New Testament" and enjoined his hearers to read them.[28] Augustine expressed a similar sentiment in *On Faith and the Creed.* The creed exists, he explained, so that "individuals who are but beginners and sucklings among those who have been born again in Christ, and who have not yet been strengthened by most diligent and spiritual handling and understanding of the divine Scriptures, should be furnished with a summary, expressed in few words, of those matters of necessary belief which were subsequently to be explained to them in many words."[29]

In actual usage creeds sometimes did assume a normative importance of their own in the patristic era. This is because it was more convenient and conclusive to apply the "summary" than to go through the labyrinth of interpretation which Scriptures sometimes required. Having such a point of reference could work both to the advantage and to the disadvantage of individual interpreters. On the one hand, it did pose a point of dis-

---

25. Athanasius, *Defence of the Nicene Definition* 21, in Nicene and Post-Nicene Fathers, 2nd ser., 4:164.

26. See Oscar Cullmann, *The Earliest Christian Confessions,* trans. J. K. S. Reid (London: Lutterworth, 1949), pp. 18-34.

27. See J. N. D. Kelly, *Early Christian Creeds,* 3rd ed. (London: Longmans, Green, and Co., 1950), pp. 30-31, 51-52.

28. Cyril of Jerusalem, *Catecheses* 4.33.

29. Augustine, *On Faith and the Creed* 1.1, in Nicene and Post-Nicene Fathers, 1st ser., 3:321.

cipline which would cut off speculations. On the other hand, by delineating what were counted essential items, it laid out a path that interpreters, once they knew the danger points, could safely tread.

In conclusion, I am in relative agreement with the concept of the authority of tradition which is suggested by the one-source model of the *Dogmatic Constitution on Divine Revelation.* As I understand this concept, the church's authority originates in the divine self-disclosure in nature, in general history, in salvation history, but above all, in Jesus of Nazareth. For what we know of the last mode of God's self-disclosure, we are dependent upon tradition. This tradition flows as a single continuous stream from the beginning on. It is embedded, however, in numerous traditions. It is embedded in the canonical Scriptures. But all of these, insofar as they are valid, have their source in this tradition. The safekeeping of this tradition lies in the hands of the magisterium, however defined.

In several vital points Protestants will be likely to question the concept of the authority of tradition presented in this constitution. A fundamental one is the ascription of infallibility to either tradition, Scriptures, or the church's magisterium. Where Protestants have conferred infallibility, they have done so only upon the Scriptures. Even this stands in direct opposition to the Protestant principle, viz., that no institution with which human beings have contact can claim to have the last word. That which is utterly reliable is the Word of God, God's self-disclosure. A second point concerns the location of the magisterium. Baptists especially, influenced as they are by the Reformation, the Renaissance, and the Enlightenment, will insist upon the right of each Christian or group of Christians to search for and interpret God's Word.[30] A third point has to do with the interrelation of the three poles of authority — tradition, Scriptures, and magisterium. The issue here is shaped by the way in which we define tradition. If defined both narrowly as the essential deposit of revelation and broadly as what the church teaches on the basis of the Word of God, then the tradition contained in the Scriptures will have to be assigned a superior place. It is, insofar as we can find a *primary* source, *the* primary source against which

30. I say this with an awareness that those who now control the Southern Baptist Convention seriously dispute this view. The convention in June 2000 generated a very strong reaction, including the severing of ties by a number of Baptist congregations, when it deleted from a revised Baptist Faith and Message the statement that Jesus Christ is the rule by which Scriptures are to be interpreted. Conservative leaders asserted that they would guide interpretation. In short, they would be the Southern Baptist magisterium!

all other traditions, even those within the Scriptures, have to be tested. This conception concurs with the Protestant view that the church always stands in need of reform.

What does this say to the question of Baptist attitudes toward councils, including the Second Vatican Council, whose perspective on tradition I have critiqued? Councils, especially the ecumenical councils, have played a major role in interpreting the Christian tradition in the broad sense all through the centuries. As we survey the history of Christian reliance on the councils, we can see near unanimity among Christians, Baptists included, that we should look to some councils for guidance, but we also see strong differences of opinion as to which councils should have the major say in helping us lay hold on the Christian tradition and apply it today. Because Christians differ so dramatically in their assessment of councils, it would not be wise to consider any council, not Nicaea or Chalcedon or Vatican II, as possessing *final* authority. None should be considered infallible and inerrant. We must acknowledge the conditioning of each by time and circumstances, which may make some of their decisions irrelevant for us in our time and circumstances. What we can draw from them is insight into the way we must take the deposit we have received and make it relevant to people who live in very different settings and contexts than the first recipients of this message. All Christians may learn much from what the Church Fathers sought to do at Nicaea in 325 when they framed that much-used creed, even what they did at Nicaea in 787 when they repudiated iconoclasm and affirmed the use of icons, and, yes, what Roman Catholic bishops planned to do through the Second Vatican Council to achieve the vision of Pope John XXIII for an "updated" church better equipped to engage a postmodern world. All of those, however, must come under the searchlight of the Word of God.

Alexander Campbell and the Apostolic Tradition

WILLIAM TABBERNEE

In one of his most poignant autobiographical statements, Alexander Campbell (1788-1866),[1] one of the founders of the Christian Church (Disciples of Christ),[2] reveals both the origins and content of the basic conviction which shaped his theological method and permeated his writings: "My faith in creeds and confessions of human device was considerably shaken while in Scotland, and I commenced my career in this country under the conviction that nothing that was not as old as the New Testament should be made an article of faith, a rule of practice or a term of communion among Christians."[3] The comment about Scotland relates to ten months Alexander spent in Glasgow following a shipwreck which delayed him, his mother, and his six younger brothers and sisters on their journey from Ireland to Pennsylvania. They had set out to join Thomas Campbell (1763-1854), Alexander's father, a Presbyterian minister who had also served as the headmaster of a school in Ireland before emigrating to North America in 1807. The delay in their journey enabled Alexander to enroll in his father's alma mater, the University of Glasgow. Alexander had already received a rigorous classical and religious education — most recently from

---

1. See Robert Richardson, *Memoirs of Alexander Campbell: Embracing a View of the Origin, Progress and Principles of the Religious Reformation which He Advocated*, 2 vols. (Philadelphia: J. B. Lippencott, 1868-70).

2. See Winfred E. Garrison and Alfred T. DeGroot, *The Disciples of Christ: A History* (St. Louis: Bethany Press, 1958).

3. *Christian Baptist* 2, no. 2 (6 September 1824): 14.

his father, who had made him a co-teacher in his school by the age of seventeen and had left him in charge of the school when he himself left for Pennsylvania. Already proficient in Greek and Latin, Alexander enrolled in an advanced New Testament Greek class as well as taking courses such as Latin, French, and natural science. He even kept a diary written in Latin during his year as a student at the university.

While in Glasgow, Alexander also spent considerable time with Greville Ewing, a former Presbyterian minister who had provided hospitality for the Campbell family after their shipwreck. Ewing was in charge of a seminary founded by Robert and James Haldane. The Haldanes, also former Presbyterians, had established a number of independent churches organized on "New Testament principles" — including congregational autonomy and the weekly observance of the Lord's Supper.

Discussions with Ewing and others influenced Alexander greatly. He became convinced of the necessity of "restoring New Testament Christianity," unaware that his father had come to a similar conclusion in North America. At almost the very same time, Thomas Campbell was defending himself against the charge that he had taught "that a church has no divine warrant for holding Confessions of Faith as terms of communion."[4] According to his accusers, Campbell had expressed the view that confessions of faith should not be used as means by which a person could be admitted to the communion table to receive the bread and wine of the Lord's Supper. The charge had originally been brought against him by William Wilson before the Chartiers Presbytery on 27 October 1807.[5] Wilson was a fellow Presbyterian minister who had accompanied Campbell on some of his itinerant preaching assignments[6] following his formal appointment to serve within the Chartiers Presbytery in southwestern Pennsylvania on 18 May 1807[7] — only five days after his arrival in Pittsburgh from Ireland.

After the charge had become a formal libel, Wilson, during the second phase of Campbell's heresy trial before the presbytery on 10-11 February 1808, testified that, at Conemaugh, "at the usual time of fencing the table,"

---

4. "Minutes of the Chartiers Presbytery," entry for 6 January 1808, in William Hubert Hanna, *Thomas Campbell: Seceder and Christian Union Advocate* (Cincinnati: Standard Publishing Co., 1935), pp. 40-41.

5. "Minutes of the Chartiers Presbytery," entry for 27 October 1807, in Hanna, p. 33.

6. See Richardson, 1:224.

7. "Minutes of the Associate Synod of North America," entries for 16 and 18 May 1807, in Hanna, pp. 29-30.

Campbell had proposed that the following should be the only "terms of communion": "1st. The scriptures; . . . 2d. The Westminster Confession of Faith; and this not particularly but generally. . . . 3d. A testimony: but this not particularly but generally."[8] What Wilson, and many of the other witnesses at Campbell's trial, objected to was that Campbell added the qualifying phrase "not particularly but generally" to explain the way he believed people should adhere to church documents such as the Westminster Confession of Faith[9] and the Declaration and Testimony.[10] Wilson and others testified that Campbell had supported his (in their view liberal and erroneous) position by declaring that "confessions" and "testimonies" had only "human authority" and contained items which could not be proven and others which were difficult to understand — especially by young people.[11]

It is important to note that although Campbell obviously disagreed radically with his fellow ministers about the precise way confessions or testimonies should be used as a "term of communion," he, at this time, had not rejected them altogether. He simply argued that some latitude should be granted in the way in which people subscribed to such documents. They were not to be equated with Scripture but subordinated to Scripture. They should also be understood and interpreted in light of Scripture. For example, John Wilkens, one of the other witnesses (apparently more favorably disposed toward Campbell), reported Campbell as declaring: "Not that I have anything against confessions, creeds or testimonies: for they are

8. "Minutes of the Chartiers Presbytery," entry for 10 February 1808, in Hanna, pp. 55-56.

9. Westminster Assembly, *The Humble Advice of the Assembly of Divines, Now by the Authority of Parliament Sitting at Westminster: Concerning Part of a Confession of Faith, Presented by Them Lately to Both Houses of Parliament* (London: Printed for the Company of Stationers, 1846). See also S. W. Curruthers, *The Westminster Confession of Faith: Being an Account of the Preparation and Printing of Its Seven Leading Editions; to Which Is Appended the Critical Text of the Confession with Notes Thereon* (Manchester: Aikman and Son, 1937).

10. Associate Presbytery of Pennsylvania, *Declaration and Testimony: For the Doctrine and Order of the Church of Christ, and Against the Errors of the Present Times* (Philadelphia: R. Aitken, 1784). Testimonies were formally approved documents expounding and defending particular interpretations of the articles contained in confessions (such as the Westminster Confession); see Thomas Campbell, *Declaration and Address of the Christian Association of Washington* (Washington, Pa.: Christian Association of Washington, 1809), appendix, pp. 43-44.

11. "Minutes of the Chartiers Presbytery," entries for 10-11 February 1808, in Hanna, pp. 56-63.

laudable and praiseworthy, and I believe done with a good design."[12] Similarly, Nathaniel Robinson testified that Campbell had said: "Brethren, I wish you not to mistake me here that I should be thought to disapprove of creeds or confessions . . . or testimonies, for I approve them as much as any, only use them in their own proper place; for I think they are an excellent help for the strengthening of our faith."

Other witnesses had heard Campbell state that confessions and testimonies were "excellent means of communicating our doctrinal ideas to one another" and that "confessions and testimonies were either like gold or silver tried, as far as agreeable to God's word."

It is clear, therefore, that Campbell had no inherent objections to creeds, confessions, and testimonies per se — he was only protesting against what he considered to be their inappropriate use by his contemporaries. It is also apparent that he had in mind the *post-Reformation documents* which were the subordinate standards of the Presbyterian Church — not the apostolic creed or the creeds of the ecumenical councils of the first five centuries of the Christian church. Similarly, later, Alexander Campbell almost invariably used the term "creed" when referring to the Westminster Confession of Faith.[13]

The process of defending himself during his heresy trial caused Thomas Campbell to "harden" his position to the extent that he came to advocate that creeds, confessions, and testimonies should have no role whatsoever in determining whether a person was fit to receive communion. His written appeal to the Associate Synod of the Seceder Presbyterian Church in North America contains the statement that "nothing should be made a term of communion in the Christian Church which is not as old as the New Testament; or that is not expressly revealed or enjoined therein."[14]

12. This and the following quotations in this and the next paragraph are from "Minutes of the Chartiers Presbytery," entry for 11 February 1808, in Hanna, pp. 58, 59-60, 62, and 61-62, respectively.

13. See, for example, *Christian Baptist* 2, no. 8 (7 March 1825): 55; 2, no. 11 (6 June 1825): 76, 79, 80; 3, no. 4 (7 November 1825): 23.

14. "Minutes of the Associate Synod of North America," entry for 26 May 1808, in Hanna, p. 79. For further details about Thomas Campbell's heresy trials, see William Tabbernee, "'Unfencing the Table': Creeds, Councils, Communion, and the Campbells," *Mid-Stream* 35, no. 4 (October 1996): 418-21.

Nothing That Is Not "as Old as the New Testament"

The striking similarity between the autobiographical statement made by Alexander Campbell in 1824 and the words Thomas Campbell used to defend himself in 1808 shows the way in which the content of the conviction, which father and son had reached independently, ended up being expressed in common, memorable language. This language, first formulated by Thomas Campbell, became a vehicle by which Alexander Campbell was able to communicate their shared conviction. Before long the movement they founded articulated this conviction through slogans, such as "No Creed but Christ" or "No Book but the Bible," which, while powerful rhetorical devices, simplified and distorted what the Campbells believed and taught. Many of their contemporaries assumed, and even more members of the Christian Church (Disciples of Christ) since their day assume, that the Campbells simply disregarded anything that was not "as old as the New Testament." A careful reading of their publications, however, shows this to be a totally false assumption.

This essay concentrates on the way Alexander Campbell understood and utilized the data provided by the post–New Testament writers of the first five centuries of Christianity, but it is worth noting that Thomas Campbell also took pains to help his readers not to draw erroneous conclusions about his own views. As early as 1809 he clarified the position he took on creeds: "As to creeds and confessions, although we may appear . . . to oppose them, yet this is to be understood only in *so far* as they oppose the unity of the church, by containing sentiments not expressly revealed in the word of God; or by the way of using them, become the instruments of a human or implicit faith; or, oppress the weak of God's heritage; where they are liable to none of those objections, we have nothing against them. It is the *abuse* and not the *lawful use* of such compilations that we oppose."[15] Similarly, Alexander Campbell occasionally railed against the *misuse* of creeds such as the Niceno-Constantinopolitan Creed as "tests of fellowship" or "terms of communion."[16] By this he meant that the content of these creeds should not be used as the substance of a doctrinal examination to determine whether a person could be considered an orthodox, "faithful," Christian worthy to belong to a particular denomination, con-

---

15. Thomas Campbell, *Declaration and Address*, postscript, pp. 24-25.
16. *Christian Baptist* 5, no. 1 (6 August 1827): 7.

gregation, or Christian "fellowship" and/or whether that person was worthy to receive the Lord's Supper in that denomination, congregation, or Christian "fellowship." For him Christian fellowship depended simply upon a person's confession "that God has anointed Jesus of Nazareth as the only Saviour of sinners."[17] According to Campbell, "The belief of this ONE FACT, and submission TO ONE INSTITUTION expressive of it, is all that is required of Heaven to admission into the church."[18] Consequently for Campbell, irrespective of how helpful creeds were as summaries of other facts about Jesus "from his birth to his coronation in heaven,"[19] they contained more than the simple fact which incorporation into the church universal and admission to communion required. Hence they were potentially divisive and counterproductive to Christian unity and to what today is called "eucharistic hospitality." The only "term of communion," according to Campbell, is assent to the biblical confession that "Jesus is the Christ, the Son of the living God" (Matt. 16:16).[20]

Despite his insistence that even the creeds of the ecumenical councils must not be used to exclude people from Christian fellowship and from the Lord's Supper, Campbell nevertheless frequently drew on such creeds to explain and defend orthodox Christology and trinitarian theology.[21] In particular, he liked the Apostles' Creed as a brief summary of the apostolic faith: "in every word true."[22] Obviously, although these creeds were not "as old as the New Testament," they were valid and helpful tools for Christian faith and piety — not to be misused but certainly not to be dismissed or discarded. Anything "younger than the New Testament" could indeed be beneficial to Christian faith and practice. It simply should not be used to put additional obstacles in the way of Christian unity and communion.

17. Alexander Campbell, *The Christian System in Reference to the Union of Christians and Restoration of Primitive Christianity as Plead by the Current Reformation,* 2nd ed. (Bethany, Va.: Alexander Campbell, 1839; reprinted St. Louis: Christian Publishing Co., 1890), p. 121.

18. Alexander Campbell, *Christian System,* p. 122.

19. Alexander Campbell, *Christian System,* p. 111.

20. Alexander Campbell, *Christian System,* p. 110.

21. See, for example, the *Millennial Harbinger* (hereafter cited as *MH*) (1845): 415-17; (1846): 216-25, 388-91.

22. *MH* (1855): 74. He pointed out, however, that its nomenclature could be corrected and some of its language (in English translation) modernized. See also M. Eugene Boring, *Disciples and the Bible: A History of Disciples Biblical Interpretation in North America* (St. Louis: Chalice, 1997), p. 74 and n. 22.

The Church Fathers

Just as Alexander Campbell could (and did) recite the Apostles' Creed verbatim,[23] he could (and did!) quote, cite, summarize, or allude to the works of the early Christian writers commonly referred to as the "Church Fathers." Indeed, his extensive use of "patristic material" during his discussions of a wide range of topics demonstrates that he had much more than a superficial knowledge of this post–New Testament literature. He referred to it almost as readily as he did to Scripture, especially when treating issues such as baptism,[24] the Lord's Supper,[25] and ministry,[26] but also when discussing less controversial topics such as preaching[27] and the canon of Scripture.[28] A section of one of his "tracts for the people" on baptism[29] reads like a (mini)"patrology,"[30] i.e., a systematic study of the Fathers of the church.[31] Campbell divides the Fathers into three major categories: the "Apostolic Fathers" ("viz. Barnabas, Clement of Rome, Hermas, Ignatius, and Polycarp");[32] the "Ante-Nicene Fathers" ("those who were conspicuous at or before the Council of Nice");[33] and "Post-Nicene Fathers."[34]

In the first of a number of "extras" published as extended appendices to the *Millennial Harbinger* on specific topics, Campbell proposed twelve propositions on the topic "Remission of Sins."[35] The eleventh proposition reads: "All the Apostolical [*sic*] Fathers, as they are called; all the pupils of the Apostles; and all the ecclesiastical writers of note, of the first four christian centuries, whose writings have come down to us; allude to, and speak

23. For example, see *MH* (1855): 74.

24. For example, see *MH* (1848): 181-82, 241-52.

25. For example, see *MH* (1848): 181-92, 241-49, and Alexander Campbell, *Christian System*, pp. 347-48.

26. For example, see *MH* (1843): 37, 145-52.

27. For example, see Alexander Campbell, *Christian System*, pp. 315, 318-19.

28. For example, see *MH* (Extra [no. 3]) (1831): 38; *MH* (1837): 21.

29. *MH* (1848): 181-92 (*Tract* no. 23; *Baptism* no. 14).

30. *MH* (1848): 184-85.

31. For a modern example of a "patrology," see Johannes Quasten, *Patrology*, vols. 1-3; vol. 4, ed. A. Di Berardino (Westminster, Md.: Christian Classics, 1956-86).

32. *MH* (1848): 185 (cf. 242).

33. *MH* (1848): 185 ("Nice," of course, here means Nicaea).

34. *MH* (1848): 185.

35. *MH* (Extra [no. 1]) (1830): 1-60. The page numbers in the following text are to this issue of *MH*.

of, christian immersion, as the 'regeneration' and 'remission of sins' spoken of in the New Testament" (p. 42). Campbell's explanation and discussion of this proposition (pp. 42-47) shows comprehensive familiarity both with the writings of the Church Fathers themselves and with what, for Campbell, was the best contemporary patristic scholarship. He commences his discussion with a clear statement about his methodology: "This proposition I shall sustain by the testimony of those who have examined all Christian antiquity, and by citing the words of those usually called the Apostolic Fathers, and other distinguished writers of the first four hundred years" (p. 42). In other words, Campbell not only utilized the ancient writings themselves, but he also entered into a meaningful discussion with (or with the views of) those he considered the best patristic scholars of his day. His first step, however, was to allow his readers to hear for themselves the testimony of the Church Fathers by quoting these Fathers verbatim in English translation.

For example, in "Remission of Sins," the topic of this "extra," having dealt with data from the New Testament in his first ten propositions, Campbell starts his discussion of the patristic data (under proposition 11) with extensive quotations from chapter 11 of the *Epistle of Barnabas* (p. 43). Campbell was well aware that, even though attributed to the *apostle* Barnabas, this letter was probably not written by the historic companion of Paul and Luke. He introduces his quotation from *Barnabas* by stating: "We shall first summon one whose name is familiar throughout christendom. Whether the writing be genuine or spurious, it is on all hands admitted to be a fragment of the highest antiquity" (p. 42). For Campbell, irrespective of whether *Barnabas* came from the pen of Barnabas or from the pen of someone writing in Barnabas's name, the indisputable antiquity of the epistle made it a useful source for determining what early "ecclesiastical writers of note" (p. 42) believed about remission of sins (and its relationship to baptism) (see p. 43).

In examining patristic data, Campbell appears to have made for himself a "checklist" of sources which he read (or reread) when treating various topics. For example, after quoting and discussing the significance of *Barnabas* for the topic "Remission of Sins," Campbell deals with other patristic data under the following subheadings printed in bold type:

CLEMENT AND HERMAS (pp. 43-44)
JUSTIN MARTYR (pp. 44-45)

TERTULLIAN (pp. 45-46)
ORIGEN (pp. 46-47)
CYPRIAN (p. 47)

In the opening sentence of the section subtitled "Clement and Hermas," Campbell declares: "The former gives no testimony on the subject" (p. 43). That Campbell had not come to this conclusion without doing the appropriate research is obvious from a subsequent statement in this section: "Having closely and repeatedly examined the Epistles of Clement;[36] of Polycarp, to the Philippians; of Ignatius, to the Ephesians; that to the Magnesians; that to the Trallians, to the Romans, the Philadelphians, the Smyrnians, and his Epistle to Polycarp; together with the Catholic Epistle of Barnabas, and the genuine works of Hermas, I can affirm that the preceding extracts are the only passages, in all these writings, that speak of immersion" (p. 43). The "preceding extracts" are two quotations from *The Shepherd of Hermas* (*Similitudes* 16; *Mandates* 4.3) (p. 43). Campbell's "checklist" for the "Apostolic Fathers" obviously comprised each of the works cited above.

Campbell's early "checklist" for the ante-Nicene Fathers appears to have been less comprehensive and more representative. In his discussion of proposition 11 of "Remission of Sins," he, as already noted, devotes subsections to Justin Martyr, Tertullian, Origen, and Cyprian (pp. 44-47). In this particular instance he quotes, or summarizes, extracts from the writings of the first three of these Fathers as translated by William Wall in the latter's *History of Infant Baptism*[37] — including quoting some of Wall's commentary. Campbell was vehemently opposed to the position in favor of infant baptism which Wall held, and he wrote a lengthy review, in three parts, of Wall's book (and of the works of some other scholars on infant baptism).[38]

---

36. Campbell appears to have considered both *1 Clement* and *2 Clement* to be genuine; see *A Debate on the Roman Catholic Religion Held in the Sycamore-Street Meeting House, Cincinnati, from the 13th to the 21st of January, 1837, Between Alexander Campbell, Bethany, Virginia and the Right Reverend John B. Purcell, Bishop of Cincinnati* (Cincinnati: J. A. James, 1837), p. 13.

37. William Wall, *The History of Infant Baptism: Being an Impartial Collection of all such Passages in the Writers of the Four First Centuries as Do Make For, or Against It . . .* , 3 vols. (London: F. C. and J. Rivington, 1819).

38. *MH* (1848): 181-92 (*Tract* no. 23; *Baptism* no. 14); *MH* (1848): 241-52 (*Tract* no. 24; *Baptism* no. 14); *MH* (1848): 301-12 (*Tract* no. 25; *Baptism* no. 16); reprinted as chapters 3–5 of

Part of Campbell's reason for quoting the Fathers via Wall's compendium was strategic. In his polemic against the practice of infant baptism, he wanted to "summon a very learned Paidobaptist antiquarian who [could] bring forward every writer and Father, down to the fifth century," so that he could "interrogate him concerning his own convictions after he had spent years in rumaging [sic] all christian antiquity" (p. 44).[39] No doubt another part of the reason he often quoted some of the Fathers via the English translations made by others was that, by citing the source of such quotations, he gave his readers (relatively) easy access to a means of double-checking his use of the patristic material and (hopefully) access to material to which he himself had only alluded. In the "tract for the people" which contains the first part of his review of Wall's book, for example, Campbell states:

> And, although in possession of the principal records of both Grecian and Roman Fathers and their opinions, I generally prefer to quote their opinions and statements from Taylor's "Ancient Christianity," because now a popular work; and because he has with great fidelity and ability examined and reported the views of the Greek and Roman Fathers on the subjects named; and especially because his antagonists, the Oxford Tract Theologians, with all their armor on, have not, so far as I have learned, presumed to cavil at his array of patristic authority and opinions.[40]

When making a particular point, Campbell did not hesitate to argue from the Greek or Latin original. During one of his numerous discussions of infant baptism, he takes issue with those who, in his view, mistranslate part of

---

book 6 of Alexander Campbell, *Christian Baptism: With its Antecedents and Consequents* (Bethany, Va.: Alexander Campbell, 1853), pp. 339-77.

39. It is interesting to note that, when Campbell republished the essay "Remission of Sins" in his *Christian System* (pp. 191-258), he kept his "interrogation of Dr. Wall" (pp. 233-38). Conversely, in his subsequently published *Christian Baptism*, he reprints most of his discussion of the patristic evidence originally included under proposition 11 of "Remission of Sins," including the quotations of the Fathers from Wall, but he deletes the "interrogation" (pp. 268-71).

40. *MH* (1848): 182-83 (*Tract* no. 24; *Baptism* no. 14). The work referred to by Campbell is Isaac Taylor, *Ancient Christianity: And the Doctrines of the Oxford Tracts for the Times*, 2 vols. (London: Jackson and Walford, 1839, 1840). Campbell's comment suggests that he used a later edition, possibly the fourth edition, also published in London by Bohn in 1844. A partial reprint of the original edition was published by H. Hooker in Philadelphia in 1840.

Justin Martyr's *First Apology.* Campbell gives his own translation: "Several persons among us of sixty and seventy years old, of both sexes, who were discipled (or made disciples) to Christ in or from their childhood, do continue uncorrupted (or virgins) (1 *Apol.* 15.6)."[41] Campbell's translation and his commentary on that translation make the point that this sentence from Justin's *Apology* does not provide evidence for infant baptism. He stresses that the text states that these sixty- and seventy-year-old Christians had been disciples "'From childhood' — not from infancy. In the original Greek of Justin it is *ek paidoon,* which indicates from ten to fifteen [years], rather than from eight days to two years."[42] Irrespective of whether we agree with the conclusions Campbell drew from his study of Justin's Greek text, it is clear that he was perfectly capable of reading and translating the Greek, which many of the early Fathers wrote — even if he normally utilized the English translations of these Greek texts in his own writings.

Similarly, Campbell was able to read and translate the Latin Fathers when need arose. In fact, he was so fluent in Latin that, in his public debate with John B. Purcell, Roman Catholic bishop of Cincinnati, in January 1837, he frequently quoted the Fathers and the ecclesiastical decrees of the early church in Latin.[43] This debate, perhaps more than any other of Alexander Campbell's works, demonstrates the comprehensive knowledge he had of patristic material, as almost every page of the printed version of his side of the debate abounds with multiple quotations of, summaries of, and allusions to the Fathers.[44] From his debate with Bishop Purcell, it is clear that by 1837, in respect of the ante-Nicene Fathers, he no longer restricted himself to his earlier "checklist." In his review of William Wall's book published in 1848, he lists Papias, Justin Martyr, Irenaeus, Clement of Alexandria, Tertullian, Origen, and Cyprian as the most conspicuous of the ante-Nicene Fathers.[45]

According to Campbell, in addition to the five *Apostolic* Fathers, "There are in all *forty-two* Fathers, a majority of which were *Ante-Nicene,* while the others are called *Post-Nicene.*" Among the most conspicuous of the latter, Campbell lists "Lactantius, Eusebius, Athanasius, Cyril of Jerusalem, Hilary, Basil, the two Gregories, Nazianzan and Nyssen, Ambrose,

41. *MH* (1848): 243.
42. *MH* (1848): 243.
43. For example, see *A Debate,* pp. 36, 116, 155, 224.
44. *A Debate,* pp. 36, 116, 155, 224, and passim.
45. *MH* (1848): 185.

Jerome, Augustin, Chrysostom, Cyril of Alexandria, and Theodoret."[46] Throughout his many published works, however, Campbell quoted many more of the Fathers, as well as other patristic material, than those listed above.

Campbell's study of the Fathers probably commenced while he was still a teenager, learning Greek and Latin from his father in Ireland. It is not unreasonable to suppose that Thomas gave Alexander passages from the Fathers to read and translate. Young Alexander certainly devoured books, staying up late and rising at four each morning to continue his studies.[47]

After their experiences in Glasgow, the Campbell family finally arrived in western Pennsylvania in 1809, and Thomas resumed tutoring Alexander to prepare him for ministry. Alexander's Latin diary reports that his daily regimen included getting up at 4:00 A.M. in order to commence with two hours of Scripture study followed by: "One hour to read Greek — from 8 to 9 in the morning. One hour to read Latin — from 11 to 12 in the morning. One half hour to [read] Hebrew — between 12 and 1 p.m."[48] Apart from chores and other duties, Alexander's daily routine allowed for considerable additional self-education: "Other reading and studies as occasion may serve. Church history, and divers other studies, are intended to constitute the principal part of my other literary pursuits. These studies in all require four and a half hours."[49] Whether or not he was always able to keep to his schedule, Alexander set himself a strict pattern of education, including the study of church history, of which the study of the early Church Fathers undoubtedly occupied a large part, and which served him well for the future. He developed a method of keeping meticulous notes on his reading of the Fathers, which he was able to utilize years later when he had less time to do research.[50] During his later busy career of pastoral ministry, editing and publishing journals such as the *Christian Baptist* and the *Millennial Harbinger*, and being president of Bethany College, he nevertheless found some time to read (or reread) the Greek and Latin Fathers. In the tract which includes the patrology-like summary mentioned above, Campbell reports: "Since writing my last essay on this subject [i.e., baptism], I have read, with more or less attention, some hundreds of pages, many of which, though read in former years, were again read

46. *MH* (1848): 185.
47. Richardson, 1:76.
48. In Richardson, 1:278.
49. In Richardson, 1:278-79.
50. See, for example, *MH* (1848): 252.

as though entirely new, that I might repose in the full assurance that I give a faithful view of the testimony and opinions of the authors."[51]

"Facts" and "Opinions"

Alexander Campbell, influenced by the Enlightenment, distinguished between "facts" and "opinions" and made this distinction a hermeneutical principle not only for his systematic theology[52] but also for his historical theology and ecclesiology. According to him, the works of the Greek and Latin Fathers provided both "facts" and "opinions" about a wide variety of topics relevant to Christian faith and practice. In reporting what the Fathers say on these topics, Campbell almost invariably separates the data into what he considers to be "historic testimony" regarding the Fathers' own time periods (i.e., "the facts") and the view these Fathers had about the facts to which they testified (i.e., "their opinions"). The following statement, penned as part of another "tract for the people" on baptism,[53] is typical: "We must logically and morally discriminate between the testimony of the Greek and Roman Fathers concerning facts and events extant or transpiring in their own times, and their own opinions touching those facts and events."[54]

Campbell recognized that "facts" should not be confined to events or practices but should also extend to beliefs — even though this could blur the sharpness of the distinction between "facts" and "opinions." He acknowledged that "It is as much a fact that a certain opinion was entertained or propagated by a Tertullian, an Origen, or a Cyprian, as that such men lived in the third century. It may also be a fact that they entertained such an opinion, or that they did not." His conclusion is significant hermeneutically: "[B]ut neither the fact of their entertaining or not entertaining any given opinion, is any proof to us or to their contemporaries of the truth or falsehood of such an opinion."[55] For Campbell, therefore, that

---

51. *MH* (1848): 182.

52. See Tabbernee, "Unfencing the Table," pp. 426-27, and Tabbernee, "Alexander Campbell's 'Teacher-Bishops' and the Role of 'Scholar-Pastors' among Contemporary Disciples of Christ," *Mid-Stream* 38, no. 1-2 (January/April 1999): 103-4.

53. *MH* (1848): 241-52 (*Tract* no. 24; *Baptism* no. 15).

54. *MH* (1848): 241; cf. *MH* (Extra [no. 1]) (1830): 43-44; *MH* (Extra [no. 3]) (1831): 37-38; *MH* (1848): 182.

55. *MH* (1848): 241.

the testimony of some of the Church Fathers reveals the fact that infant baptism was practiced in the early church or even the fact that some of these early Fathers were of the opinion that infant baptism was a legitimate Christian practice, even if he himself held the opposite opinion, did not mean that the *testimony* of these Fathers was invalid.

All that Campbell required for "admitting the testimony of Greek and Latin Fathers"[56] on a given subject was a threefold test:

> 1st. That the works assigned to those Fathers be proved to be the genuine and unadulterated works of the men whose names they bear.[57]
>
> 2d. That their whole testimony be regarded as equally worthy of all acceptation.
>
> 3d. And that their whole testimony be heard on any particular fact which they attest.[58]

If an author's works passed tests 1 and 2 and the historian carefully applied test 3, the testimony was deemed to provide valid historical data — irrespective of whether it accorded with Scripture or with Campbell's interpretation of Scripture. Such data were facts to be reckoned with and not to be disregarded. That Campbell tried to be scrupulously careful (and honest) in his use of the patristic sources is clear from a number of statements of which the following on infant baptism are but a sample:

> [H]ave I not always admitted that in Origen's time infants were immersed? Have I not affirmed, upon the testimony of Tertullian and Origen, that in Tertullian's time infants in some cases began to be immersed!![59]

> We concede, without a demur, that in the Greek and the Roman church, whether in Africa, Asia, or Europe, infant baptism . . . not only existed, but in triumph reigned for more than twelve hundred years.[60]

---

56. *MH* (1843): 149.

57. As noted above, in respect of works such as the *Epistle of Barnabas*, Campbell was prepared to use them if it could be shown that they were genuinely ancient.

58. *MH* (1843): 149 (cf. 182).

59. *MH* (Extra [no. 3]) (1831): 38.

60. *MH* (1848): 247.

"Corroboration" and "Germination"

The primary issue for Campbell was not whether the data provided by the Church Fathers were authentic and valid but whether they were authoritative for the kind of Christian "movement" he and the other early "Disciples of Christ" were establishing in the first half of the nineteenth century.

As is clear from the autobiographical statement quoted at the beginning of this essay, Campbell, like his father, held the New Testament to be the ultimate authority for Christian faith and practice. For both men the New Testament writings constituted the definitive witness to the teachings of Christ and those of the apostles, including the apostle Paul. Unaware of (later) scholarly opinions that some of the books of the New Testament may have been composed "in the name" of Paul or Peter by members of "their circle" or that the author of the book of Revelation or, at least, the Johannine Epistles may not have been John "the apostle," the Campbells simply equated "canonicity" with "apostolicity." That is, they adopted the prevailing view that the primary criterion for determining which books should be considered part of "the New Testament" and thus authoritative for the church was whether or not these books had been written by one of the apostles — with the proviso (as in the case of Mark and Luke) that the works of close associates of the apostles (who were deemed to have gained much of the content of what they wrote from these apostles) could also be included. Unlike some of their contemporaries, however, both Campbells were adamant that the end of the "apostolic age" also defined the boundary between authoritative and non-authoritative documents. The apostolic documents contained in the New Testament were authoritative; the postapostolic documents of the post–New Testament era were not.

As is equally clear from Alexander Campbell's (perhaps surprisingly) frequent use of the post-apostolic documents of the era of the successors of the apostles, he certainly did not reject the writings of the Church Fathers as irrelevant or unimportant. Instead, he considered them to have a crucial, albeit secondary, role in helping contemporary Christians determine what they could believe, how they should organize themselves, how they should worship, and what they should practice. Rather than viewing the "apostolic witness" of the *apostles themselves* and the "apostolic tradition" of the *successors of the apostles* as totally incompatible, Campbell saw a twofold, overlapping affinity between the New Testament witness and the testimony of the Church Fathers.

The first way in which Campbell could hold on to the ultimate authority of the New Testament while incorporating much of the post–New Testament data was through the concept of corroboration. His clearest statement on the subject was written as early as 1831:

> Though no article of christian faith, nor item of christian practice, can, legitimately, rest upon any testimony, reasoning, or authority out of [i.e., "beyond"] the sacred writings of the Apostles, *were it only one day after their decease;* yet the views and practices of those who were the co-temporaries or the pupils of the Apostles and their immediate successors may be adduced as corroborating evidence of the truths taught, and the practices enjoined by the Apostles; and as such, may be cited; still bearing in mind that where the testimony of the Apostles ends, christian faith[61] necessarily terminates.[62]

According to Campbell, a great deal of what the "successors of the apostles" taught corroborated, and therefore provided additional evidence for, beliefs and practices already revealed through Scripture. The writings of the Church Fathers confirmed and illuminated authentic Christian faith and practice, but according to Campbell, it neither established nor authorized these.

The second way he could hold in balance his view of the primacy of Scripture and the crucial importance of "the apostolic tradition" was through the concept of germination. Campbell was prepared to acknowledge that, in some instances, such as in the case of episcopacy, it is possible to see the "development of New Testament germs."[63] Campbell had no difficulty with reconciling the threefold ministerial structure (bishop-presbyters-deacons) of the second and third centuries with the twofold structure (elders/bishops-deacons) of the first-century church as recorded in the New Testament. The threefold structure for him was simply a modest development of a ministerial organization already authorized by Scripture. He saw no substantial incompatibility between the New Testament order of ministry and the order developed "in the first ages [by which] every church had its bishops and deacons, of which bishops one was emphatically *the* Bishop, or Chairman President."[64] He also believed, however, that

61. That is, "*authoritative* Christian faith."
62. *MH* (Extra [no. 3]) (1831): 37-38.
63. *MH* (1843): 149 (cf. 151).
64. *MH* (1843): 152.

the concept of germination could sprout unwarranted aberrations, such as "bishops" in the sense of "*diocesan* bishops." Campbell, on the basis of the testimony of the Fathers, was ready to (and unsuccessfully[!] did) use the term "bishop" for local church ministers,[65] but was not prepared to consider the validity of "one bishop for fifty or a hundred churches":[66] "[T]here is neither Bible nor paternal [i.e., patristic] authority for any one of the popular forms of Episcopalianism, hierarchical or Methodistical."[67]

Campbell, while not willing to subscribe to a diocesan model of episcopacy, was very willing to adopt the model of episcopacy he found in the earliest of the Church Fathers, viz., one minister per church with the title "bishop," who presided over the presbyters and was elected by them and by the laity of the congregation.[68] He saw in this model, if churches with (diocesan) bishops would adopt it also, a potential means of forging "a bond of union and cooperation"[69] between currently separated Christian groups.

Conclusion

For Alexander Campbell there was always a creative tension between two related goals which brought the movement he led into being. "Restoration of New Testament Christianity" was never an end in itself. It was supposed to be the means by which Christian unity could be achieved. Ahead of his time, therefore, Campbell saw that the "ecumenical imperative" could (and should) provide ways by which churches with differing understandings about practices such as episcopacy could move closer together by

65. See Alexander Campbell, *Christian System*, pp. 83-84, 90, and Tabbernee, "Alexander Campbell's 'Teacher-Bishops,'" especially pp. 104-10.

66. *MH* (1843): 151.

67. *MH* (1843): 152. "Methodistical" here is obviously Campbell's way of producing a form of the word "Methodist" to parallel the "hierarchical" in this sentence. The "hierarchical" form of "Episcopalianism" designated for Campbell the kind of episcopal structure exhibited in the Roman Catholic, Orthodox, and Episcopalian churches wherein the position of (diocesan) bishop is but one (normally the lowest) rank in a hierarchy of bishops consisting also of archbishops, cardinals, metropolitans, patriarchs, and/or popes. The "Methodistical" form of "Episcopalianism" designated for Campbell the kind of ecclesiastical structure in which the (diocesan/conference) bishop is the highest-ranking cleric.

68. *MH* (1843): 151-52.

69. *MH* (1843): 152.

finding common ground in the apostolic tradition, redefined to incorporate both the primary witness of Scripture and the corroborative and even "germinative" testimony of the Church Fathers.[70]

Despite Campbell's rhetoric against creeds and in favor of making nothing normative which was not at least as old as the New Testament, it is clear from a closer examination of the totality of his writings that the "*early* church," not merely the "*New Testament* church," was extremely important to him. His knowledge of the apostolic tradition, including the tradition of the early church as recorded in the writings of the Church Fathers (apostolic, ante-Nicene, and post-Nicene), was profound, and he utilized this patristic knowledge consistently and effectively. A superficial reading of Campbell, focusing on his popular slogans such as "No Creed but Christ" or "No Book but the Bible,"[71] has produced a distorted view of his teachings and methodology within the three major contemporary "denominations" which have arisen out of the movement he founded. In North America these "denominations" are the Christian Church (Disciples of Christ), the Independent Christian Churches, and the Church of Christ.[72]

An inadequate insight into Campbell's patristic knowledge has also tended to produce within the "denominations" he founded an unwarranted bias against the validity and importance of utilizing the apostolic tradition as well as Scripture to understand Christian faith and to shape contemporary Christian worship and practice. A renewed emphasis on following Alexander Campbell's footsteps through patristic territories will not only result in a more accurate view of his own thought on many issues, but will also enrich our contemporary understanding of Christian faith and practice through being able to incorporate those aspects of the apostolic tradition still relevant today.

---

70. See also William Tabbernee, "Restoring Normative Christianity: *Episkopē* and the Christian Church (Disciples of Christ)," *Mid-Stream* 37, no. 2 (April 1998): 157-63.

71. See Tabbernee, "'Unfencing the Table,'" especially pp. 421, 425-26.

72. In Great Britain, Australia, and New Zealand, the generic designation "Churches of Christ" is still used to apply to all three branches of the movement.

Contributors

Dr. D. Jeffrey Bingham, Professor of Historical Theology, Southwestern Baptist Theological Seminary, Texas (Southern Baptist)

Dr. Everett Ferguson, Professor Emeritus of Church History, Abilene Christian University, Abilene, Texas (Church of Christ)

Dr. E. Glenn Hinson, Professor of Spirituality and John Loftis Professor of Church History Emeritus, Baptist Theological Seminary at Richmond, Richmond, Virginia (Baptist)

Rev. Dr. Frederick W. Norris, Dean E. Walker Professor of Church History and Professor of World Mission/Evangelism, Emmanuel School of Religion, Johnson City, Tennessee (Christian Church)

Dr. Phyllis Rodgerson Pleasants, Professor of Church History, Baptist Theological Seminary at Richmond, Richmond, Virginia (Baptist)

Dr. Gerald W. Schlabach, Associate Professor of Theology, University of Saint Thomas, Saint Paul, Minnesota (Mennonite)

Rev. Dr. William Tabbernee, President and Stephen J. England Professor of Christian Thought and History, Phillips Theological Seminary, Tulsa, Oklahoma (Disciples of Christ)

Rev. Dr. Daniel Williams, Professor of Religion in Patristics and Historical Theology, Baylor University, Waco, Texas (American Baptist)

Index